Irish Christian Handbook
Lámhleabhar Chríostaí na hEireann

Articles by:
R A Diebold, M C Considère-Charon,
L J Francis and J E Greer

Edited by:
Val Hiscock, Peter Brierley, Boyd Myers
and Lindsey Mansfield

1992

MARC Europe's object is to assist Christian leaders with factual information, surveys, management skills, strategic planning and other tools for evangelism and growth. MARC Europe also publishes and distributes books on related subjects.

Copyright: © MARC Europe, 1992. All rights reserved. No part of this publication may be reproduced or transmitted in any form or by any means, electronic or mechanical, including photocopying, recording, or any information storage and retrieval system, without permission in writing from the publisher. This book is sold subject to the condition that it shall not, by way of trade or otherwise, be lent, re-sold, hired out or otherwise circulated without the publisher's prior consent in any form of binding or cover other than that in which this is published and without a similar condition including this condition being imposed on the subsequent purchaser.

The addresses in this publication are put at the disposal of the users of this Handbook subject to the express condition that the user by the single fact of buying the publication takes upon himself or herself the obligation not to multiply and/or circulate the addresses or to have them multiplied or circulated without the copyright holder's express written consent.

Although the details in this Handbook have been compiled with the utmost care, responsibility for their accuracy cannot be accepted. Details are up-to-date April 1992. The Editor welcomes any additions, corrections and changes. Editorial address: MARC Europe, Vision Building, 4 Footscray Road, Eltham, London SE9 2TZ.

Typeset and printed in Great Britain for MARC Europe by Stanley L. Hunt (Printers) Ltd., Midland Road, Rushden, Northants NN10 9UA.

British Library Cataloguing in Publication Data
Irish Christian Handbook
   1. Ireland. Christian church
   1. Hiscock, Valerie
   2. Brierley, Peter
   3. Myers, Boyd
   4. Mansfield, Lindsey
   274.15

ISBN 0 947697 97 7

ACKNOWLEDGEMENTS

We are so grateful for all the help, encouragement and enthusiasm received for this Handbook, from the initial suggestion of its compilation through to its present form.

The idea of a Christian Handbook reflecting the total Christian presence throughout the whole of Ireland, North and South, has been welcomed by many. We are grateful to Mary Lawson for her initial work in consolidating details, Robert Diebold for his most helpful exploratory research, Ingrid Knapp for her suggestions and support, Canon Edgar Turner for his advice on the Church of Ireland figures, Laura Diggins for organising the advertisements, and many others who have helped with numerous suggestions. We appreciate, as always, the very careful work of the typesetter at our printers.

The Editors,
April 1992.

AMENDMENTS

The information in this Handbook was as correct and up-to-date as was possible at the time it went to print. Some has appeared in the companion volume *UK Christian Handbook 1992/93 Edition*, but data relating to the Irish Republic is, for the most part, new. As with any first edition of a book of reference, if there are errors, omissions or corrections the editors would be very grateful to learn of them. Please contact them at this address:

    Irish Christian Handbook
    c/o MARC Europe
    Vision Building
    4 Footscray Road
    Eltham, London SE9 2TZ

    ☎ 081-294 1989 (from N Ireland)
    ☎ 0044-81 294 1989 (from the Republic)

CONTENTS

	Page
Acknowledgements	
Amendments	

Forewords
- by Archbishop Robin Eames — 4
- by Bishop Brendan Comiskey — 5
- by The Right Rev Dr Rodney Sterritt — 7
- by Rev J Winston Good — 8
- by Rev Robert Dunlop — 9

Statistics and Diagrams — 10

Articles
- The Church in Ireland by R A Diebold — 11
- Southern Irish Protestantism by M C Considère-Charon — 15
- The Teenage Voice by The Revd Professor Leslie Francis and The Revd Dr John E Greer — 20
- Information Collection, Notes and Definitions and Abbreviations — 24

Summary Church and Population Tables
- Summary All Churches (Table 1) — 25
- Irish Population (Table 2) — 26
- Proportions in Northern Ireland and the Republic (Tables 3, 4) — 28-29

Denominational Tables
- Anglican Churches (Table 5) — 30
- Baptist Churches (Table 6) — 31
- Roman Catholic Churches (Table 7) — 32
- Independent Churches (Table 8) — 33-34
- Methodist Churches (Table 9) — 35
- Orthodox Churches (Table 10) — 36
- Pentecostal/Holiness Churches (Table 11) — 37
- Presbyterian Churches (Table 12) — 38
- Other Protestant Churches (Table 13) — 39

Other Churches and Religions Tables
- Non-Trinitarian Churches (Table 14) — 41-42
- Other Religions (Table 15) — 43

Community and Historical Tables
- Religious Community (Table 16) — 45
- Church Membership 1900-2000 (Tables 17-19) — 46, 49

Marriage Tables
- Northern Ireland (Table 20) — 50
- Republic of Ireland (Table 21) — 52

Notes and Definitions — 54

Accommodation
- Conference and Other Centres
  - Northern Ireland — 55
  - Republic of Ireland — 56
- Retreat Houses
  - Northern Ireland — 59
  - Republic of Ireland — 59

Books
- Titles and Size of Bookshops (Tables 22, 23) — 63
- Bookshops
  - Northern Ireland — 63
  - Republic of Ireland — 66
- Libraries — 68
- Publishers and Other Literature Producers and Distributors — 68

Counties of Ireland Map — 70

Churches and Evangelism
- Church Headquarters — 71
- Church and Other Organisations — 82
- City and Town Missions — 82
- Evangelistic Agencies — 83

Overseas
- Notes and Definitions, Tables — 87
- Missionary Societies
  - Protestant — 88
  - Roman Catholic — 91
- Index: Irish Missionaries by Country — 101
- Missionary Support Organisations — 106
- Statistical Tables — 108

Services
- Audio-Visual, Film and Video Producers and Suppliers — 109
- Benevolent Organisations — 110
- Counselling and Information Organisations — 110
- Educational Agencies — 112
- Musical and Theatrical Services — 112
- Professional Christian Groups — 112
- Radio and TV Programme Producers — 113
- Reconciliation Groups — 113
- Relief and Development Agencies — 115
- Social Service and Welfare Organisations — 116
- Theological Colleges and Bible Schools by Denomination — 118
  - Northern Ireland — 118
  - Overseas — 119
  - Republic of Ireland — 119
- Training Centres and Services — 120
- Youth Organisations — 121

Summary Table (Table 30) — 123

Index — 125

FOREWORD

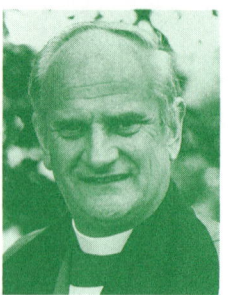

The Most Rev Robin Eames
Archbishop of Armagh
Primate of All Ireland and Metropolitan

It is a massive task to undertake a compilation of the statistical data of the main Christian Churches in Ireland. This ancient island, known worldwide for its saints and scholars, for the witness of St Patrick and the early Irish Christians and for the missionaries sent from its heart, still has today a strong and faithful Christian community.

From Armagh, where St Patrick built his first cathedral in AD445, to every corner of this troubled island, clergy and laity are serving God through every kind of ministry — not always in churches and cathedrals, but always with a commitment and a conviction that is intrinsically Irish.

In the pages of this book will be found data about the present membership — and future projections — of the 'mainline' churches and a host of the smaller religious communities in Ireland, both North and South. In addition there is much helpful information on such matters as the numbers of clergy, the numbers of church buildings, trends in religious marriages, etc. Because of the wealth of information about bookshops, conference centres and the many social agencies of the various churches the *Handbook* will be a ready source of reference for all who wish to know what literature and facilities are available — and where.

In view of the huge nature of the task and the virtual impossibility of being both accurate and complete, the authors are worthy of our thanks for this comprehensive production.

+ Robert Armagh.

FOREWORD

The Most Rev Brendan Comiskey
Bishop of Ferns

The *Irish Christian Handbook* is a newcomer on the scene but I suspect that it will become a "must" on the shelf of the person whose business it is to relate to, and understand better, the different Christian churches and their related organisations in Ireland.

The purpose of the book is to provide material which helps as a reference to Irish Churches and organisations, and to give an overview of the key church statistics which are essential to strategic planning and change. It is envisaged that this *Handbook* will be continually updated in a manner similar to its British counterpart. In brief, between the covers of this one book is contained information which one would otherwise have to cull from a dozen sources.

I found the articles on the Churches fair and informative. Naturally I would be more familiar with the various points made about my own Church, but I welcomed the calm, dispassionate treatment afforded the other denominations.

A chapter entitled, "Southern Irish Protestantism in Perspective" might serve as a good sample of what might be found in this book. Firstly, it deals with demographic trends within the Church of Ireland and then offers a research design and analysis of the trends.

A sample of some of the findings: 45% of Church of Ireland members live in rural areas and 55% are town dwellers; they enjoy a relatively privileged economic position which is confirmed by the small number of unemployed people (2%); 97% of the respondents stated that they have Catholic friends; more Church of Ireland women tend to reach a higher level of education than men; only 1% play Gaelic football or hurling; 72% go to church every Sunday; the majority of those surveyed believe that "Protestant values" are still different from "Catholic values"; the majority confessed a relatively low interest in politics.

The *Handbook* contains a veritable treasure-trove of statistics: population numbers and proportions, rates of change, denominational tables, diocesan boundaries, a listing of "Independent Churches", community and historical tables, marriage tables for Northern Ireland and the Republic, conference and retreat houses for both parts of the island, religious bookshops, publishers and libraries, etc., etc.

The supply of information is so great that one might entitle this *Handbook* "All I ever wanted to know about the Churches in Ireland but didn't know where to find!" Or, if I did, I didn't relish the prospect of wading through a different directory for each Church or agency.

This is a valuable book and an essential resource, a brave undertaking, that deserves support.

FOREWORD

The Right Rev Dr Rodney Sterritt
*Moderator of the General Assembly
Presbyterian Church in Ireland, 1991*

The *Irish Christian Handbook* contains a wealth of material relating to the Church, and to the many Agencies associated with its life and work.

When thinking of the Church we must remember that it is not an Institution, but an ever growing company of people — called into a special relationship with God through Jesus Christ, and entrusted with the task of sharing in His Mission to the world.

The variety of Agencies listed in the *Handbook* indicates something of the nature of this Mission and of the resources available to facilitate this work today.

The latest available statistics are presented and analysed, enabling us to recognise changing patterns in religious life. This provides us with an opportunity to reflect on our faithfulness to our calling in Jesus Christ. It also enables us realistically to evaluate our strengths and weaknesses, to establish priorities in Mission, and hopefully, enable us to be better stewards of the resources God has given us.

The *Handbook* is interesting and informative. It is a convenient and comprehensive reference book and as such will be of great value to the Church.

FOREWORD

Rev J Winston Good
1991 President of the Conference of the Methodist Church of Ireland

I have been greatly encouraged with the wealth of information and detail found within the pages of this new *Irish Christian Handbook*. I have been intrigued as I have read the proofs. There is such a lot of very useful information about the present day Churches in Ireland and their work which reaches far over the seas all around the world. I am sure that many a reader will find many things about the Irish Church scene which were unknown previously.

The statistical survey relating to membership is very interesting and perhaps can prove to be a basis for a further study into trends with children and thus Junior Members. The Tables giving information about marriage trends is also very helpful. All the lists of services and accommodation available through Ireland provided by the Churches are very valuable.

I would hope that not only will the *Irish Christian Handbook* prove to be a grand source of relevant information but provide realistic statistical and informative appraisal of Church based resources throughout Ireland giving a basis from which the Churches can move forward. We may read from within these pages facts about ourselves which hopefully will spur us on to seek to use our plant in terms of human power, various facilities and many resources which are evidently available to us.

FOREWORD

Rev Robert Dunlop
Chairman, Lausanne Committee of Ireland

Reliable information has always been an important part of mission strategy in the Christian church. In welcoming the *Irish Christian Handbook* I believe that its usefulness will become apparent and apposite in several areas as the data is unpacked, analysed and discussed at congregational level.

The statistical material throws light on trends and tendencies as far as numbers are concerned. It is descriptive rather than prescriptive in style. This has many advantages in Ireland. With this new ecclesiastical *literary smorgasboard* available for consultation the Irish churches have access to a rich vein of reflective data. This information has important demographic, sociological and cultural dimensions. When placed alongside the historical analyses and comments it serves to provide valuable interpretative material.

It is my prayer that the publication of the *Handbook* will stimulate goal-setting and strategic planning by Christian leaders, churches and organisations committed to the task of sharing God's Good News with the Irish people. A sturdy spiritual search is developing across the island and it is our hope that the valuable material in this *Handbook* will encourage the churches to catch the rising tide and launch out into the deep as fisherfolk for Christ.

STATISTICS AND DIAGRAMS

	Page
Anglican Churches:	
community 1900-2000, Fig 29	47
map of diocesan boundaries, Fig 40	75
members, ministers & churches, 1980-1995, Table 5	30
proportional changes, 1980-1995, Fig 5 & 6	30
Baptist Churches:	
members, ministers & churches, 1980-1995, Table 6	31
membership 1900-2000, Fig 32	48
proportional changes, 1980-1995, Fig 7 & 8	31
Bookshops:	
average turnover, size & titles, 1991, Table 23	63
by size & number of titles, Table 22	63
Roman Catholic churches:	
map of diocesan boundaries, Fig 39	72
mass attendance, ministers & churches, 1980-1995, Table 7	32
membership 1900-2000, Table 18	46
& Fig 30	47
proportional changes, 1980-1995, Fig 9 & 10	32
Christian organisations summary table, Table 30	123
Church members – see also respective denomination	
members, ministers & churches, 1980-1995, Table 1	25
proportional changes, 1980-1995, Fig 2, 3 & 4	27
proportions by denomination, 1980-1995, Table 3	28
rates of change:	
by selected denominations, 1900-2000, Table 17	46
per annum, 1980-1995, Table 4	29
Counties of Ireland map, Fig 38	70
Independent Churches:	
members, ministers & churches, 1980-1995, Table 8	33
proportional changes, 1980-1995, Fig 11 & 12	34
Marriage statistics, 1900-2000:	
Northern Ireland:	
by church, Fig 35	51
summary & ratios, Table 20	50
trends, Fig 34	51
Republic of Ireland:	
by church, Fig 37	53
summary & ratios, Table 21	52
trends, Fig 36	53

	Page
Methodist Churches:	
map of district boundaries, Fig 41	78
members, ministers & churches, 1980-1995, Table 9	35
membership 1900-2000, Fig 31	48
proportional changes, 1980-1995, Fig 13 & 14	35
Missionary personnel:	
by society type, Table 25	87
continental proportions 1992, Table 24	87
& map, Fig 43	87
countries with largest numbers 1992, Table 26 & 27	108
largest Catholic societies, Table 29	108
largest Protestant societies, Table 28	108
Non-Trinitarian Churches:	
members, ministers & churches, 1980-1995, Table 14	41
proportional changes, 1980-1995, Fig 23 & 24	42
Other Protestant Churches:	
members, ministers & churches, 1980-1995, Table 13	39
proportional changes, 1980-1995, Fig 21 & 22	40
Orthodox Churches:	
members, ministers & churches, 1980-1995, Table 10	36
proportional changes, 1980-1995, Fig 15 & 16	36
Other religions:	
members, leaders & buildings, 1980-1995, Table 15	39
proportional changes, 1980-1995, Fig 25 & 26	44
Pentecostal/Holiness Churches:	
members, ministers & churches, 1980-1995, Table 11	37
proportional changes, 1980-1995, Fig 17 & 18	37
Population statistics, 1976-2006:	
change, Fig 1	26
in thousands, Table 2	26
Presbyterian Churches:	
communicants 1900-2000, Table 17 & Fig 33	49
map of presbytery boundaries, Fig 42	80
members, ministers & churches, 1980-1995, Table 12	38
proportional changes, 1980-1995, Fig 19 & 20	40
Religious community, 1980-1995, Table 16	45
proportional changes, 1980-1995, Fig 27 & 28	44

THE CHURCH IN IRELAND

R A Diebold
Retired journalist

GENERAL OVERVIEW
When Ireland was politically divided in 1922 into the Republic of Ireland and Northern Ireland, the major churches continued to be organised as single units covering both the north and south.

It is estimated that about 95% of the Republic's population is Catholic while about 65% of the Northern Ireland population is Protestant. The major Protestant denominations include the Church of Ireland, Presbyterian and Methodist Churches.

The Churches play an important part in the life of Ireland, being involved closely with education and health care. The preponderance of schools in both north and south are owned and managed by churches or religious orders although largely financed by public funds. Many hospitals and clinics are run by religious orders.

Although the Catholic Church has no special standing in the Irish State (a clause which recognised "the special position" of the Catholic Church was removed from the Constitution by the Irish electorate in a referendum in 1972), the laws of the Republic still are a matter of controversy in such church-related matters as divorce, abortion and contraception. Divorce is not recognised in the Republic and the sale or distribution of contraceptives is rigidly controlled. Abortion remains a most contentious issue; few are ever performed in the Republic, while an estimated 1,500 women annually from the Irish Republic go to England for the operation.

Ecumenism
Ecumenism has continued as elsewhere, with enormous progress during the 1960s and 1970s, followed by the present period of reflection on the fundamental issues which unite and divide the Churches. To outsiders, Irish ecumenism may not be evident amid the violence which goes on in Northern Ireland. But that violence today has nothing to do with religion and little to do with politics. Theoretically the issue concerns the differing political and cultural identities of the two communities — the nationalists (predominantly Catholic) who identify with the Republic, and the unionists (largely Protestant) who consider themselves as British. In reality, while the political dialogue continues in hope, the organisations of violence engage in their activities without any real mandate from either community.

While the social tension has strewn the route towards ecumenism with obstacles, almost every parish in Northern Ireland can offer examples of the crossing of denominational boundaries in a spirit of real ecumenical commitment. And in the Republic, major surveys carried out in the 1970s and 1980s showed that four out of five Catholics (80%) approved of participating in inter-faith services, and there was an increase between 1974 and 1984 in the number willing to accept inter-faith marriages.

There are many inspiring examples of joint witness of Irish Christians in the struggle for peace, promotion of social justice and relief of poverty and distress. Small groups meet in many places to study the Bible and the life and teaching of different Christian churches.

At a national level, the leaders of the four main churches — Catholic, Church of Ireland, Methodist and Presbyterian — have been meeting several times a year for nearly two decades to discuss inter-church problems and to plan ecumenical action. In few countries in the world do the leaders of the churches meet so frequently. Joint studies have been undertaken not only of the issues which divide Irish Christians but also on such social problems as alcoholism, drug abuse, rural underdevelopment and environment.

Education
In the Republic, the primary education system is denominationally based. The leader of the local church is the patron of the school, delegating management of the school to a board of management. Teachers are appointed by the Board, approved by the Department of Education and paid by the State. The local community provides the site for the school and the State pays $7/8$ of the building costs and approximately 80% of the operating costs, the remainder of which is paid by the community through parish collections. Education in primary schools is free, with fewer than 4% of primary pupils attending private schools which charge fees.

Secondary education in the Republic is in voluntary Secondary Schools, which accommodate about 70% of the post-primary population, Vocational Schools and Community Schools. The majority of secondary schools are owned and managed by religious orders. Catholic lay people run a small number of schools. The State pays the major portion of teacher salaries and education in 97% of these schools is free. Religious education is a recognised subject of secondary school curriculum although it is not a subject for the public examinations.

In Northern Ireland, the primary schools are in two categories: Controlled Schools — all Protestant and 100% State financed: and Maintained Schools — all Catholic, parish-owned, with an 85% capital grant from the State and equipped by the local educational authority. Primary education is free, with only a tiny proportion of primary school children attending fee-paying schools.

About 70% of children over the age of 11 in Northern Ireland are educated in secondary intermediate schools (high schools) with both Controlled and Maintained sectors funded similarly to primary schools. Some 30% of post-primary children are educated in grammar schools, which again have a Controlled sector with 100% capital grant and Voluntary sector which includes schools owned by Catholic and other Christian churches. There are few comprehensive schools in Northern Ireland, although St Louise's School in Belfast is the largest girls' comprehensive in Europe.

Although there has been a move in recent years towards ecumenism in the teaching of religion in the respective schools, the matter of integrated schools is so complex that it remains to date in the realm of research projects and pilot schemes to find effective ways to bring together Protestant and Catholic children at school level.

Denominational Populations

The Catholic Church in Ireland as a whole has continued to increase in numbers, rising from 3,171,000 in 1961 to 3,890,000 in 1989. The major Protestant denominations, on the other hand, have diminished in population from 959,000 in 1961 to 795,000 in 1981, according to Census figures from both the Republic and Northern Ireland. Meanwhile the other religions, including non-Trinitarian churches as well as non-Christian religions, have grown from 77,780 in 1961 to 125,792 in 1981.

Mainly because of the Northern "troubles", respondents in the Census have become increasingly reluctant to reveal their religious preference, and that number, North and South, has increased tenfold from 30,790 in 1961 to 385,132 in 1981. This decrease in the numbers stating their religion, plus the increase in "Other" religions, may account for the fall-off in the Protestant denominations. (While these non-stating statistics are taken from Census reports, the source for the Catholic figures is the Irish Catholic Directory whose Summary of Diocesan Statistics can be taken to represent the entire Catholic population.)

Marriage

In Northern Ireland, 19 out of 20 weddings in 1920 took place in church, a proportion which will have fallen to 16 out of 20 by the year 2000. In 1920, roughly one third of these were Church of Ireland, Presbyterian and Catholic. By 2000 almost half of the church weddings will be Catholic, with only one in six being Anglican, one quarter Presbyterian and one in eight being in other denominations (see Figure 33 on Page 00). Figure 34 shows how the number of people married in different churches has varied since 1900. The number of Methodist marriages has increased substantially since the end of the Second World War, while religious marriages in other denominations have increased significantly since 1970.

In the Republic of Ireland virtually all marriages are religious, though even here non-church weddings will account for 6% of the total by the year 2000. The church weddings are solidly Catholic, although if recent trends continue for another decade the Catholic proportion will decline from 97% in 1970 to 90% in 2000 (see Figure 35).

The number of Protestant marriages has increased steadily since the mid-1960s (Figure 36 on Page 51).

Divorce

While the numbers of marriages both North and South have held a fairly steady average for the past three decades, the number of divorces granted in Northern Ireland rose sharply in the 1970s and '80s to exceed the 1960 figure by 1,000%. This is partly due to two liberalisations of the law. With 9,901 marriages in the North in 1960, there were just 108 divorces. By 1970 the numbers rose to 12,297 marriages with 309 divorces, and in 1980 there were 9,923 marriages with 896 divorces. In 1986 the figure had gone to 10,343 marriages and 1,669 divorces and levelled off in 1988 to 9,958 marriages and 1,550 divorces. About a quarter of these divorces were to Roman Catholics.

In the Republic, where divorce is prohibited by the Constitution, marriages averaged around 17,000 a year from 1960 to 1988. While the number of divorces applied for or granted abroad is not documented, the Catholic Church's Regional Marriage Tribunals during 1988-1989 received a total of 915 applications for annulment of marriage; out of 256 cases passed on to the National Marriage Appeal Tribunal, 212 annulments were granted. Of these, 97 were cases in which a "vetitum" was imposed on one or both parties, prohibiting them from re-marriage.

The Catholic Marriage Advisory Council, under the patronage of the Hierarchy, operates 55 centres throughout Northern Ireland and the Republic, to give counselling by trained staff in pre-marriage courses, one-to-one situations, fertility awareness and natural family planning methods. (While the sale of contraceptive devices now is legal throughout Ireland, and sterilisation operations are conducted, the Church does not recognise any other but "natural" birth control.) To place children, whether or not born out of wedlock, the Central Council of Catholic Adoption Societies has 19 societies — one in Derry, six in Dublin and the remainder throughout the Republic.

CATHOLIC CHURCH SURVEYS ON RELIGIOUS PRACTICE AND BELIEFS

Two major surveys, in 1974 and 1984, were commissioned by the Irish Bishops' Conference of the Roman Catholic Church in Ireland, measuring the religious beliefs, practices and moral attitudes of Catholics in the Republic.

The later survey showed several signs of improvement in the level of religious practice in the decade following 1974. However, the findings showed that there were growing difficulties with Church teachings, mainly in the areas of sexual morality and some doctrinal areas such as Papal Infallibility.

Although it found a small drop, from 91% to 87%, in the overall attendance of Catholics at Sunday Mass, the survey also found that in 1984 almost one in three went to mass more than once weekly, compared with one in four in 1974. There was also improvement in the quality of participation at Mass, with the numbers who received Communion weekly rising from 28% in 1974 to 38% in 1984.

The survey found that over the ten years there had been a slight increase, from 80% to 84% in the proportion of people who prayed daily. There was also a growth in those who prayed as a family, and in those for whom praying was an experience of being in touch with God.

In both surveys, married people had a higher weekly Mass attendance rate than the single. While the attendance rate of rural Catholics was constant at 94% over the decade, there was a drop from 86% to 77% in urban areas.

The area of religious practice showing the sharpest drop over the decade was the frequency of Confession. The proportion who go once a month dropped from 47% in 1974 to 26% in 1984. The number going to Confession about three times a year also fell, from 90% to 76%.

Changes in Beliefs

In doctrinal beliefs, the basic beliefs in the existence of God and the resurrection of Christ are fully accepted by the vast majority of Catholics. However, there were growing doubts about Papal Infallibility, up from 18% in 1974 to 30% in 1984; and the proportion who fully believe in the concept of hell fell from 51% to 41%, and belief in the Devil from 50% to 45%.

In the area of sexual morality, the survey examined attitudes in three areas — contraception, abortion and pre-marital sex. Here the general shift was away from absolute condemnation to having reservations in certain circumstances.

On contraception within marriage 15% said it was "always wrong", 25% said it was "generally or always right", and the remainder felt it was "generally wrong" or "depends on the circumstances". Reasons given by those who made exceptions were: "If they have too many children", "If the woman's health is in danger" and "It's up to the couple to decide". Replies made to the survey clash with actual practice. Since the sale of contraceptives became legal in the Republic in 1980, the birth rate has plummeted.

On abortion, a substantial majority, 68%, considered abortion to be "always wrong", although this number was down from 74% in 1984. Those who felt it was "generally wrong" or "depends on the circumstances" increased from 23% in 1974 to 30% in 1984. They gave as extenuating circumstances "If the mother's health is in danger" or "In the case of rape/incest". The number who thought it was generally or always right remained at 1% in both surveys.

On pre-marital sex, attitudes softened in the decade, with a substantial decrease, from 71% to 46%, in the number who thought it was "always wrong". There was a significant increase from 18% to 41% in the number who believed it was "generally but not always" wrong. There was no change in the 9% who felt it was "generally or always right".

Towards Divorce

There was a shift during the decade in favour of divorce being allowed. The 54% who in 1974 felt divorce should never be allowed dropped to 43% in 1984, and the number favouring divorce rose from 41% to 48%. The number of "don't knows" also increased, from 5% to 9%.

The survey examined people's attitudes to endangering life (killing or seriously injuring another, driving recklessly, drinking to excess) and judgements regarding the rights of others (stealing, cheating, rejection of minority groups etc). The findings showed that, while the majority condemned these behaviours as "always wrong", there was an increase in those who said "it depends on the circumstances". The report noted with some concern that among the extenuating circumstances listed, "revenge" was prominent.

In the earlier survey, substantial attention was paid to the 21-25 age group whose level of belief, practice and quality of moral judgements differed widely from those of older respondents, and fears were expressed that the level of belief and practice would continue to deteriorate among this young group. However, the 1984 survey found that, in fact, there had been a small increase of 2% in the number of this group attending weekly Mass, and an even larger increase from 49% to 55% in the number taking Communion once a month.

Both surveys showed that Catholics place a high value on membership of the Church. In general, the 1984 survey showed that, in the area of religious beliefs, there had been a movement over the decade from full acceptance of various church teachings to qualified acceptance or uncertainty.

THE EFFECT OF DENOMINATIONS ON THE STANDARD OF LIVING

Since the Continuous Household Survey was only first carried out in Northern Ireland in 1983, it would be impossible to deduce from that how much the considerable margin between Catholic and Protestant families has narrowed since the present "troubles" erupted in 1969. It is safe to conclude, however, that the differences in opportunity, income and lifestyle have been diminished to some extent by the numerous reforms imposed since that time. But the fact remains that, overall, Catholics generally have a slightly lower standard of living than Protestants in Northern Ireland, as evinced by the most recent CHS in 1987.

Unemployment, which has been greatly exacerbated by the violence, remains the most pressing problem faced by both denominations, with 80% of Catholics and 76% of Protestants giving that problem top priority. The troubles are given second priority by 59% of Catholics against 68% of Protestants. Some 30% of Catholics and 28% of Protestants see the high cost of living as the third in importance, and 17% of Catholics as against 14% of Protestants put low wages in fourth place. In diminishing order are bad housing (6% Catholics, 5% Protestants), and Inflation (5% Catholics, 4% Protestants).

Protestants in the 1985-87 sample were significantly more likely to be working and less likely to be unemployed compared to Catholics. There were 45% of Catholic males and 62% of Protestant males employed, against 25% of Catholic males unemployed to 10% of Protestant males unemployed (not including inactive, that is, the retired, in training, disabled, etc). A smaller difference was evident in females of the two denominations. Half the population in the west is Catholic, whereas only 40% of the jobs are there. Poorer educational qualifications, often biased towards the less marketable arts subjects, and an understandable reluctance to take up employment in the security services among Catholic males, makes the vast employment differential between the two communities easy to explain.

In occupations, Catholics were significantly less likely than Protestants to hold either professional/managerial or other non-manual posts with 5% of Catholics in the professional/managerial sector compared to 11% of Protestants, and 21% of Catholics in non-manual employment compared to 29% of Protestants. Conversely, Catholics were over-represented in the semi- and unskilled manual occupational groups.

Catholic households remain larger than those of Protestants, with an average household size of 3.4 and 2.7 respectively. More than a quarter (29%) of Catholic households, compared to one-eighth of Protestant holds, contained five or more persons. Average household sizes remained stable over the period 1983/84-1985/87. Catholic women interviewed during 1986 and 1987 reported a higher number of births (average 2.8) than did Protestant women (average 2.0).

More than half of working and unemployed groups (53%) had no educational qualifications. The proportion having no qualifications was higher among unemployed adults (63%) than those in employment (42%), and higher among Catholics (58%) than among Protestants (50%) in the sample. At all levels of educational achievement, however, Catholics were twice as likely to be unemployed as similar Protestants.

In income, the distribution differed perceptibly between each of the religious groups. More than one-fifth (21%) of Protestants reported annual earnings of £10,000 or more compared with 13% of Catholic households, while 37% of Catholics earned less than £4,000 a year compared with 31% of Protestants. The higher long-term unemployment rate among Catholics was reflected in the comparison of proportions receiving Supplementary Benefit — 37% of Catholic as against 20% of Protestant families. Moreover, the proportion of Catholic families in receipt rose significantly between 1983-84 (32%) and 1985-87, while the proportion of Protestant families remained relatively stable.

Catholic families still display a consistently lower level of ownership than Protestant households for all consumer durables with the exception of televisions. The disparity remains most pronounced in the case of freezers, telephones, cars/vans, small electrical items and microwave ovens. In type of household tenure, 58% of Protestant, compared with 49% of Catholic homes were owner occupied, while 44% of Catholic as against 34% of Protestant homes were rented from the Northern Ireland Housing Executive. Moreover, overcrowding in Catholic homes (13%) tended to be more prevalent than in Protestant homes (4%).

No such comparisons were available in the Republic of Ireland, where the 1987 Household Budget Survey compares only urban and rural households, and makes no comparison by religious denomination. The question of denomination in the Republic, where only a tiny minority of population is other than Catholic, is less likely to arise regarding employment, income, lifestyle, ownership, etc.

However, a comparison of the Republic with Northern Ireland in housing shows a greater preponderance of home ownership south of the Border, with more than three-quarters in the Republic (77%) compared to over half (57%) in the North, and only 14% rented from Local Authorities in the Republic as against 36% rented from the NIHE. Privately rented and rent-free accommodation North and South were fairly comparable in proportion.

Ownership of a few consumer durables was higher in Northern Ireland than in the Republic. Residents of Northern Ireland had more personal computers (10%) than those in the Republic (6%), more tumble driers (30% as against 22%) and video recorders (28% compared to 21%). Ownership of other items such as microwave ovens, refrigerators, washing machines, dishwashers, cars/vans were largely comparable North and South.

SOUTHERN IRISH PROTESTANTISM IN PERSPECTIVE

M C Considère-Charon
Professor agrègè

Readers might wonder why one should wish to investigate the Protestant minority in the Republic. The term minority whenever it is mentioned suggests the idea of opposition or even conflict with a majority which supposedly imposes its views, logic and rules. However, a short glance at the Protestant minority in the Republic of Ireland does not reveal anything of the kind but on the contrary peaceful and fairly good relations with the Roman Catholic majority.

This apparent absence of conflict should suggest that the Protestant minority is fully integrated in the overall society and experiences no frustration or resentment towards the majority group.

This ideal picture is, however, contradicted by a few facts and figures. First, a short glance at the census figures is enough to understand that the Protestant minority does not show any signs of vitality and is even facing problems.

Secondly, a few cases that come up occasionally, such as the controversy around the last Protestant hospital in Dublin – the Adelaide Hospital – reveal the presence of a few bones of contention between the two communities. Our purpose is to try and give a realistic picture of the minority, its difficulties, concerns and aspirations in that part of Ireland which is both so close and so far from the border.

This article takes as its focal point the results of a survey that was carried out by the author between July 1989 and September 1990.

Our survey concerned a sample of 687 Church of Ireland members on 50 different parishes scattered all over the Republic who agreed to fill out a questionnaire that was handed to them by their ministers (see map of the parishes at the end of this article).

The data were computerised at the INSEE (Institut National des Statistiques et Etudes Economiques) in Strasbourg and then carefully analysed.

Our approach is coloured by different readings and similar tests of public opinion (see bibliography). It is also based on the figures from the different censuses which have taken place since independence.

For stylistic reasons the terms Protestant, Anglican and Church of Ireland member are used interchangeably although strictly speaking the respondents of our survey should be embraced under the term "Church of Ireland".

DEMOGRAPHIC TRENDS

It seemed to us that the easiest way to test the vitality of a social group is to study its demographic evolution over a number of decades. Concerning the Anglican minority it seemed obvious that we should start with the first census that occurred after the emergence of the new state (in 1926).

In 1861 the Protestants accounted for 8.5% of the total population of the 26 counties which now constitute the Republic. By 1961 the percentage had fallen to 3.7% and by 1981 only 2.8% of the population were Protestant.

This decline was much more dramatic during the decades that immediately followed the treaty of 1922 than during the second half of the twentieth century.

The exceptional size of the minority's decline revealed by the census figures of 1926 can be seen as an aftermath of the treaty. Under its terms the British armed forces were withdrawn and the Royal Irish Constabulary and the Dublin metropolitan police were disbanded. They were essentially composed of Anglicans who decided to transfer to Britain or Northern Ireland.

Various incidents which ranged from raids, attacks on property and eviction notices to murders also prompted the exodus of the minority who believed there was no future for them in the new state.

In the following decades peace was restored and the rate at which the Church of Ireland declined slowed dramatically.

Demographic evolution of the minority and majority populations

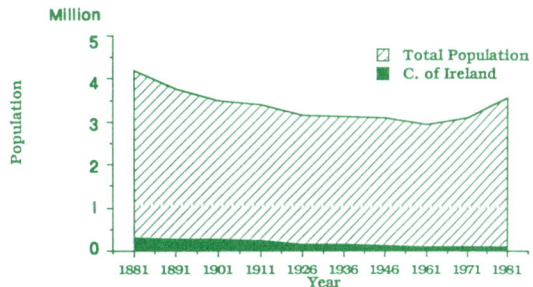

Source: Department of Cartography, University College, Dublin.

Between 1971 and 1981 the total Protestant population dropped by 2.4%. This decline would not be so alarming if it had also affected the Catholic majority. However, Figure 5 reveals that over the last twenty years the Catholic population has substantially increased. The decline in the Protestant community seems to be due to three main factors: emigration, mixed marriages and a low birth rate.

Emigration

It appears that emigration was the chief cause of the decline in the minority's population before the 1960s. The rate of emigration considerably slackened in the 1960s as a result of the new government policies which stimulated the rate of economic growth. Parallel to this reduction of emigration, a process of immigration took place whereby a growing number of English Anglicans came to live in Ireland and joined the Church of Ireland.

Mixed Marriages

Ever since the 1940s a growing number of mixed marriages, that is, marriages of Church of Ireland members with Roman Catholic partners, took place. In accordance with Canon Law, the Roman Catholic Church discouraged mixed marriages. If they did occur, the Ne Temere decree stipulated firstly, that official dispensation had to be granted by the Roman Catholic hierarchy, and secondly, that the children of those mixed marriages had to be brought up as Roman Catholics. This meant that they were to be cut off from the Protestant community.

After the second Vatican Council, the Roman Catholic Church grew more tolerant towards mixed marriages and in 1970 the Motu Proprio, or edict from Rome, no longer made written promises from the Roman Catholic partner mandatory and even allowed that under certain circumstances marriages could be conducted in non-Catholic churches.

Birth Rate, Marriage Rate and Fertility Rate

Leaving aside the topics of emigration and mixed marriages it seems that the Church of Ireland population has been undergoing a process of natural decrease since 1926 for the very obvious reason that the number of deaths has exceeded the number of births.

The minority's birth rate and fertility rate strike the observer as being relatively low compared with those of the majority. Thus, the average number of children for 100 married women in 1961 was 361 for the Roman Catholics and only 228 for the Anglicans. At first glance it would appear that the marriage practices of the Irish Anglicans were the major cause of their relatively low birth rate. The low nuptiality of Irish Anglicans in the South has been due to their small and scattered numbers, the consequent lack of suitable partners and their unwillingness to marry Roman Catholics. All these factors contribute to the establishment of an ageing community whose members may lack confidence in the future.

Some Church of Ireland officials went as far as saying that the two alternatives for Southern Irish Protestants were extinction or the ghetto. In other words, the only way for the community to escape extinction is to retreat both mentally and literally within its own sphere.

RESEARCH DESIGN AND ANALYSIS OF THE RESULTS

We believed that the best way to gain a better awareness of the present position of the minority was through the selection of a sample of Church of Ireland members scattered all over the country. This sample was selected randomly from several parishes (see map of parishes).

1,600 questionnaires were distributed and the response rate of 43% resulted in 687 questionnaires being filled out and returned to the author.

The questionnaire was designed to collect data relating to the personal, social and cultural identity of the respondents, their attitude to their environment and finally their opinions on various issues of national importance.

Our purpose was two-fold:

Firstly, to define the degree of distinctiveness of the Protestant minority as regards their occupations, interests, hobbies and education as well as their attitudes and opinions.

Secondly, to assess their degree of internal cohesion as a social group and integration into the nation as a whole.

Gender and Marital Status

Of the 687 individuals 328 (48%) were men and 359 (52%) were women.

Information on marital status suggests that women tend to marry later than men. The number of single women in their sixties is higher than that of men due to war losses and a higher emigration rate among men in the 1940s. These findings confirm the trends that were defined previously.

Number of Children

The average number of children per family is 2.2. Although this fertility rate is higher than in most European countries it indicates that Church of Ireland women are not as fertile as Roman Catholic women in Ireland, although the most recent figures suggest the difference is disappearing.

Occupational Status

The professional breakdown is as follows:

	%
Housewives	23
Farmers	21
Executives and professionals	17
Retired people	16
State-employed or clerks	9
Shopkeepers	5
Students	4
Workers	3
Unemployed	2

The high percentage of farmers is striking but is in keeping with the high proportion of rural parishes in our survey — 45% of the population live in rural areas while 55% are town-dwellers. The high percentage of executives and professionals and the low number of clerks and state-employed people reveal the well-known preference of the Protestant minority for the private sector. They also reveal the relatively privileged economic position of the Church of Ireland members which is confirmed by the small number of unemployed people. (An analysis of the 1981 Census, however, shows a higher Protestant unemployment rate than Catholic for almost every occupational class outside the higher status ones.)

Most parishioners declare that they belong to the middle class. What is much more surprising is that most respondents (including retired people and widows) say that their financial situation has improved over recent years. This is probably due to the Irish government policy in favour of pensioners and the series of measures in their favour in such areas as housing, travelling and so on. What emerges from these findings is that on a socio-economic level the Protestant minority appears to be in a rather comfortable position, especially in urban areas.

Some farmers, however, admit having occasional financial difficulties but in many cases they seem to survive these times because of a second source of income from a part-time or even full-time job.

Most respondents (70%) admit that their religion is not an obstacle when looking for a job. Those who believe it can be an obstacle believe that this is only the case in the public sector regarding employment in teaching or nursing jobs.

Other interests

It was hypothetised that the educational level of those questioned would be relatively high, due to a tradition of high educational standards and the Protestant minority's attachment to education. Also, we expected to find a high proportion of traditionally Protestant activities and sports. Our findings would either confirm or reject the notion of a distinctive minority group.

The number of people reading a daily newspaper is high (76%). Half read the *Irish Times* while most of the others either read the *Irish Independent* or the *Cork Examiner*. A small proportion (5%) read an English newspaper and fewer still read the *Irish Press* or a tabloid. This reveals the taste of the minority for a high quality national press. The *Irish Times* has traditionally been read by the minority members. It was once considered to be the newspaper of the minority, but since Independence it has enlarged its readership and has taken up a moderate, middle of the road attitude. One respondent said that he liked the *Irish Times* "because there he could find all the Church of Ireland wedding notices and obituaries".

The vast majority of people have a particular interest or pastime outside work, which confirms a relatively high degree of openness.

Twenty per cent of the respondents devote part of their free time to parish activities. Those doing so are largely housewives and retired people.

A further 20% mentioned gardening or flower-arranging as a major source of interest. This interest reveals a certain degree of freedom from household chores and also an aesthetic concern. Seventeen per cent of the respondents mentioned an intellectual or artistic interest, and 10% are involved in charity work. These two interests were traditionally found among the social and cultural Church of Ireland elite. Besides these interests, many people mention another type of interest such as bowls, cards etc . . .

Among the 551 people who practise or have practised one or several sports, a large number play tennis, table tennis or badminton. These sports seem to be traditionally played by Protestants as there are often clubs where they can be practised within the parish. As for the team sports, hockey and rugby are still commonly practised (29%) as they are traditionally taught in Protestant schools. Sixteen per cent mention golf, riding or cricket which could still be considered as "British" by the Roman Catholics and the practice of which suggests a relatively high standard of living.

Only 1% play traditionally Catholic sports such as hurling and gaelic football.

However, we were surprised to find that a high proportion of people (37%) practised "other sports", that is, sports that cannot be labelled "Protestant" or "Catholic".

Two-thirds of the respondents belong to at least one association, which reveals a certain amount of vitality.

Forty-two per cent of the people mention an association either connected with the parish or with their church on a wider scale.

More than half (52%) belong to a local non-denominational club — either a sports club, a cultural club or an association connected with their town.

One-fifth say they belong to a professional, unionist or political association. It is interesting to note that only 4% belong to either the Orange Lodge or a Masonic Lodge.

When asked about the confessional membership in their clubs or associations 36% said their association is predominantly Protestant; 35% that it is predominantly Roman Catholic; and 29% that it is fairly mixed.

These findings suggest that although the respondents often seem attached to a Protestant cultural heritage, they do not have a "ghetto" mentality.

Many respondents made a point of having two kinds of interests: one that ensured frequent contact with their co-religionists and another that enabled them to meet people outside their minority circles.

Social Life and Communications Network

An overwhelming majority of people (97%) said that they have Roman Catholic friends; 88% have contact with Protestants abroad — mostly in England, Northern Ireland and to a lesser extent in countries like Australia, the United States and Canada.

Education

The level of education attained by the parishioners is as follows: 17% have a primary level of education; 52% have a secondary level of education and 31% have a university or other tertiary level of education.

More women tend to reach a higher level of education than men.

The schools attended by parishioners' children are, in most cases, Protestant.

The small minority of parents who send their children to Roman Catholic schools gave several reasons for this. For some, it is more convenient as the Catholic school is close to their homes so their children do not have to be boarders. For others, it is a much cheaper option. Some parents said that the Roman Catholic schools maintain higher standards or that the Protestant school in their locality did not offer the syllabus their child had chosen.

When asked whether their children were or had been taught Irish at school 95% of the answers concerning primary education were positive as were 90% of those relating to secondary education.

Frequency of Attendance at Formal Religious Worship
The majority of the parishioners (72%) go to church every Sunday. However, this percentage is much higher than the actual level of attendance as the respondents were regular churchgoers whom the minister could contact easily. The ministers, when asked about the proportion of regular churchgoers, suggested a figure between 30 and 50 per cent. Of those not attending a Sunday service regularly, one third said that this was due to practical reasons, such as the church being too far away. The remainder did not explain the reasons behind their non-attendance.

ATTITUDINAL AND OPINION-TYPE QUESTIONS

Priority to Class or Religion
When asked, "Do you think you have more in common with a person of the same class as yourself but of a different religion?" the answers were split evenly.

Older respondents and those under 25 years of age tend to consider religion to be more important than class. The reasons are fairly obvious: older people are naturally more attached to their cultural heritage, while a segregated school system has meant that teenagers mix largely with members of their own denomination.

Protestant Values
The respondents were asked whether they believed that Protestant values were still different from Roman Catholic values.

The majority of people gave positive answers. It was made clear in the personal comments added to questionnaires that Protestant values such as honesty, hard work, free enterprise and freedom of conscience do not seem to be enjoyed by the Roman Catholic majority.

Ecumenism
Perceptions of the ecumenical movement were as follows: 36% consider it to be a good thing; 12% see it as a threat; 50% believe it can be both good and bad. The reserves expressed by half of the respondents reveal a fear that most ecumenical initiatives might essentially benefit the Roman Catholic majority and endanger the cohesion of the minority group.

Perception of the Position of the Roman Catholic Church
Sixty-five per cent of the parishioners believe that the position and influence of the Roman Catholic Church in the Republic are "far too important".

Twenty-seven per cent believe it is "a little too important" and 5% that it is "just right". The perception of the role of the Catholic Church seems to depend on the local attitude towards Roman Catholic clergy.

Political Representation and Expression of the Minority
Seventy-nine per cent of the parishioners believe that the Protestant minority is under-represented in public life. Only one member of the Dail and two senators are Protestant.

Of the 543 who declared that the minority was under represented, 525 said that it should voice its opinion more. It is true that ever since the emergence of the new state the minority has tended to keep a low profile. It seems that more and more Protestants now believe that they should change their attitude and become more involved in local and national politics.

Discrimination
When asked, "Do you believe that Protestants in the Republic are the victims of any kind of discrimination?" a small majority answered "No". Some of those who answered "Yes" made it clear that discrimination was often subtle and could be met in the public services or in establishments such as schools, hospitals and so on run by Roman Catholics. In such a context the Roman Catholic religion was regarded as the norm and any person who was of a different confession felt like the "odd man out".

Degree of Political Unrest
When asked whether they were interested in politics the majority of parishioners confessed a relatively low interest.

Political Party Preference
Sixty-three per cent confessed their regular support to a party. We may assume that the majority of Protestants tend to favour Fine Gael. However, in the farming areas, a few respondents mentioned that they were members of Fianna Fail.

Opinion on Controversial Issues
Concerning issues such as divorce, contraception and information about abortion which have divided the country and where the options of the government seemed to many to have been dictated by the Roman Catholic hierarchy, 45% of the people questioned said they differed a lot from the majority viewpoint, 39% a little and 12% not at all.

Protestants find themselves in an awkward position regarding these matters as they run the risk of appearing permissive. Many older people said they shared the majority's views. Many parishioners across the age groups said legislation about divorce should be introduced and contraception should be made available to all. However, they were against abortion in all cases, except when the life of the mother was in danger.

The Northern Ireland Conflict
The question about possible solutions to the conflict in Northern Ireland was meant to test the degree of cohesion in the Protestants' perception of the conflict and also their sense of kinship with the Northern Protestants. The answers revealed many different perceptions of the situation. 13% believe in a united Ireland; 20% believe in a federated Ireland; 14% believe in an independent Ireland; 13% believe in the Anglo-Irish agreement; 18% believe Northern Ireland should be maintained within the United Kingdom and 18% say that they see no solution to the conflict.

At the heart of the constitutional problem lies the dilemma of whether to coax Ulster towards an all-Ireland framework or to maintain it within the United Kingdom, according to the wishes of the majority of Northern Protestants. The advocates of a United Ireland may argue that in a United Ireland the minority would numerically and therefore politically benefit from the influx of Northern Protestants. Those who reject such a solution suggest that the antagonistic sentiments and attitudes in Northern Ireland would not augur well for the stability of the new state that would emerge from a reunification of the two parts of the island.

The final question asked the parishioners whether or not they were happy living in Ireland. An overwhelming majority (98%) answered "Yes".

The picture we can draw from these results is less straightforward and less clear cut than might otherwise be expected. The two communities, Protestant and Roman Catholic, are far less polarised than they used to be. Some of the respondents insisted that they never thought about religion in their social context.

Protestants do not offer uniform views — there are a wide variety of perceptions and opinions within the community.

We can conclude that the Protestant minority may lack confidence in its future but it does not appear to be too badly off in Irish society. Relations with Roman Catholics are emphasised as being very good, especially in rural areas.

The degree of cohesion seems to vary according to age group and area. Those over fifty-five are likely to have a deeper sense of polarisation from the majority than those in other age groups. Surprisingly, social polarisation is apparent among those under twenty-five as a result of segregated schooling.

There seems to be a hard core of interaction and cultural affinity, with "contour lines" of variation shading almost imperceptibly into the majority group. There is a broad consensus concerning relations with the majority group. Most people agree that the domination of the Roman Catholic ethos which has persisted through the decades is more the expression of the Roman Catholic hierarchy than that of individuals who seem to be drawing closer to the minority. But one parishioner did say, "unfortunately Home rule is still Rome rule!".

However, many areas of common ground seem to have developed between the two groups. Religion is no longer the only significant predictor of attitudinal variations. Socio-economic status provides an important cross-cutting influence.

Map of Parishes covered by the Survey

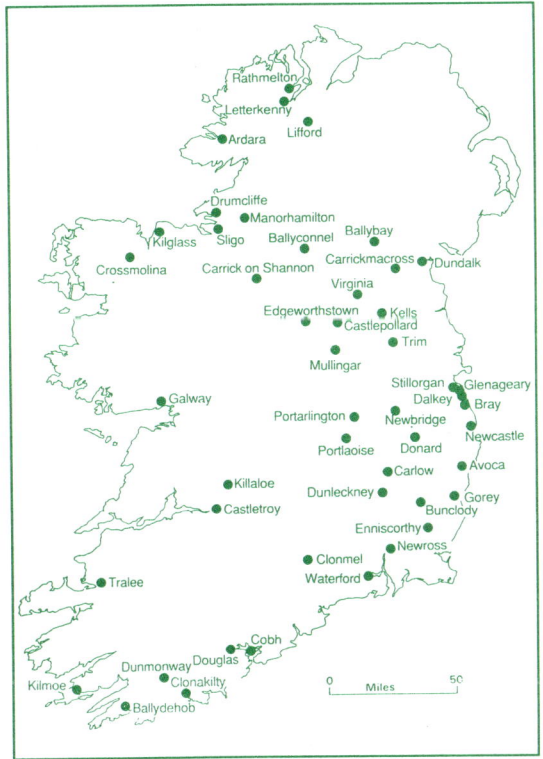

Source: Department of Cartography, University College, Dublin.

Bibliography

K Bowen, *Protestants in a Catholic State, Ireland's privileged minority.* Dublin: Gill and Macmillan. 1983.
E Moxon-Browne, *Nation, Class and Creed in Northern Ireland.* J F B Printing Ltd, Camberley, Surrey. 1983.
M Mac Greil, *Prejudice and Tolerance in Ireland.* Dublin: College of Industrial Relations.
J White, *Minority Report: The Protestant Community in the Irish Republic.* Dublin: Gill and Macmillan. 1975.

A copy of the questionnaire used is available through MARC Europe.

THE TEENAGE VOICE

The religious profile of pupils attending Catholic and Protestant secondary schools in Northern Ireland

The Revd Professor
Leslie J Francis
D I James Professor of Pastoral
Theology and Mansel Jones
Fellow Trinity College,
Carmarthen, and St David's,
University College, Lampeter,
Dyfed

The Revd Dr John E Greer
Reader in Education
University of Ulster
Co Londonderry

INTRODUCTION

Over the past three decades John Greer has conducted a detailed programme of empirical research on adolescent religion in Northern Ireland. These studies include the long term monitoring of the religious belief of sixth formers through a foundation study conducted in 1968[1] and replicated in 1978[2] and 1988[3]; the charting of religious attitudes and thinking[4] and religious development[5] among Belfast pupils; the examination of parental influence,[6] religious experience,[7] moral cultures,[8] openness to members of the other religious community,[9] difficulties in belief,[10] and religion in rural Ulster.[11]

The present article summarises the findings of John Greer's recently completed comparison of the religious practices, beliefs and attitudes of pupils attending Catholic and Protestant secondary schools. Fuller details of this study were published in *Journal of Empirical Theology*.[12]

THE STUDY

Ten Protestant and ten Catholic secondary schools agreed to administer a confidential questionnaire to three classes each of about twenty pupils, one form 4, one form 5 and one form 6. A total of 1,177 pupils participated. The twenty schools appear generally representative of the two different sectors.

The questionnaire included three well tested psychometric instruments, known to function reliably and validly among Catholic and Protestant pupils in Northern Ireland: a scale of attitude towards Christianity,[13] a scale of rejection of Christianity,[14] and a scale of Christian moral values.[15] Other questions were concerned with religious practices and beliefs.

The present analysis draws attention to the different religious profile of four groups of pupils: males attending Protestant schools, males attending Catholic schools, females attending Protestant schools, and females attending Catholic schools.

Church attendance

Table 1 makes it clear that 87% of male and 95% of female pupils attending Catholic schools attend church most Sundays. In the Protestant schools the proportion falls to 39% of male and 55% of female pupils.

Table 1: Frequency of church attendance

	Protestant		Catholic	
	Male %	Female %	Male %	Female %
About once a week or more	39	55	87	95
Once or twice a month	17	12	6	3
A few times a year	23	20	6	2
Never	20	13	0	0

Personal prayer

Table 2 demonstrates that pupils attending Catholic schools are more likely to engage in a daily pattern of

Table 2: Frequency of personal prayer

	Protestant		Catholic	
	Male %	Female %	Male %	Female %
Daily	11	27	38	49
Sometimes	46	50	47	49
Never	43	23	15	3

prayer than pupils attending Protestant schools. In both types of school, female pupils are more likely to engage in a daily pattern of prayer than male pupils.

Bible reading

Table 3 indicates that pupils attending Protestant schools give more attention to Bible reading than pupils

Table 3: Frequency of personal Bible reading

	Protestant		Catholic	
	Male %	Female %	Male %	Female %
Daily	6	13	0	3
Sometimes	37	52	35	48
Never	58	35	65	49

attending Catholic schools. In both types of school female pupils give more attention to Bible reading than male pupils.

Belief in God
Table 4 confirms that pupils in Catholic schools are more likely to be completely confident in the existence of God than pupils in Protestant schools and that girls are more likely to be completely confident in the existence of God than boys.

Table 4: Degrees of belief in God

	Protestant		Catholic	
	Male %	Female %	Male %	Female %
Completely confident that God exists	35	50	44	61
Fairly sure that God exists	30	26	39	31
Uncertain whether God exists	23	17	15	7
Fairly sure that God does not exist	6	4	2	0
Completely confident that God does not exist	7	4	0	0

Experience of God
Table 5 presents the proportions of pupils who report that they have had something which they would describe as an experience of God. Females are more likely to report an experience of God than males and pupils in Catholic schools are more likely to report such experiences than pupils in Protestant schools.

Table 5: Experience of God

	Protestant		Catholic	
	Male %	Female %	Male %	Female %
Have had experience of God	26	38	34	56
Have not had experience of God	74	62	67	44

Importance of religion in life
Table 6 demonstrates that pupils attending Catholic schools attribute a higher level of importance to the place of religion in their lives than pupils attending Protestant schools. Female pupils attribute a higher level of importance to religion than male pupils.

Table 6: The importance of religion in life

	Protestant		Catholic	
	Male %	Female %	Male %	Female %
Very important	13	23	23	31
Pretty important	23	30	43	55
A little important	40	32	30	14
Not important	23	14	5	0

Attitude to God
Table 7 displays four of the statements assessing attitude to God, alongside the percentages of male and female pupils in Protestant and Catholic schools who either "agree" or "agree strongly" with these statements. These statistics demonstrate that male pupils in Catholic schools have a less favourable attitude to God than female pupils in Catholic schools; female pupils in Protestant schools have a less favourable attitude than male pupils in Catholic schools; and male pupils in Protestant schools have a less favourable attitude than female pupils in Protestant schools.

Table 7: Attitude to God

	Protestant		Catholic	
	Male %	Female %	Male %	Female %
God helps me to lead a better life	32	48	61	71
God means a lot to me	38	55	65	84
I believe that God helps people	58	75	78	89
God is very real to me	43	56	62	75

Attitude to Jesus
Table 8 displays four of the statements assessing attitude to Jesus. These statistics demonstrate that attitude to Jesus follows a similar trend to attitude to God.

Table 8: Attitude to Jesus

	Protestant		Catholic	
	Male %	Female %	Male %	Female %
I know that Jesus helps me	39	53	62	83
I want to love Jesus	41	58	77	89
I know that Jesus is very close to me	26	42	45	70
I believe that Jesus still helps people	59	69	72	86

Attitude to prayer
Table 9 displays four of the statements assessing atti-

Table 9: Attitude to prayer

	Protestant		Catholic	
	Male %	Female %	Male %	Female %
Prayer helps me a lot	26	47	52	72
I think praying is a a good thing	48	69	69	85
I believe that God listens to prayers	49	67	57	80
I think people who pray are stupid	7	5	4	3

tude to prayer. While nearly three-quarters (72%) of the female pupils in Catholic schools feel that prayer helps them a lot, the proportion falls to a quarter (26%) of the male pupils in Protestant schools.

Attitude to church
Table 10 displays four of the statements assessing atti-

Table 10: Attitude to church

	Protestant		Catholic	
	Male %	Female %	Male %	Female %
The church is very important to me	28	44	53	69
I think going to church is a waste of my time	31	18	11	10
I think church services are boring	62	38	44	32
Sermons in church are a boring waste of time	42	25	32	17

tude to church. While 69% of female pupils in Catholic schools rate the church as very important to them, the proportion falls to 28% of male pupils in Protestant schools. While 32% of female pupils in Catholic schools rate church services as boring, the proportion rises to 62% of male pupils in Protestant schools.

Attitude to religious education
Table 11 displays three of the statements assessing atti-

Table 11: Attitude to religious education

	Protestant		Catholic	
	Male %	Female %	Male %	Female %
I like school lessons about God very much	24	34	36	47
I think saying prayers in school does no good	42	32	26	16
Religious education in school is uninteresting and ineffective	46	33	24	16

tude to religious education. Less than half (47%) of female pupils in Catholic schools report that they like school lessons about God very much. The proportion falls to a quarter (24%) of male pupils in Protestant schools.

Rejection of belief
Table 12 displays four of the statements assessing rejection of belief. Belief in God is found hard by 36% of male pupils in Protestant schools, 27% of female pupils in Protestant schools, 27% of male pupils in Catholic schools and 14% of female pupils in Catholic schools.

Table 12: Rejection of belief

	Protestant		Catholic	
	Male %	Female %	Male %	Female %
I do not believe that there is any life after death	21	18	10	9
I see too much innocent suffering to believe in a good God who is all powerful	33	26	22	17
I find it hard to accept that the miracles of Jesus actually happened	35	26	23	21
I find it hard to believe in God	36	27	27	14

Rejection of religion
Table 13 displays four of the statements assessing

Table 13: Rejection of religion

	Protestant		Catholic	
	Male %	Female %	Male %	Female %
Religion is out of touch with my experience and interests	43	22	22	13
In the past religion has done more harm than good to mankind	25	14	17	9
Money and enjoyment are more important to me than religion	42	23	22	14
God is something which people create for themselves	22	16	19	12

rejection of religion. Money and enjoyment are seen as being more important than religion by 42% of male pupils in Protestant schools, 23% of female pupils in Protestant schools, 22% of male pupils in Catholic schools and 14% of female pupils in Catholic schools.

Christian moral values
Table 14 displays the ten items included in the scale of Christian moral values, alongside the percentages of male and female pupils in Protestant and Catholic schools who regard these practices to be either "always wrong" or "usually wrong but excusable in certain circumstances". These statistics demonstrate that females are more likely to espouse traditional Christian moral values than males, and that pupils in Catholic schools are more likely to espouse traditional Christian moral values than pupils in Protestant schools. For example, abortion is judged to be wrong, within these terms, by 64% of male pupils in Protestant schools, 77% of female pupils in Protestant schools, 90% of male pupils in Catholic schools and 97% of female pupils in Catholic schools.

Table 14: Christian moral values

	Protestant		Catholic	
	Male %	Female %	Male %	Female %
Gambling	55	71	49	69
Drinking alcohol	38	43	28	43
Drunkenness	77	78	81	86
Stealing	94	96	93	98
Drug taking	84	93	91	93
Sexual intercourse before marriage	27	46	42	65
Abortion	64	77	90	97
Artificial birth control	24	26	54	58
Suicide	75	77	83	86
Divorce	58	56	75	80

DISCUSSION

How do the results of this investigation relate to the dual system of education in Northern Ireland? It may be noted first that the figures relating to religious practice, belief, experience and attitudes which were recorded for Protestants and Catholics indicated significant and consistent differences but not complete contrast. For example, about half of Protestants and nine out of ten Catholics attended church weekly, and by general European standards these figures indicate frequent attendance. Throughout the investigation significant differences between members of the two traditions were noted, but these were observed against a background of broad similarity and agreement on issues like stealing and taking drugs. On this evidence it would be wrong to regard all Protestant pupils as secular or as non-Christians, just as it would be inaccurate to regard all Catholic pupils as committed, freely assenting, uncritical members of the church.

Having said that, it must also be recognised that the religious ethos or atmosphere in, for example, a girls' Catholic school in which 95% attend church on Sunday and less than 2% attend occasionally or never, must be different from that in a boys' Protestant school in which 39% attend church weekly and 43% attend occasionally or never. It seems likely that the assumption about pupils' faith, the level of sacramental involvement, the background knowledge of the Christian tradition, the interest in religious matters would be very different in these two types of school, and these must be important factors in deciding on legitimate aims, how religion is taught and what seems appropriate content in such varied settings. The two groups of pupils studied and compared in this research were clearly different and this must have been reflected in their behaviour and performance in classroom, assembly hall and other less formal situations in school and local community.

In relation to religious practice, belief, experience, attitude and moral judgement, the present study provides empirical confirmation of the real differences in pupils' religious profiles communicated by the dual system of schools in Northern Ireland. In this way it could be used by protagonists to argue in support of a separate Catholic culture or of a separate Protestant culture which needs its own schools through which distinctive values and beliefs are transmitted to the next generation. However, the empirical confirmation of real differences communicated by the dual system could also be used in quite a different way, namely to argue for the development of effective ways in which the evil consequences of division in society may be overcome. Schools are part of the divided society in Northern Ireland and they help to perpetuate the divisions in society. Research studies such as this must surely make clear both the nature and magnitude of the divisions and also the need for healing and reconciliation in the field of education.

REFERENCES

1. J E Greer, *A Questioning Generation*, Belfast, Church of Ireland Board of Education, 1972.
2. J E Greer, The persistence of religion: a study of adolescents in Northern Ireland, *Character Potential*, 9, 139-149, 1980.
3. J E Greer, The persistence of religion in Northern Ireland: a study of sixth form religion, 1968-1988, *Collected Original Resources in Education*, 13, 2 fiche 20, G9, 1989.
4. J E Greer, Religious attitudes and thinking in Belfast pupils, *Educational Research*, 23, 177-189, 1981.
5. J E Greer, Growing up in Belfast: a study of religious development, *Collected Original Resources in Education*, 6, 1, fiche 1, A14, 1982.
6. J E Greer, Religious belief and church attendance of sixth form pupils and their parents, *Irish Journal of Education*, 5, 98-106, 1971.
7. J E Greer, The religious experience of Northern Irish pupils, *The Irish Catechist*, 6, 2, 49-58, 1982.
8. J E Greer, Moral cultures in Northern Ireland, *Journal of Social Psychology*, 123, 63-70, 1984.
9. J E Greer, Viewing "the other side" in Northern Ireland: openness and attitude to religion among Catholic and Protestant Adolescents, *Journal for the Scientific Study of Religion*, 24, 275-292, 1985.
10. J E Greer, *Hardest to Accept*, Coleraine, University of Ulster Faculty of Education Resource Centre, 1988.
11. J E Greer and J Long, Religion in rural Ulster, *Education North*, 1, 2, 15-19, 1989.
12. J E Greer and L J Francis, The religious profile of pupils in Northern Ireland: a comparative study of pupils attending Catholic and Protestant secondary schools, *Journal of Empirical Theology*, 3, 35-50, 1990.
13. L J Francis and J E Greer, Measuring attitudes towards Christianity among pupils in Protestant secondary schools in Northern Ireland, *Personality and Individual Differences*, 11, 853-856, 1990; J E Greer and L J Francis, Measuring attitudes towards Christianity among pupils in Catholic secondary schools in Northern Ireland, *Educational Research*, 33, 100-103, 1991.
14. J E Greer and L J Francis, Measuring "rejection of Christianity" among 14-16 year old adolescents in Catholic and Protestant schools in Northern Ireland, *Personality and Individual Differences*, in press.
15. L J Francis and J E Greer, Measuring Christian moral values among Catholic and Protestant adolescents in Northern Ireland, *Journal of Moral Education*, 21, 59-65, 1992.

Note

The Revd Dr John E Greer is currently working on a new survey among secondary school pupils concerned with the relationship between attitudes towards religion and science.

INFORMATION COLLECTION

Prior to the production of this edition, each organisation listed was sent a form asking for up-to-date details of its work. Organisations not previously listed (because newly formed or unintentionally omitted from earlier volumes) were sent similar forms. Twenty-five different forms were used varying slightly according to the kinds of information requested.

Reminders by letter and telephone were subsequently made to ensure that the data is as up-to-date and as accurate as possible. Information received up to April 1992 has been included.

Categories
The basic details of each organisation listed in this volume are shown once, under the most appropriate category. As many have activities in more than one group, a number will be found in more than one category, by special arrangement.

Scope
While every effort has been made to include all organisations relevant to this publication, the inclusion of an organisation does not necessarily mean agreement by the Editors with its work.

NOTES AND DEFINITIONS

Church Statistics Tables 1-15

Membership figures were given in answer to the following request:
"Total number of adult (aged 15 and over) members/adherents in Ireland." Definitions of membership vary according to the church denomination or religious group in question. Adult church membership is defined as appropriate to each particular group, whilst because there is no comparable equivalent to the Protestant definitions of membership, Roman Catholic adult mass attendance figures have mostly been used.
Ministers are full-time active clergy, or ordained officials, including those in administration, chaplaincies etc.

Churches are those religious buildings in regular use, normally wholly owned by the organisations. Numbers of buildings do not necessarily correspond to the number of congregations or groups within the particular denomination so the number of congregations has been used in some tables as indicated.
Revised figures refer to changes from the 1992/93 edition of the *UK Christian Handbook*.
Estimates indicated by footnotes are editorial estimates, rather than ones made by the individual denominations themselves, which are not identified in these tables.

ABBREVIATIONS

CC = Registered with the Charity Commission
Co = County
E = Estimated
M = Men
n/a = Not answered, not available, not applicable, or available only on request
W = Women
† = No return received
☎ = Telephone
📠 = Faxphone

CHURCH AND POPULATION TABLES
Summary of All Churches

Table 1a: Northern Ireland 1980-1995

Church	Members					Ministers					Churches				
	1980	1985	1988	1990	1995E	1980	1985	1988	1990	1995E	1980	1985	1988	1990	1995E
Methodist	43,159	42,607	43,130	43,424	43,310	127	112	115	115	113	231	209	219	215	206
Independent	13,597	15,468	17,634	19,382	21,836	66	85	108	119	144	280	296	334	366	396
Baptist	7,545	8,339	8,470	8,570	8,795	84	92	97	101	109	91	95	95	95	98
Pentecostal	4,404	7,078	8,600	9,469	11,805	39	67	70	76	84	73	74	77	80	87
Others	3,049	2,775	2,709	2,807	3,010	44	48	50	50	54	51	54	53	52	53
Total Free Church	71,754	76,267	80,543	83,652	88,756	360	404	440	461	504	726	728	778	808	840
Roman Catholic[1]	373,020	353,019	342,514	326,010	307,010	568	549	545	542	530	431	420	424	424	420
Presbyterian	353,910	339,961	330,772	325,195	310,625	469	473	475	489	481	542	542	541	543	542
Anglican	166,783	159,770	155,760	154,755	152,740	330	364	340	300	310	462	440	450	475	465
Orthodox	97	117	128	133	152	0	0	0	0	0	0	0	0	0	0
TOTAL	965,564	929,134	909,717	889,745	859,283	1,727	1,790	1,800	1,792	1,825	2,161	2,130	2,193	2,250	2,267
Percentage of population[2]	63%	59%	58%	56%	53%										

Table 1b: Republic of Ireland 1980-1995

Church	Members					Ministers					Churches				
	1980	1985	1988	1990	1995E	1980	1985	1988	1990	1995E	1980	1985	1988	1990	1995E
Methodist	4,680	4,620	4,675	4,700	4,690	25	25	25	26	26	65	65	65	65	65
Independent	3,930	4,530	5,047	5,389	6,050	12	20	26	31	37	93	108	116	123	137
Baptist	483	567	614	650	725	17	17	19	19	20	17	17	19	20	20
Pentecostal	250	300	343	380	435	8	9	12	12	13	9	10	10	10	10
Others	1,167	1,279	1,344	1,382	1,488	11	11	11	11	11	14	15	16	16	17
Total Free Church	10,610	11,296	12,023	12,501	13,388	73	82	93	99	107	198	215	226	234	249
Roman Catholic[1]	2,850,020	2,820,030	2,800,050	2,790,050	2,760,050	3,751	3,401	3,144	3,384	3,236	2,071	2,081	2,087	2,091	2,101
Presbyterian	14,818	14,142	13,719	13,438	12,757	41	44	44	44	44	112	112	112	112	112
Anglican	55,000	53,000	52,000	51,000	49,000	245	241	240	235	230	663	655	650	650	640
Orthodox	350	350	350	350	350	3	3	3	3	3	3	3	3	3	3
TOTAL	2,930,698	2,898,818	2,878,142	2,867,339	2,835,545	4,113	3,771	3,524	3,765	3,620	3,047	3,066	3,078	3,090	3,105
Percentage of population[2]	85%	82%	81%	81%	81%										

Table 1c: Total All Ireland 1980-1995

Church	Members					Ministers					Churches				
	1980	1985	1988	1990	1995E	1980	1985	1988	1990	1995E	1980	1985	1988	1990	1995E
Methodist	47,839	47,227	47,805	48,124	48,000	152	137	140	141	135	296	274	284	280	271
Independent	17,527	19,998	22,681	24,771	27,886	78	105	134	150	181	373	404	450	489	533
Baptist	8,028	8,906	9,084	9,220	9,520	101	109	116	120	129	108	112	114	115	118
Pentecostal	4,654	7,378	8,943	9,849	12,240	47	79	82	88	97	82	84	87	90	97
Others	4,216	4,054	4,053	4,189	4,498	55	59	61	61	65	65	69	69	68	70
Total Free Church	82,266	87,563	92,566	96,153	102,144	433	486	533	560	611	924	943	1,004	1,042	1,089
Roman Catholic[1]	3,223,040	3,173,049	3,142,564	3,116,060	3,067,060	4,319	3,950	3,689	3,926	3,766	2,502	2,501	2,511	2,515	2,521
Presbyterian	368,728	354,103	344,491	338,633	323,382	510	517	519	533	525	654	654	653	655	654
Anglican	221,783	212,770	207,760	205,755	201,740	575	605	580	535	540	1,125	1,095	1,100	1,125	1,105
Orthodox	447	467	478	483	502	3	3	3	3	3	3	3	3	3	3
TOTAL	3,896,262	3,827,952	3,787,859	3,757,084	3,694,828	5,840	5,561	5,324	5,557	5,445	5,208	5,196	5,271	5,340	5,372
Percentage of population[2]	78%	75%	74%	73%	72%										

[1] Mass attendance   [2] Based on figures given in Table 2

Table 2 — **Irish Population in Thousands**

The percentages represent the proportion of men in that age group

Northern Ireland	1976	%	1981	%	1986	%	1991	%	1996	%	2001	%	2006	%
0-14	442	51.5	413	51.3	397	51.3	394	51.4	392	51.2	376	51.7	357	51.5
15-19	131	50.4	146	51.9	144	51.9	129	51.9	126	51.2	129	51.9	126	52.1
20-29	205	51.3	227	51.6	253	51.9	261	52.4	247	52.5	228	52.1	229	52.7
30-44	257	50.3	274	50.0	289	49.7	306	49.2	327	49.9	350	50.3	346	49.8
45-64	304	48.1	294	47.5	295	47.9	305	48.2	320	48.9	337	48.8	362	49.0
65 or over	175	40.0	184	39.6	189	39.3	194	39.1	198	39.8	202	40.3	205	39.9
TOTAL	1,514	49.2	1,538	49.0	1,567	49.0	1,589	49.1	1,610	49.2	1,622	49.4	1,625	49.3
Republic of Ireland														
0-14	994[1]	51.2	1,044	51.3	1,025	51.3	963	51.2	861	51.5	794	51.5	754	51.5
15-19	301[1]	51.1	326	51.1	331	51.3	333	51.2	324	51.3	298	51.4	262	51.6
20-29	460[1]	50.8	522	50.7	545	50.1	546	51.0	489	51.6	494	51.6	475	51.6
30-44	533[1]	50.9	592	51.2	664	50.7	668	50.0	744	50.0	734	50.4	712	51.0
45-64	598[1]	50.1	590	49.9	592	50.0	618	50.1	691	50.2	770	49.9	848	49.4
65 or over	351[1]	45.3	369	44.8	384	43.9	395	43.2	395	42.5	395	42.4	405	42.6
TOTAL	3,237	50.2	3,443	50.2	3,541	49.4	3,523	49.7	3,504	49.9	3,485	49.9	3,456	49.9
All Ireland														
0-14	1,436	51.3	1,457	51.3	1,422	51.3	1,357	51.3	1,253	51.4	1,170	51.6	1,111	51.5
15-19	432	50.9	472	51.3	475	51.5	462	51.4	450	51.3	427	51.6	388	51.8
20-29	665	51.0	749	51.0	798	50.7	807	51.5	736	51.9	722	51.8	704	52.0
30-44	790	50.7	866	50.8	953	50.4	974	49.7	1,071	50.0	1,084	50.4	1,058	50.6
45-64	902	49.4	884	49.1	887	49.3	923	49.5	1,011	49.8	1,107	49.6	1,210	49.3
65 or over	526	43.5	553	43.1	573	42.4	589	41.8	593	41.6	597	41.7	610	41.7
TOTAL	4,751	49.9	4,981	49.8	5,108	49.3	5,112	49.5	5,114	49.7	5,107	49.7	5,081	49.7

Source: *Office of Population Censuses and Surveys* for Northern Ireland and *Central Statistics Office* for the Republic of Ireland

[1] As there was no Census in the Republic in 1976, these figures are based on a linear regression of data from the 1966, 1971, 1979 and 1981 Censuses.

Fig 1: Population change in Ireland

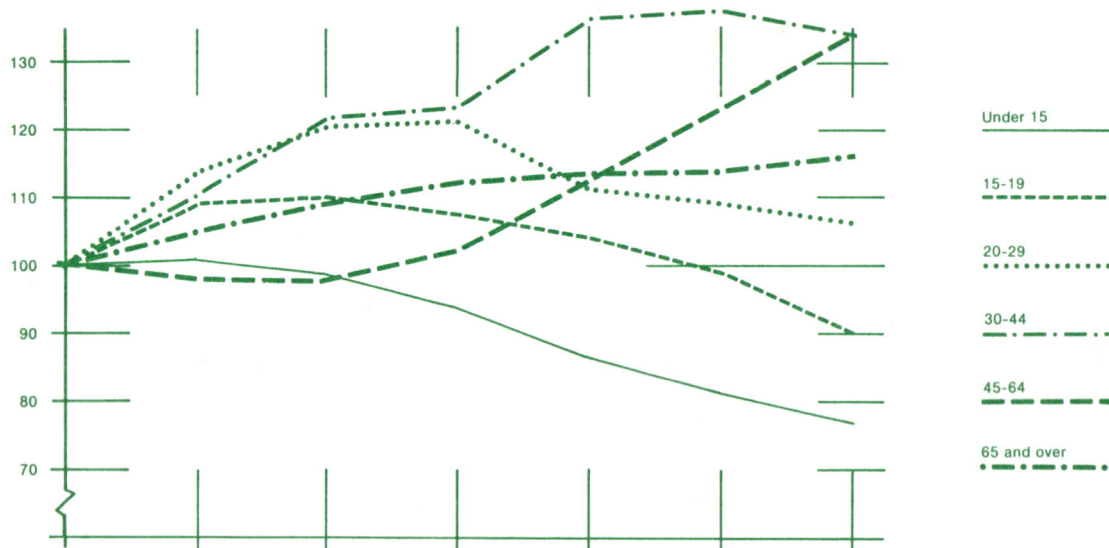

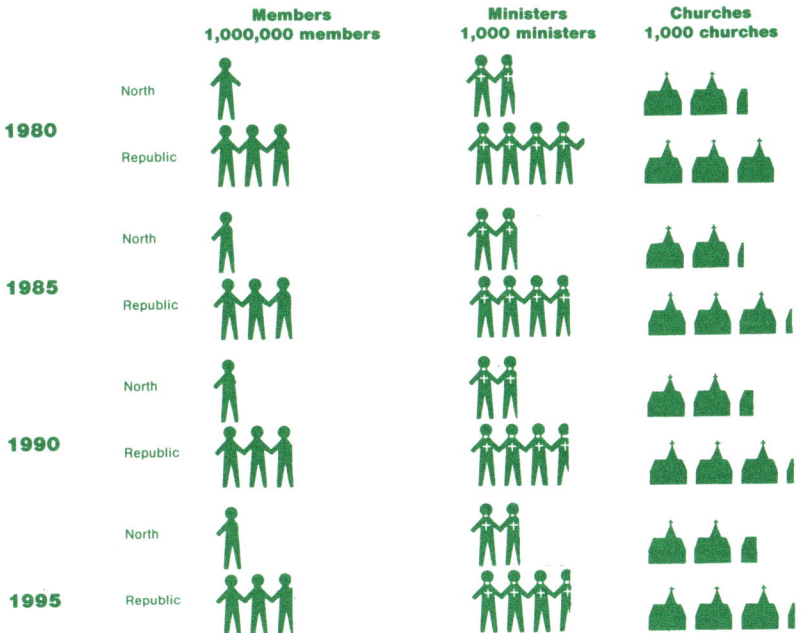

Fig 2: Members, Ministers, Churches for Northern Ireland & the Republic

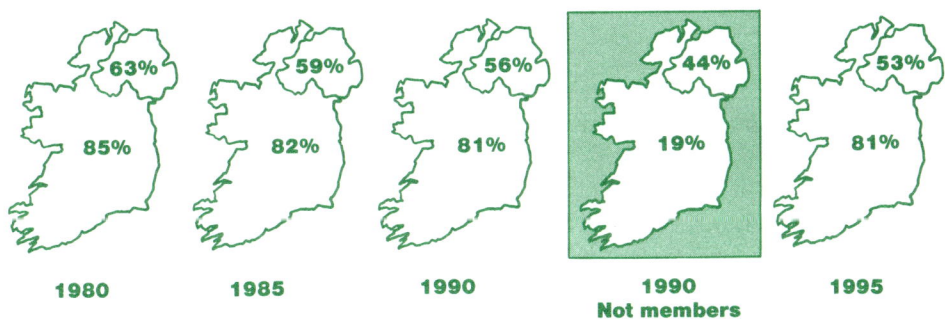

Fig 3: Proportion of population who are church members

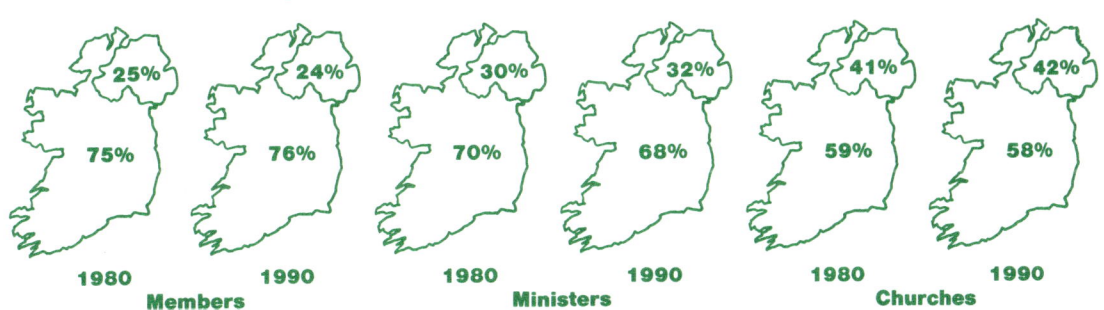

Fig 4: Proportions in the two countries 1980 and 1990

Table 3a: **Proportions of the whole church, Northern Ireland**

Church	Members				Ministers				Churches			
	1980	1985	1990	1995E	1980	1985	1990	1995E	1980	1985	1990	1995E
	%	%	%	%	%	%	%	%	%	%	%	%
Methodist	5	4	5	5	7	6	6	6	11	10	10	9
Independent	1	2	2	3	4	5	7	8	13	14	16	18
Baptist	1	1	1	1	5	5	6	6	4	4	4	4
Pentecostal	0	1	1	1	2	4	4	5	3	3	4	4
Others	0	0	0	0	3	3	3	3	3	3	2	2
Total Free Church	7	8	9	10	21	23	26	28	34	34	36	37
Roman Catholic	39	38	37	36	33	31	30	29	20	20	19	19
Presbyterian	37	37	37	36	27	26	27	26	25	25	24	24
Anglican	17	17	17	18	19	20	17	17	21	21	21	20
Orthodox	0	0	0	0	0	0	0	0	0	0	0	0
TOTAL	100	100	100	100	100	100	100	100	100	100	100	100

Table 3b: **Proportions of the whole church, Republic of Ireland**

Church	Members				Ministers				Churches			
	1980	1985	1990	1995E	1980	1985	1990	1995E	1980	1985	1990	1995E
	%	%	%	%	%	%	%	%	%	%	%	%
Methodist	0	0	0	½	½	½	1	1	2	2	2	2
Independent	0	0	0	½	½	½	1	1	3	4	4	4½
Baptist	0	0	0	0	½	½	½	½	½	½	½	1
Pentecostal	0	0	0	0	0	0	¼	¼	0	0	0	0
Others	0	0	0	0	½	½	¼	¼	½	½	½	½
Total Free Church	0	0	0	1	2	2	3	3	6	7	7	8
Roman Catholic	97	97	97	97	91	90	90	89	68	68	68	68
Presbyterian	1	1	1	0	1	1	1	1	4	4	4	4
Anglican	2	2	2	2	6	7	6	7	22	21	21	20
Orthodox	0	0	0	0	0	0	0	0	0	0	0	0
TOTAL	100	100	100	100	100	100	100	100	100	100	100	100

Table 3c: **Proportions of the whole church, All Ireland**

Church	Members				Ministers				Churches			
	1980	1985	1990	1995E	1980	1985	1990	1995E	1980	1985	1990	1995E
	%	%	%	%	%	%	%	%	%	%	%	%
Methodist	1	1	1	1	2	2	2	3	6	5	5	5
Independent	½	½	1	1	1	2	3	3	7	8	9	10
Baptist	½	½	½	½	2	2	2	2	2	2	3	3
Pentecostal	0	0	½	½	1	2	1	2	2	2	2	2
Others	0	0	0	0	1	1	1	1	1	1	1	1
Total Free Church	2	2	3	3	7	9	9	11	18	18	20	21
Roman Catholic	83	83	83	83	74	71	71	69	48	48	47	46
Presbyterian	9	9	9	9	9	9	10	10	13	13	12	12
Anglican	6	6	5	5	10	11	10	10	21	21	21	21
Orthodox	0	0	0	0	0	0	0	0	0	0	0	0
TOTAL	100	100	100	100	100	100	100	100	100	100	100	100

Table 4a: Rates of change per annum, Northern Ireland

Church	Members			Ministers			Churches		
	1980-85	1985-90	1990-1995	1980-85	1985-90	1990-1995	1980-85	1985-90	1990-1995
	%	%	%	%	%	%	%	%	%
Methodist	−0.3	+0.4	−0.1	−2.5	+0.5	−0.4	−2.0	+0.6	−0.9
Independent	+2.6	+4.6	+2.4	+5.2	+7.0	+3.9	+0.4	+4.3	+1.6
Baptist	+2.0	+0.5	+0.5	+1.8	+1.9	+1.5	+0.9	+1.8	+0.6
Pentecostal	+10.0	+6.0	+4.5	+11.4	+2.6	+2.0	+0.3	+1.6	+1.7
Others	−1.9	+0.2	+1.4	+1.8	+0.8	+1.6	+1.1	−0.8	+0.4
Total Free Church	+1.2	+1.9	+1.2	+2.3	+2.7	+1.8	+0.1	+2.3	+0.8
Roman Catholic	−1.1	−1.6	−1.2	−0.7	−0.3	−0.4	−0.5	+0.2	−0.2
Presbyterian	−0.8	−0.9	−0.9	+0.2	+0.7	−0.3	0.0	0.0	0.0
Anglican	−0.9	−0.6	−0.3	+2.0	−3.8	+0.7	−1.0	+1.5	−0.4
Orthodox	+3.8	+2.6	+2.7	–	–	–	–	–	–
OVERALL	−0.8	−0.9	−0.7	+0.7	0.0	+0.4	−0.3	+1.2	+0.2

Table 4b: Rates of change per annum, Republic of Ireland

Church	Members			Ministers			Churches		
	1980-85	1985-90	1990-1995	1980-85	1985-90	1990-1995	1980-85	1985-90	1990-1995
	%	%	%	%	%	%	%	%	%
Methodist	−0.3	+0.3	0.0	0.0	+0.8	0.0	0.0	0.0	0.0
Independent	+2.9	+3.5	+2.3	+10.8	+9.2	+3.6	+3.0	+2.6	+2.2
Baptist	+4.6	+3.7	+2.8	0.0	+2.2	+1.0	0.0	+2.2	0.0
Pentecostal	+3.7	+4.8	+2.7	+2.4	+5.9	+1.6	+2.1	0.0	0.0
Others	+1.8	+1.6	+1.5	0.0	0.0	0.0	+1.4	+1.3	+1.2
Total Free Church	+1.5	+2.1	+1.4	+2.4	+3.8	+1.6	+1.7	+1.6	+1.3
Roman Catholic	−0.2	−0.2	−0.2	−1.9	−0.1	−0.9	+0.1	+0.1	+0.1
Presbyterian	−0.9	−1.0	−1.0	+1.4	0.0	0.0	0.0	0.0	0.0
Anglican	−0.7	−0.8	−0.8	−0.3	−0.5	−0.4	−0.2	−0.2	−0.3
Orthodox	0.0	0.0	0.0	0.0	0.0	0.0	0.0	0.0	0.0
OVERALL	−0.2	−0.2	−0.2	−1.7	0.0	−0.8	+0.1	+0.1	+0.1

Table 4c: Rates of change per annum, All Ireland

Church	Members			Ministers			Churches		
	1980-85	1985-90	1990-1995	1980-85	1985-90	1990-1995	1980-85	1985-90	1990-1995
	%	%	%	%	%	%	%	%	%
Methodist	−0.3	+0.4	−0.1	−2.1	+0.6	−0.9	−1.5	+0.4	−0.7
Independent	+2.7	+4.4	+2.4	+6.1	+7.4	+3.8	+1.6	+3.9	+1.7
Baptist	+2.1	+0.7	+0.7	+1.5	+1.9	+1.5	+0.7	+1.9	+0.5
Pentecostal	+9.7	+5.9	+4.4	+10.9	+2.2	+2.0	+0.5	+1.4	+1.5
Others	−0.8	+0.7	+1.4	+1.4	+0.7	+1.3	+1.2	−0.2	+0.6
Total Free Church	+1.3	+1.9	+1.2	+2.3	+2.9	+1.8	+0.4	+2.2	+0.9
Roman Catholic	−0.3	−0.4	−0.3	−1.8	−0.1	−0.8	0.0	+0.1	0.0
Presbyterian	−0.8	−0.9	−0.9	+0.3	+0.6	−0.3	0.0	0.0	0.0
Anglican	−0.8	−0.7	−0.4	+1.0	−2.4	+0.2	−0.5	+0.5	−0.4
Orthodox	+0.1	+0.1	+0.1	0.0	0.0	0.0	0.0	0.0	0.0
OVERALL	−0.4	−0.4	−0.3	−1.0	0.0	−0.4	0.0	+0.6	+0.1

DENOMINATIONAL TABLES

Anglican Churches

Table 5a: Northern Ireland 1980-1995

Church	Members					Ministers					Churches				
	1980	1985	1988	1990	1995E	1980	1985	1988	1990	1995E	1980	1985	1988	1990	1995E
Church of England	2,503[3]	2,500[1]	2,500[1]	2,500[1]	2,500	–	–	–	–	–	–	–	–	–	–
Church of Ireland[4]	164,000[2]	157,000	153,000[1]	152,000[1]	150,000	330	364	340	300[5]	310	462	440	450	475	465
Scottish Episcopal Church	280[3]	270[1]	260[1]	255[1]	240	0	0	0	0	0	0	0	0	0	0
TOTAL	166,783	159,770	155,760	154,755	152,740	330	364	340	300	310	462	440	450	475	465

Table 5b: Republic of Ireland 1980-1995

Church	Members					Ministers					Churches				
	1980	1985	1988	1990	1995E	1980	1985	1988	1990	1995E	1980	1985	1988	1990	1995E
Church of England	–	–	–	–	–	–	–	–	–	–	–	–	–	–	–
Church of Ireland[4]	55,000[2]	53,000[1]	52,000[1]	51,000[1]	49,000	245[1]	241	240	235[1,5]	230	663[1]	655[1]	650	650[1]	640
Scottish Episcopal Church	–	–	–	–	–	–	–	–	–	–	–	–	–	–	–
TOTAL	55,000	53,000	52,000	51,000	49,000	245	241	240	235	230	663	655	650	650	640

Table 5c: Total All Ireland 1980-1995

Church	Members					Ministers					Churches				
	1980	1985	1988	1990	1995E	1980	1985	1988	1990	1995E	1980	1985	1988	1990	1995E
Church of England	2,503	2,500	2,500	2,500	2,500	–	–	–	–	–	–	–	–	–	–
Church of Ireland[4]	219,000[2]	210,000	205,000	201,000	192,000	575	605	580	535	540	1,125	1,095	1,100	1,125	1,105
Scottish Episcopal Church	280	270	260	255	240	0	0	0	0	0	0	0	0	0	0
TOTAL	221,783	212,770	207,760	205,755	201,740	575	605	580	535	540	1,125	1,095	1,100	1,125	1,105

[1] Estimate   [2] Membership is taken as about 58% of the community figure given in the Census of Population. In 1981, the latest available figure, the Census figure was 376,838   [3] Taken from the Northern Ireland Census 1981   [4] These figures relate to adult members only   [5] In addition, there are 340 Non-Stipendiary Ministers in Northern Ireland and 97 in the Republic of Ireland

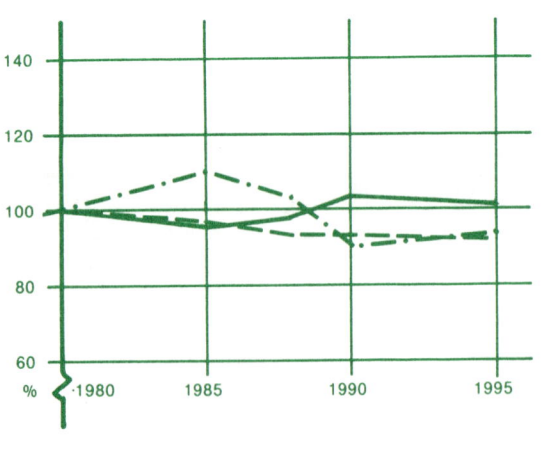

Fig 5: Proportional changes in Anglican Churches Northern Ireland 1980-1995

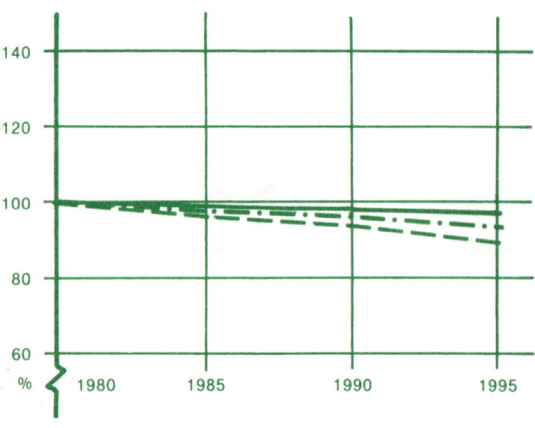

Fig 6: Proportional changes in Anglican Churches Republic of Ireland 1980-1995

——— Members   — · — · — Ministers   ———— Churches

Baptist Churches

Table 6a: Northern Ireland 1980-1995

Church	Members					Ministers					Churches				
	1980	1985	1988	1990	1995E	1980	1985	1988	1990	1995E	1980	1985	1988	1990	1995E
Baptist Union of Ireland	7,475	8,269	8,400[1]	8,500	8,725	81	89	94[1]	98	106	88	92	92	92	95
Grace Baptist Assembly	–	–	–	–	–	–	–	–	–	–	–	–	–	–	–
Other Baptist Churches[2]	70[1]	70[1]	70[1]	70[1]	70	3	3	3	3	3	3	3	3	3	3
TOTAL	7,545	8,339	8,470	8,570	8,795	84	92	97	101	109	91	95	95	95	98

Table 6b: Republic of Ireland 1980-1995

Church	Members					Ministers					Churches				
	1980	1985	1988	1990	1995E	1980	1985	1988	1990	1995E	1980	1985	1988	1990	1995E
Baptist Union of Ireland	273	352	396	430[1]	500	9[1]	9[1]	11[1]	11[1]	12	9	9	11	12	12
Grace Baptist Assembly	60[1]	65[1]	68[1]	70[1]	75	2	2	2	2	2	2	2	2	2	2
Other Baptist Churches[2]	150[1]	150[1]	150[1]	150[1]	150[1]	6	6	6	6	6	6	6	6	6	6
TOTAL	483	567	614	650	725	17	17	19	19	20	17	17	19	20	20

Table 6c: Total All Ireland 1980-1995

Church	Members					Ministers					Churches				
	1980	1985	1988	1990	1995E	1980	1985	1988	1990	1995E	1980	1985	1988	1990	1995E
Baptist Union of Ireland	7,748	8,621	8,796	8,930	9,225	90	98	105	109	118	97	101	103	104	107
Grace Baptist Assembly	60	65	68	70	75	2	2	2	2	2	2	2	2	2	2
Other Baptist Churches[2]	220	220	220	220	220	9	9	9	9	9	9	9	9	9	9
TOTAL	8,028	8,906	9,084	9,220	9,520	101	109	116	120	129	108	112	114	115	128

[1] Estimate [2] Including Independent Baptists such as Calvary Bible, Galway Bay, Lifegate in Templeogue, Raheray Fellowship, Victory Baptist in Dublin, and the Westside Baptist Fellowship churches

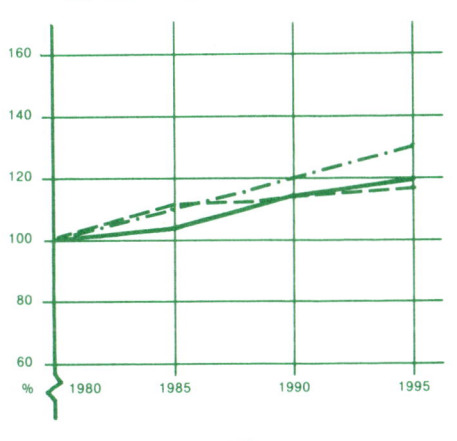

Fig 7: Proportional changes in Baptist Churches Northern Ireland 1980-1995

Fig 8: Proportional changes in Baptist Churches Republic of Ireland 1980-1995

Roman Catholic Churches

Table 7a: Northern Ireland 1980-1995

Church	Mass Attendance					Ministers					Churches				
	1980	1985	1988	1990	1995E	1980	1985	1988	1990	1995E	1980	1985	1988	1990	1995E
Church in Northern Ireland	373,000[2]	353,000[1]	342,500[3]	326,000[1]	307,000	568	549	545	542	530	431	420	424	424	420
Croatian	12[1]	12	6[1]	0	0	0	0	0	0	0	0	0	0	0	0
Hungarian	8	7	8	10	10	0	0	0	0	0	0	0	0	0	0
Tridentine	–	–	–	–	–	–	–	–	–	–	–	–	–	–	–
TOTAL	373,020	353,019	342,514	326,010	307,010	568	549	545	542	530	431	420	424	424	420

Table 7b: Republic of Ireland 1980-1995

Church	Mass Attendance					Ministers					Churches				
	1980	1985	1988	1990	1995E	1980	1985	1988	1990	1995E	1980	1985	1988	1990	1995E
Church in Republic of Ireland	2,850,000[2]	2,820,000[1]	2,800,000[3]	2,790,000[1]	2,760,000	3,750[1]	3,400[1]	3,143	3,383	3,235	2,070[1]	2,080[1]	2,086	2,090[1]	2,100
Croatian	–	–	–	–	–	–	–	–	–	–	–	–	–	–	–
Hungarian	–	–	–	–	–	–	–	–	–	–	–	–	–	–	–
Tridentine[4]	20[1]	30	50	50[1]	50[1]	1	1	1	1	1	1	1	1	1	1
TOTAL	2,850,020	2,820,030	2,800,050	2,790,050	2,760,050	3,751	3,401	3,144	3,384	3,236	2,071	2,081	2,087	2,091	2,101

Table 7c: Total All Ireland 1980-1995

Church	Mass Attendance					Ministers					Churches				
	1980	1985	1988	1990	1995E	1980	1985	1988	1990	1995E	1980	1985	1988	1990	1995E
Church in Ireland	3,223,000	3,173,000	3,142,500	3,116,000	3,067,000	4,318	3,949	3,688	3,925	3,765	2,501	2,500	2,510	2,514	2,520
Croatian	12	12	6	0	0	0	0	0	0	0	0	0	0	0	0
Hungarian	8	7	8	10	10	0	0	0	0	0	0	0	0	0	0
Tridentine	20	30	50	50	50	1	1	1	1	1	1	1	1	1	1
TOTAL	3,223,040	3,173,049	3,142,564	3,116,060	3,067,060	4,319	3,950	3,689	3,926	3,766	2,502	2,501	2,511	2,515	2,521

[1] Estimate [2] Mass Attendance taken as 89% of Catholic population [3] Mass Attendance taken as 87% of Catholic population
[4] St John's, Mount town

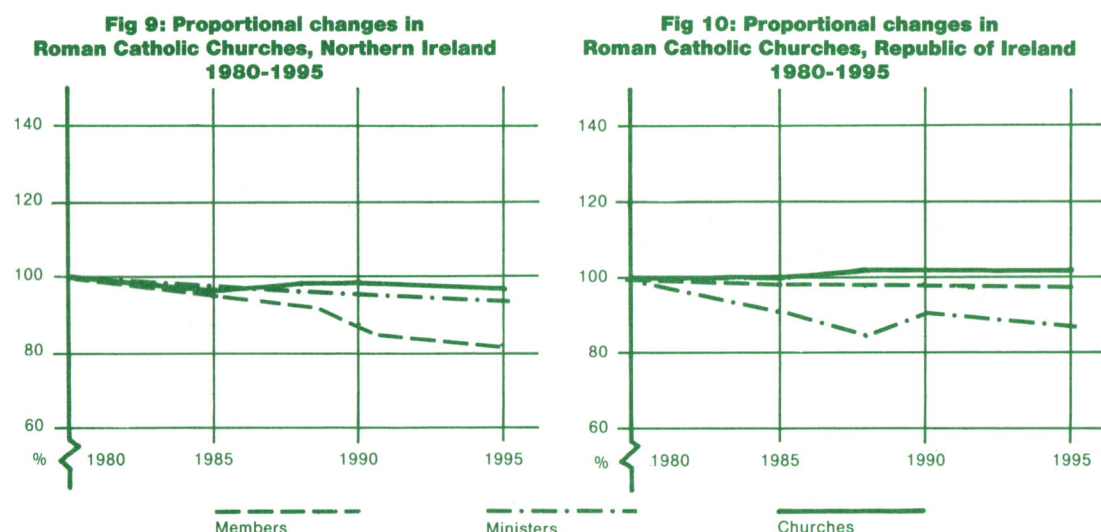

Fig 9: Proportional changes in Roman Catholic Churches, Northern Ireland 1980-1995

Fig 10: Proportional changes in Roman Catholic Churches, Republic of Ireland 1980-1995

Members — — —   Ministers — · — ·   Churches ———

Independent Churches

Table 8a: Northern Ireland 1980-1995

Church	Members					Ministers					Churches				
	1980	1985	1988	1990	1995E	1980	1985	1988	1990	1995E	1980	1985	1988	1990	1995E
Christian Brethren	7,000[1]	6,800[1]	6,400[1]	6,200[2]	5,850	22[1]	22[1]	19[1]	16[2]	14	180	179	180	181	181
Plymouth Brethren No. 4	1,000[1]	1,000[1]	1,000[1]	1,000[1]	1,000	—	—	—	—	—	30[1]	30[1]	30[1]	30[1]	30
Church of Christ	363[5]	350[1]	350[1]	350[1]	350	3	3	3	3	3	7	7	7	7	7
Fellowship of Independent Evangelical Churches	60[1]	135[1]	145[1]	150[1]	200	1	1	2	2	3	2	2	2	2	3
Evangelical Fellowship of Congregational Churches	1,218	1,110[1]	1,045[1]	1,000[1]	900	8	8	8	7	7	9	8	8	9	8
Congregational Union of Ireland	2,940[3]	2,917[3]	3,048[3]	3,136[3]	3,190	21	25	26	26	29	24	22	25	25	25
House Church Movement	500[1]	2,500[1]	4,500[1]	6,000[1]	8,400	5[1]	20[1]	40[1]	50[1]	70	10[1]	25[1]	45[1]	60[1]	80
Other Non-Denominational Churches[4]	450[1]	600[1]	1,100[1]	1,500[1]	1,900	5[1]	5[1]	10[1]	15[1]	18	15[1]	20[1]	35[1]	50[1]	60
Cooneyites[5]	26[5]	26[1]	26[1]	26[1]	26	—	—	—	—	—	1[1]	1[1]	1[1]	1[1]	1[1]
Reidites	20[1]	20[1]	20[1]	20[1]	20	—	—	—	—	—	1[1]	1[1]	1[1]	1[1]	1[1]
Liberal Catholic	20	10	0	0	0	1	1	0	0	0	1	1	0	0	0
TOTAL	13,597	15,468	17,634	19,382	21,836	66	85	108	119	144	280	296	334	366	396

Table 8b: Republic of Ireland 1980-1995

Church	Members					Ministers					Churches				
	1980	1985	1988	1990	1995E	1980	1985	1988	1990	1995E	1980	1985	1988	1990	1995E
Christian Brethren	630[1]	770[1]	875[1]	950[1]	1,100	2[1]	2[1]	3[1]	3[1]	4	18	22[1]	25[1]	27	31
Plymouth Brethren No. 4	200[1]	200[1]	200[1]	200[1]	200	—	—	—	—	—	5[1]	5[1]	5[1]	5[1]	5
Church of Christ	40[1]	40[1]	40[1]	40[1]	40	—	—	—	—	—	2[1]	2[1]	2[1]	2[1]	1
Fellowship of Independent Evangelical Churches	0	10[1]	20[1]	35[1]	45	0	1	1	1	1	0	1	1	1	1
Evangelical Fellowship of Congregational Churches	—	—	—	—	—	—	—	—	—	—	—	—	—	—	—
Congregational Union of Ireland	60[3]	60[3]	62[3]	64[3]	65	2	2	2	2	2	2	2	2	2	2
House Church Movement	150[1]	600[1]	1,000[1]	1,250[1]	1,750	3[1]	10[1]	15[1]	20[1]	25	5[1]	15[1]	20[1]	25[1]	35
Other Non-Denominational Churches[4]	300[1]	300[1]	300[1]	300[1]	300	5[1]	5[1]	5[1]	5[1]	5	10[1]	10[1]	10[1]	10[1]	10
Cooneyites[5]	2,500[1]	2,500[1]	2,500[1]	2,500[1]	2,500	—	—	—	—	—	50[1]	50[1]	50[1]	50[1]	50
Reidites	50[1]	50[1]	50[1]	50[1]	50	—	—	—	—	—	1[1]	1[1]	1[1]	1[1]	1[1]
Liberal Catholic	—	—	—	—	—	—	—	—	—	—	—	—	—	—	—
TOTAL	3,930	4,530	5,047	5,389	6,050	12	20	26	31	37	93	108	116	123	137

Independent Churches

Table 8c: Total All Ireland 1980-1995

Church	Members					Ministers					Churches				
	1980	1985	1988	1990	1995E	1980	1985	1988	1990	1995E	1980	1985	1988	1990	1995E
Christian Brethren	7,630	7,570	7,275	7,150	6,950	24	24	22	19	18	198	201	205	208	212
Plymouth Brethren No. 4	1,200	1,200	1,200	1,200	1,200	—	—	—	—	—	35	35	35	35	35
Church of Christ	403	390	390	390	390	3	3	3	3	3	9	9	9	9	9
Fellowship of Independent Evangelical Churches	60	145	165	185	245	1	2	3	3	4	2	3	3	3	4
Evangelical Fellowship of Congregational Churches	1,218	1,110	1,045	1,000	900	8	8	8	7	7	9	8	8	9	8
Congregational Union of Ireland	3,000[1]	2,977	3,110[1]	3,200	3,255	23	27	28	28	31	26	24	27	27	27
House Church Movement	650	3,100	5,500	7,250	10,150	8	30	55	70	95	15	40	65	85	115
Other Non-Denominational Churches[4]	750	900	1,400	1,800	2,200	10	10	15	20	23	25	30	45	60	70
Cooneyites[5]	2,526	2,526	2,526	2,526	2,526	—	—	—	—	—	51	51	51	51	51
Reidites	70	70	70	70	70	—	—	—	—	—	2	2	2	2	2
Liberal Catholic	20	10	0	0	0	1	1	0	0	0	1	1	0	0	0
TOTAL	17,527	19,998	22,681	24,771	27,886	78	105	134	150	181	373	404	450	489	533

[1] Estimate [2] Figures based on paper by Neil Summerton "The Christian (Open) Brethren in the British Isles in numerical context"
[3] Approximately 98% of the membership live in Northern Ireland [4] Including Churches of God and other Independent Churches
[5] Taken from the Northern Ireland Census 1981

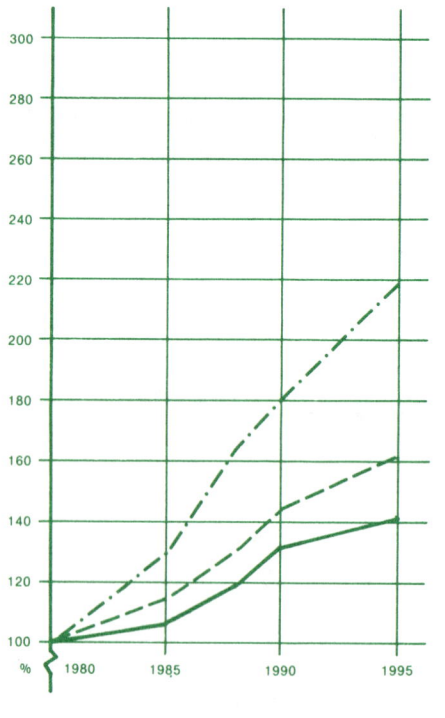

Fig 11: Proportional changes in Independent Churches, Northern Ireland 1980-1995

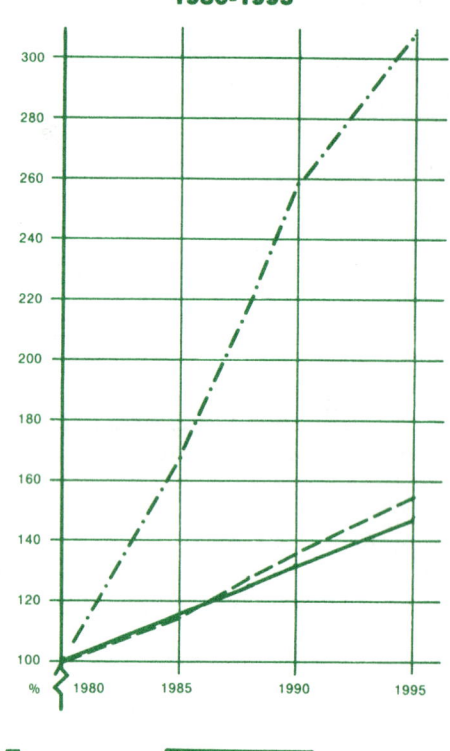

Fig 12: Proportional changes in Independent Churches, Republic of Ireland 1980-1995

——— Members   —·—·— Ministers   ——— Churches

Methodist Churches

Table 9a: Northern Ireland 1980-1995

Church	Members					Ministers					Churches				
	1980	1985	1988	1990	1995E	1980	1985	1988	1990	1995E	1980	1985	1988	1990	1995E
Methodist Church in Ireland	42,847[2]	42,280[2]	42,775[2]	43,050[2]	42,910	117[2]	103[2]	105[2]	105[2]	99	218[2]	196[2]	205[2]	201[2]	191
Free Methodist Church	212	227	255[1]	274	300	5	4	5	5	5	7	7	8	8	9
Independent Methodist	100[1]	100[1]	100[1]	100[1]	100	5[1]	5[1]	5[1]	5[1]	5	6[1]	6[1]	6[1]	6[1]	6
TOTAL	43,159	42,607	43,130	43,424	43,310	127	112	115	115	109	231	209	219	215	206

Table 9b: Republic of Ireland 1980-1995

Church	Members					Ministers					Churches				
	1980	1985	1988	1990	1995E	1980	1985	1988	1990	1995E	1980	1985	1988	1990	1995E
Methodist Church in Ireland	4,680[2]	4,620[2]	4,675[2]	4,700[2]	4,690	25[2]	25[2]	25[2]	26[2]	26	65[2]	65[2]	65[2]	65[2]	65
Free Methodist Church	—	—	—	—	—	—	—	—	—	—	—	—	—	—	—
Independent Methodist	—	—	—	—	—	—	—	—	—	—	—	—	—	—	—
TOTAL	4,680	4,620	4,675	4,700	4,690	25	25	25	26	26	65	65	65	65	65

Table 9c: Total All Ireland 1980-1995

Church	Members					Ministers					Churches				
	1980	1985	1988	1990	1995E	1980	1985	1988	1990	1995E	1980	1985	1988	1990	1995E
Methodist Church in Ireland	47,527	46,900	47,450[1]	47,750	47,600	142	128	130	131	125	283	261	270	266	256
Free Methodist Church	212	227	255	274	300	5	4	5	5	5	7	7	8	8	9
Independent Methodist	100	100	100	100	100	5	5	5	5	5	6	6	6	6	6
TOTAL	47,839	47,227	47,805	48,124	48,000	152	137	140	141	135	296	274	284	280	271

[1] Estimate [2] Estimated from a breakdown of circuits in the conference minutes

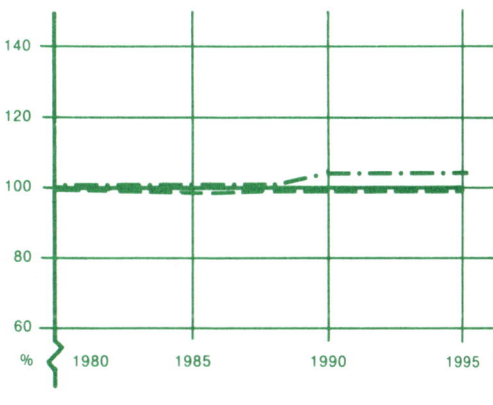

Fig 13: Proportional changes in Methodist Churches, Northern Ireland 1980-1995

Fig 14: Proportional changes in Methodist Churches, Republic of Ireland 1980-1995

Orthodox Churches

Table 10a: Northern Ireland 1980-1995

Church	Members					Ministers					Churches				
	1980	1985	1988	1990	1995E	1980	1985	1988	1990	1995E	1980	1985	1988	1990	1995E
Antiochan	5[1]	5[1]	8[1]	10[1]	0	0	0	0	0	0	0	0	0	0	0
Coptic	50[1]	50[1]	50[1]	50[1]	12	0	0	0	0	0	0	0	0	0	0
Greek Orthodox	42	47[1]	50[1]	50[1]	55	0	0	0	0	0	0	0	0	0	0
Indian (Syrian)	0	15[1]	20[1]	23	35	0	0	0	0	0	0	0	0	0	0
Russian (Moscow)	—	—	—	—	—	—	—	—	—	—	—	—	—	—	—
Russian Outside Russia	—	—	—	—	—	—	—	—	—	—	—	—	—	—	—
TOTAL	97	117	128	133	152	0	0	0	0	0	0	0	0	0	0

[1] Estimate

Table 10b: Republic of Ireland 1980-1995

Church	Members					Ministers					Churches				
	1980	1985	1988	1990	1995E	1980	1985	1988	1990	1995E	1980	1985	1988	1990	1995E
Antiochan	—	—	—	—	—	—	—	—	—	—	—	—	—	—	—
Coptic	—	—	—	—	—	—	—	—	—	—	—	—	—	—	—
Greek Orthodox	150[1]	150[1]	150[1]	150[1]	150	1	1	1	1	1	1	1	1	1	1
Indian (Syrian)	—	—	—	—	—	—	—	—	—	—	—	—	—	—	—
Russian (Moscow)	100[1]	100[1]	100[1]	100[1]	100	1	1	1	1	1	1	1	1	1	1
Russian Outside Russia	100[1]	100[1]	100[1]	100[1]	100	1	1	1	1	1	1	1	1	1	1
TOTAL	350	350	350	350	350	3	3	3	3	3	3	3	3	3	3

[1] Estimate

Table 10c: Total All Ireland 1980-1995

Church	Members					Ministers					Churches				
	1980	1985	1988	1990	1995E	1980	1985	1988	1990	1995E	1980	1985	1988	1990	1995E
Antiochan	5	5	8	10	12	0	0	0	0	0	0	0	0	0	0
Coptic	50	50	50	50	50	0	0	0	0	0	0	0	0	0	0
Greek Orthodox	192	197	200	200	205	1	1	1	1	1	1	1	1	1	1
Indian (Syrian)	0	15	20	23	35	0	0	0	0	0	0	0	0	0	0
Russian (Moscow)	100	100	100	100	100	1	1	1	1	1	1	1	1	1	1
Russian Outside Russia	100	100	100	100	100	1	1	1	1	1	1	1	1	1	1
TOTAL	447	467	478	483	502	3	3	3	3	3	3	3	3	3	3

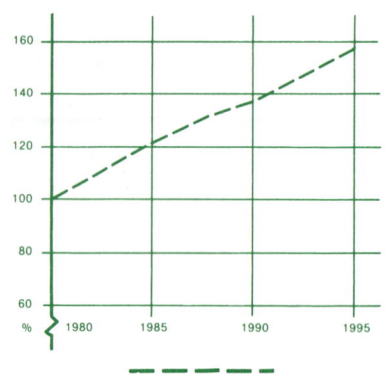

Fig 15: Proportional changes in Orthodox Churches, Northern Ireland 1980-1995

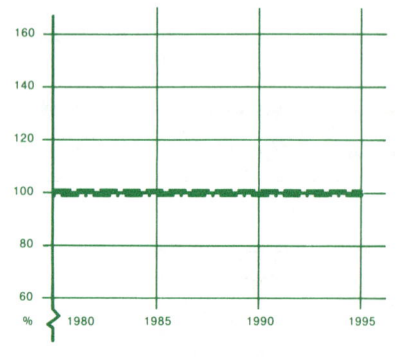

Fig 16: Proportional changes in Orthodox Churches, Republic of Ireland 1980-1995

— — — — Members   — · — · — Ministers   ———— Churches

Pentecostal/Holiness Churches

Table 11a: Northern Ireland 1980-1995

Church	Members					Ministers					Churches				
	1980	1985	1988	1990	1995E	1980	1985	1988	1990	1995E	1980	1985	1988	1990	1995E
Apostolic Church	381	398	420[1]	441	465	4	5	4	6	6	14	14	13	11	11
Assemblies of God	700	700	760[1]	800	875	9	8	10	12	14	8	7	8	10	12
Elim Pentecostal Church	2,800	5,400	6,750[1]	7,500	9,650	17	50	52	54	58	41	42	45	48	52
Church of the Nazarene	523	580	670[1]	728	815	9	4	4	4	6	10	11	11	11	12
Other Pentecostal Churches[2,3]	250	250	250	250	250	5	5	5	5	5	8	8	8	8	8
TOTAL	4,654	7,328	8,850	9,719	12,055	44	72	75	81	89	81	82	85	88	95

Table 11b: Republic of Ireland 1980-1995

Church	Members					Ministers					Churches				
	1980	1985	1988	1990	1995E	1980	1985	1988	1990	1995E	1980	1985	1988	1990	1995E
Apostolic Church	0	10[1]	20[1]	35[1]	45	0	1	2	2	2	0	1	1	1	1
Assemblies of God	50[1]	55[1]	58[1]	60[1]	65	1	1	1	1	1	1	1	1	1	1
Elim Pentecostal Church	150[1]	175[1]	200[1]	215[1]	245	5	5	7	7	8	6	6	6	6	6
Church of the Nazarene	50[1]	60[1]	65[1]	70[1]	80	2[1]	2[1]	2[1]	2[1]	2	2	2	2	2	2
Other Pentecostal Churches[2,3]	20	20	20	20	20	0	0	0	0	0	1	1	1	1	1
TOTAL	270	320	363	400	455	8	9	12	12	13	10	11	11	11	11

Table 11c: Total All Ireland 1980-1995

Church	Members					Ministers					Churches				
	1980	1985	1988	1990	1995E	1980	1985	1988	1990	1995E	1980	1985	1988	1990	1995E
Apostolic Church	381	408	440	476	510	4	6	6	8	8	14	15	14	12	12
Assemblies of God	750	755	818	860	940	10	9	11	13	15	9	8	9	11	13
Elim Pentecostal Church	2,950	5,575	6,950	7,715	9,895	22	55	59	61	66	47	48	51	54	58
Church of the Nazarene	573	640	735	798	895	11	6	6	6	8	12	13	13	13	14
Other Pentecostal Churches[2,3]	270	270	270	270	270	5	5	5	5	5	9	9	9	9	9
TOTAL	4,924	7,648	9,213	10,119	12,510	52	81	87	93	102	91	93	96	99	106

[1] Estimate [2] Including Churches of God, Emmanuel Mission, Free Church of God and Others
[3] Estimated from the Northern Ireland Census 1981

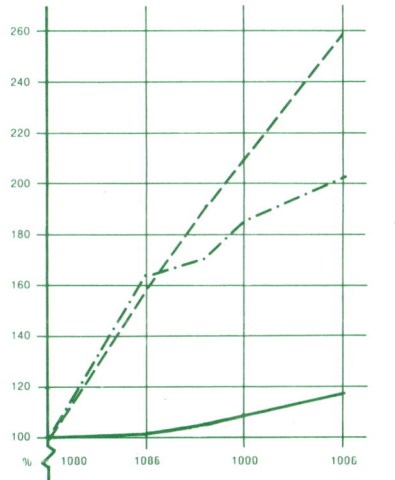

Fig 17: Proportional changes in Pentecostal/Holiness Churches, Northern Ireland 1980-1995

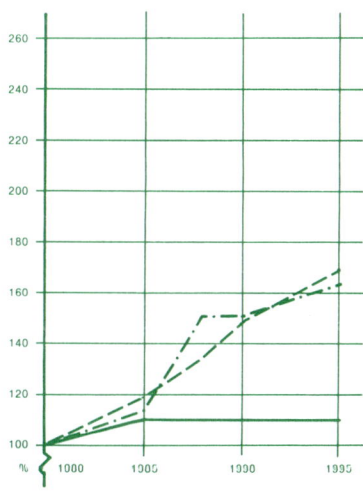

Fig 18: Proportional changes in Pentecostal/Holiness Churches, Republic of Ireland 1980-1995

Presbyterian Churches

Table 12a: Northern Ireland 1980-1995

Church	Members					Ministers					Churches				
	1980	1985	1988	1990	1995E	1980	1985	1988	1990	1995E	1980	1985	1988	1990	1995E
The Presbyterian Church in Ireland[3]	340,110[1]	323,690[1]	313,835[1]	307,269[2]	290,840	397	386	389	398	385	461	458	456	456	453
Reformed Presbyterian Church in Ireland	3,600[1]	4,500	4,500	4,500	5,000	29	30	31	32	33	36	36	36	36	36
Free Presbyterian Church of Ulster	9,700	11,319	12,000[1]	13,000[1]	14,400	35	47	48[1]	50[1]	55	35	37	38[1]	40[1]	42
Evangelical Presbyterian Church of Ireland	500[1]	452[1]	437[1]	426	385	8	10	7	9	8	10	11	11	11	11
TOTAL	353,910	339,961	330,772	325,195	310,625	469	473	475	489	481	542	542	541	543	542

Table 12b: Republic of Ireland 1980-1995

Church	Members					Ministers					Churches				
	1980	1985	1988	1990	1995E	1980	1985	1988	1990	1995E	1980	1985	1988	1990	1995E
The Presbyterian Church in Ireland[2,3]	14,658[1]	13,950[1]	13,525[1]	13,243	12,540	37	40	40	40	40	108	108	108	108	108
Reformed Presbyterian Church in Ireland	110	140[1]	140[1]	140[1]	160	2	2	2	2	2	2	2	2	2	2
Free Presbyterian Church of Ulster	10[1]	12[1]	14[1]	15	17	1	1	1	1	1	1	1	1	1	1
Evangelical Presbyterian Church of Ireland	40[1]	40[1]	40[1]	40[1]	40	1	1	1	1	1	1	1	1	1	1
TOTAL	14,818	14,142	13,719	13,438	12,757	41	44	44	44	44	112	112	112	112	112

Table 12c: Total All Ireland 1980-1995

Church	Members					Ministers					Churches				
	1980	1985	1988	1990	1995E	1980	1985	1988	1990	1995E	1980	1985	1988	1990	1995E
The Presbyterian Church in Ireland[3]	354,768	337,640[1]	327,360[1]	320,512	303,380	434	426	429	438	425	569	566	564	564	561
Reformed Presbyterian Church in Ireland	3,710	4,640	4,640	4,640	5,160	31	32	33	34	35	38	38	38	38	38
Free Presbyterian Church of Ulster	9,710	11,331	12,014	13,015	14,417	36	48	49	51	56	36	38	39	41	43
Evangelical Presbyterian Church of Ireland	540	492	477	466	425	9	11	8	10	9	11	12	12	12	12
TOTAL	368,728	354,103	344,491	338,633	323,382	510	517	519	533	525	654	654	653	655	654

[1] Estimate   [2] Approximately 4% of membership lives in Irish Republic   [3] These figures relate to adult members only
For diagrams illustrating these tables please see Page 40.

Other Protestant Churches

Table 13a: Northern Ireland 1980-1995

Church	Members					Ministers					Churches				
	1980	1985	1988	1990	1995E	1980	1985	1988	1990	1995E	1980	1985	1988	1990	1995E
Chinese	30[1]	40[1]	45[1]	50[1]	60	1	1	1	1	1	1	1	1	1	1
Church of God	1,284[3]	1,300[1]	1,300[1]	1,300[1]	1,300	20	20	20	20	20	10	10	10	10	10
Lutheran	70[2]	70	70	70	70	1	1	1	1	1	1	1	1	1	1
Mennonites	—	—	—	—	—	—	—	—	—	—	—	—	—	—	—
Moravian Church in Great Britain	358	362	389	384	400	4	4	4	3	4	5	5	5	5	5
Religious Society of Friends	764[3]	845[1]	890[1]	924[4]	1,000	—	—	—	—	—	15	15	15	15	15
Salvation Army	1,663	1,200[1]	1,050[1]	1,110	1,200	35	35[1]	36[1]	36	37	24	24	22[1]	20	19
Seventh-Day Adventists	164[5]	258[5]	265[5]	269[5]	280	3	7	8	9	11	5	8	9	10	12
Others[7,8]	250	250	250	250	250	4	4	4	4	4	7	7	7	7	7
TOTAL	4,583	4,325	4,259	4,357	4,560	68	72	74	74	78	68	71	70	69	70

Table 13b: Republic of Ireland 1980-1995

Church	Members					Ministers					Churches				
	1980	1985	1988	1990	1995E	1980	1985	1988	1990	1995E	1980	1985	1988	1990	1995E
Chinese	30[1]	40[1]	45[1]	50[1]	60	1	1	1	1	1	1	1	1	1	1
Church of God	—	—	—	—	—	—	—	—	—	—	—	—	—	—	—
Lutheran	415[2]	460[1]	485[1]	500[1]	545	3[1]	3[1]	3[1]	3[1]	3	3	3	3	3	3
Mennonites	6	10	10	10[1]	12	—	—	—	—	—	1	1	1	1	1
Moravian Church in Great Britain	—	—	—	—	—	—	—	—	—	—	—	—	—	—	—
Religious Society of Friends	642[6]	685[1]	715[1]	732[4]	775	—	—	—	—	—	8	9[1]	10	10	11
Salvation Army	56	55	60	60[1]	65	7	7	7	7	7	1	1	1	1	1
Seventh-Day Adventists	18[5]	29[5]	29[5]	30[5]	31	—	—	—	—	—	1	1	1	1	1
Others[7,8]	20	20	20	20	20	—	—	—	—	—	—	—	—	—	—
TOTAL	1,187	1,299	1,364	1,402	1,508	11	11	11	11	11	15	16	17	17	18

Table 13c: Total All Ireland 1980-1995

Church	Members					Ministers					Churches				
	1980	1985	1988	1990	1995E	1980	1985	1988	1990	1995E	1980	1985	1988	1990	1995E
Chinese	60	80	90	100	120	2	2	2	2	2	2	2	2	2	2
Church of God	1,284	1,300	1,300	1,300	1,300	20	20	20	20	20	10	10	10	10	10
Lutheran	485	530	555	570	615	4	4	4	4	4	4	4	4	4	4
Mennonites	6	10	10	10	12	—	—	—	—	—	1	1	1	1	1
Moravian Church in Great Britain	358	362	389	384	400	4	4	4	3	4	5	5	5	5	5
Religious Society of Friends	1,406	1,530	1,605	1,656	1,775	—	—	—	—	—	23	24	25	25	26
Salvation Army	1,719	1,255	1,110	1,170	1,265	42	42	43	43	44	25	25	23	21	20
Seventh-Day Adventists	182[1]	287	294[1]	299	311	3	7	8	9	11	6	9	10	11	13
Others[7,8]	270	270	270	270	270	4	4	4	4	4	7	7	7	7	7
TOTAL	5,770	5,624	5,623	5,759	6,068	79	83	85	85	89	83	87	87	86	88

[1] Estimate [2] Active membership taken as half the community [3] Taken from the Northern Ireland Census 1981
[4] Taken from Religious Society of Friends' Book of Meetings 1991 [5] Republic of Ireland estimated at 10% of total adult membership
[6] Taken from Census of Population of Ireland 1981 [7] Estimated from Population Census 1981
[8] Includes Bible Pattern Church, Faith Mission, New Life Community Church, Presbyterian Apostolic, United Church of Canada and Others

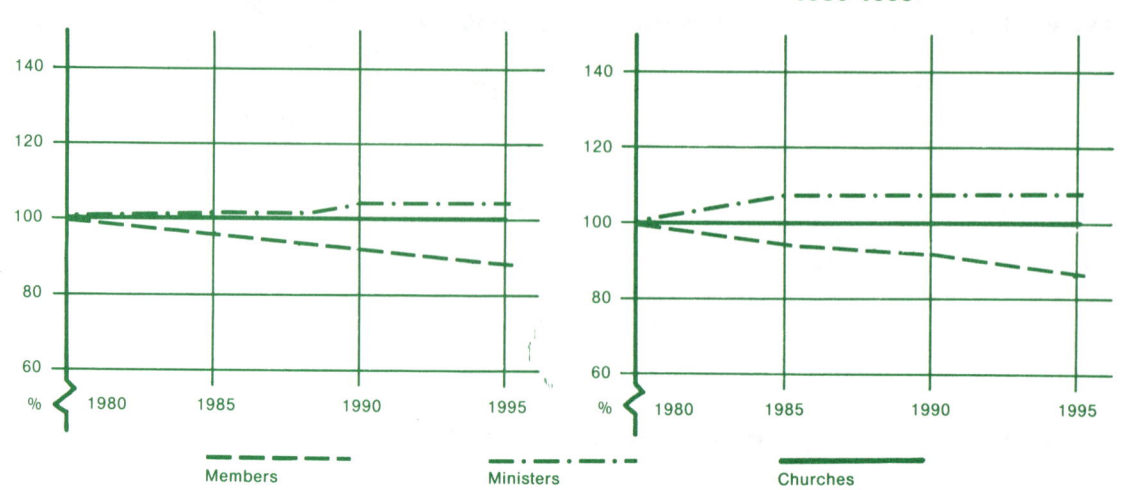
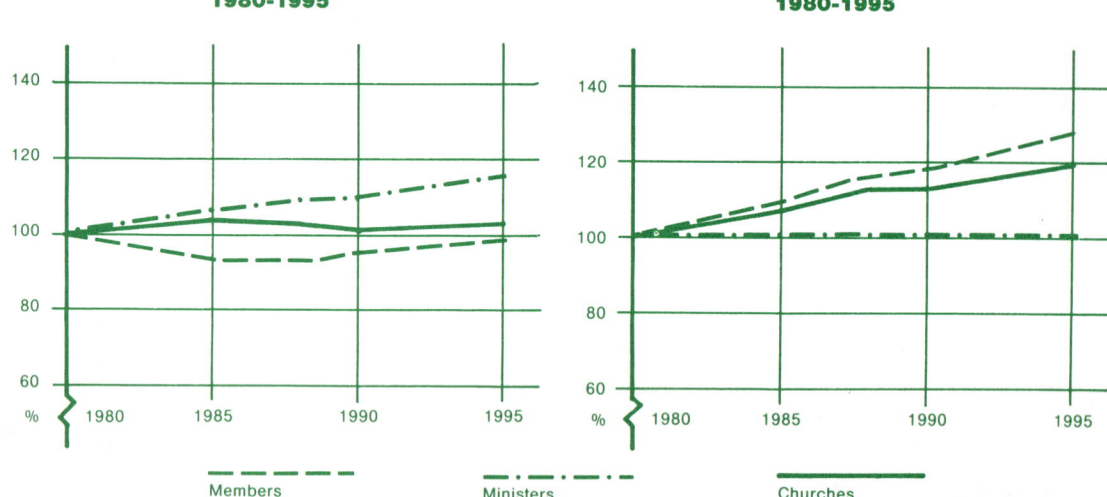

OTHER CHURCHES AND RELIGIONS TABLES

Non-Trinitarian Churches

Table 14a: Northern Ireland 1980-1995

Church	Active Members					Ministers					Churches				
	1980	1985	1988	1990	1995E	1980	1985	1988	1990	1995E	1980	1985	1988	1990	1995E
Children of God	—	—	—	—	—	—	—	—	—	—	—	—	—	—	—
Christadelphians	60[8]	70[1]	70[1]	70[1]	75	—	—	—	—	—	1	1	1	1	1
Church of Christ Scientist	200[6]	200	200	200	200	—	—	—	—	—	3	3	3	3	3
Jehovah's Witnesses	920[4]	1,200[1]	1,900[1]	2,600[1]	3,150	109	120[1]	215[1]	280[1]	335	27	27	28[1]	29	30
Church of Jesus Christ of Latter-Day Saints (Mormons)	3,746[5]	4,500[1]	6,300[1]	7,500[1]	8,955	220	300[1]	420[1]	500[1]	600	8	10[1]	15[1]	20[1]	24
Non-Subscribing Presbyterian Church[2]	4,274[3]	4,085	4,010[1]	4,050	3,900	13	16	17	16	19	32	32	32	32	32
Church of Scientology	250[1]	500[1]	800[1]	1,000	1,300	25[1]	35[1]	45[1]	50	60	1	1	1	1	1
Spiritualists	200[1,7]	250[1]	300[1]	350[1]	400	10	10	10	10	10	5[1]	5[1]	5[1]	5[1]	5
Theosophists	43	49	50	50	55	—	—	—	—	—	1	1	1	1	1
Unification Church (Moonies)	27[8]	30[1]	32[1]	35[1]	40	0	0	0	0	0	1[1]	1[1]	1[1]	1[1]	1
Unitarian and Free Christian Churches	200[1]	200[1]	200[1]	200[1]	200	5[1]	5[1]	5[1]	5[1]	5	4[1]	4[1]	4[1]	4[1]	4[1]
The Way	25[1]	25[1]	25[1]	25[1]	25	0	0	0	0	0	2	2	2	2	2
Worldwide Church of God	200	245[1]	270[1]	290	330	1	1	1	1	1	3	3	3	3	3
Others	300[1]	300[1]	300[1]	300[1]	300	10[1]	10[1]	10[1]	10[1]	10	5[1]	5[1]	5[1]	5[1]	5
TOTAL	10,445	11,654	14,457	16,670	18,930	393	497	723	872	1,040	93	95	101	107	112

Table 14b: Republic of Ireland 1980-1995

Church	Active Members					Ministers					Churches				
	1980	1985	1988	1990	1995E	1980	1985	1988	1990	1995E	1980	1985	1988	1990	1995E
Children of God	25[1]	25[1]	25[1]	25[1]	25	1[1]	1[1]	1[1]	1[1]	1	1	1	1	1	1
Christadelphians	30[1]	35[1]	35[1]	35[1]	40	—	—	—	—	—	1[1]	1[1]	1[1]	1[1]	1
Church of Christ Scientist	150[1]	150[1]	150[1]	150[1]	150	—	—	—	—	—	3	3	3	3	3
Jehovah's Witnesses	700[1]	850[1]	1,300[1]	1,800[1]	2,100	85[1]	95[1]	160[1]	210[1]	250	21	21[1]	21[1]	21[1]	21
Church of Jesus Christ of Latter-Day Saints (Mormons)	1,000[1]	1,200[1]	1,300[1]	1,400[1]	1,600	300[1]	400[1]	500[1]	600[1]	700	22	25[1]	28[1]	30[1]	34
Non-Subscribing Presbyterian Church	100	125	130	200	215	2	2	2	2	2	2	2	2	2	2
Church of Scientology	—	—	—	—	—	—	—	—	—	—	—	—	—	—	—
Spiritualists	—	—	—	—	—	—	—	—	—	—	—	—	—	—	—
Theosophists	—	—	—	—	—	—	—	—	—	—	—	—	—	—	—
Unification Church (Moonies)	25	25[1]	25[1]	25[1]	25	1	1	1	1	1	1	1	1	1	1
Unitarian and Free Christian Churches	30[1]	30[1]	30[1]	30[1]	30	1[1]	1[1]	1[1]	1[1]	1	1	1	1	1	1
The Way	25[1]	35[1]	45[1]	50[1]	60	0	0	0	0	0	1[1]	1[1]	1[1]	1[1]	1
Worldwide Church of God	—	—	—	—	—	—	—	—	—	—	—	—	—	—	—
Others	—	—	—	—	—	—	—	—	—	—	—	—	—	—	—
TOTAL	2,085	2,475	3,040	3,715	4,245	390	500	665	815	955	53	56	59	61	65

[1] Estimate [2] Including 50 Non-Subscribing Old Presbyterians in all years [3] 1981 Census figure 3,423
[4] 1981 Census Community figure 1,214 [5] 1981 Census figure 1,067 [6] 1981 Census figure 171
[7] 1981 Census figure 82 [8] 1981 Census figure

Non-Trinitarian Churches

Table 14c: **Total All Ireland 1980-1995**

Church	Members					Ministers					Churches				
	1980	1985	1988	1990	1995E	1980	1985	1988	1990	1995E	1980	1985	1988	1990	1995E
Children of God	25	25	25	25	25	1	1	1	1	1	1	1	1	1	1
Christadelphians	90	105	105	105	115	—	—	—	—	—	2	2	2	2	2
Church of Christ Scientist	350	350	350	350	350	—	—	—	—	—	6	6	6	6	6
Jehovah's Witnesses	1,620	2,050	3,200	4,400	5,250	194	215	375	490	585	48	48	49	50	51
Church of Jesus Christ of Latter-Day Saints (Mormons)	4,746	5,700	7,600	8,900	10,555	520	700	920	1,100	1,300	30	35	43	50	58
Non-Subscribing Presbyterian Church	4,374	4,210	4,140	4,250	4,115	15	18	19	18	21	34	34	34	34	34
Church of Scientology	250	500	800	1,000	1,300	25	35	45	50	60	1	1	1	1	1
Spiritualists	200	250	300	350	400	10	10	10	10	10	5	5	5	5	5
Theosophists	43	49	50	50	55	—	—	—	—	—	1	1	1	1	1
Unification Church (Moonies)	52	55	57	60	65	1	1	1	1	1	2	2	2	2	2
Unitarian and Free Christian Churches	230	230	230	230	230	6	6	6	6	6	35	35	35	35	35
The Way	50	60	70	75	85	0	0	0	0	0	3	3	3	3	3
Worldwide Church of God	200	245	270	290	330	1	1	1	1	1	3	3	3	3	3
Others	300	300	300	300	300	10	10	10	10	10	5	5	5	5	5
TOTAL	12,530	14,129	17,497	20,385	23,175	783	997	1,388	1,687	1,995	176	181	190	198	207

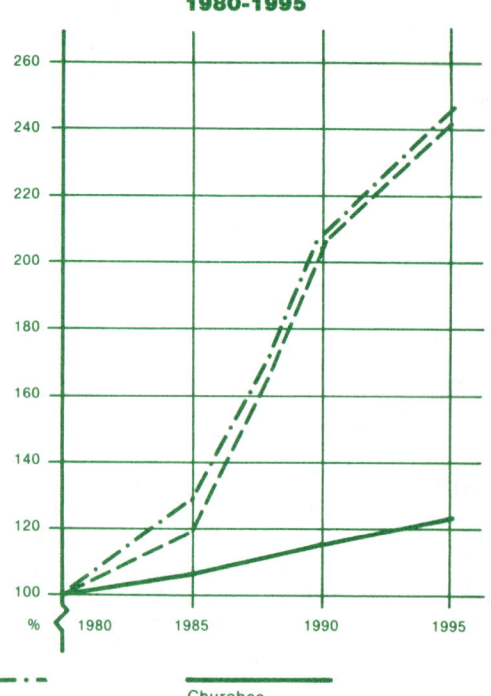

Fig 23: Proportional changes in Non-Trinitarian Churches, Northern Ireland 1980-1995

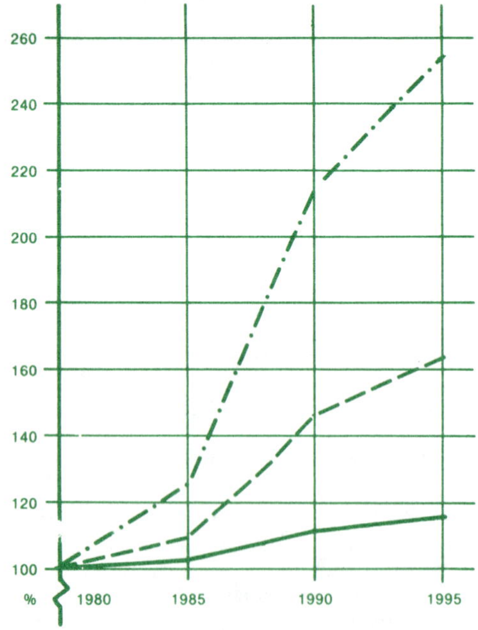

Fig 24: Proportional changes in Non-Trinitarian Churches, Republic of Ireland 1980-1995

Members   Ministers   Churches

Other Religions

Table 15a: Northern Ireland 1980-1995

Religion	Active Members					Full-time Leaders					Buildings				
	1980	1985	1988	1990	1995E	1980	1985	1988	1990	1995E	1980	1985	1988	1990	1995E
Ahmadiyya Movement in Islam[2,3]	100[1]	100[1]	100[1]	100	100	1	1	1	1	1	2	2	2	2	2
Baha'i World Faith[2,4]	150[1]	150[1]	150[1]	150[1]	150	5[1]	5[1]	5[1]	5[1]	5	5	5[1]	5[1]	5[1]	5
Buddhists[2,5]	50	50[1]	50[1]	50[1]	50	0	0	0	0	0	0	0	0	0	0
Hindus[2,6]	500	550[1]	580[1]	600[1]	650	5	5	5	5	5	1	1	1	1	1
International Society for Krishna Consciousness	0	0	50[1]	150[1]	250	0	0	5[1]	15	25	0	0	1	2	4
Jews[2,7]	400	400[1]	400[1]	400[1]	400	1	1	1	1	1	1	1	1	1	1
Muslims[2,3]	250	500	600	750	1,000	1	2	3	5	6	1	2	3	4	5
Sikhs[2,8]	50[1]	75[1]	90[1]	100	125	3	5	5	5	6	3	5	5	5	6
Others	200[1]	200[1]	200[1]	200[1]	200	–	–	–	–	–	–	–	–	–	–
TOTAL	1,700	2,025	2,220	2,500	2,925	16	19	25	37	49	13	16	18	20	24

Table 15b: Republic of Ireland 1980-1995

Religion	Active Members					Full-time Leaders					Buildings				
	1980	1985	1988	1990	1995E	1980	1985	1988	1990	1995E	1980	1985	1988	1990	1995E
Ahmadiyya Movement in Islam	–	–	–	–	–	–	–	–	–	–	–	–	–	–	–
Baha'i World Faith	20[1]	20[1]	20[1]	20[1]	20	4[1]	4[1]	4[1]	4[1]	4	4	4[1]	4[1]	4[1]	4
Buddhists	50[1]	50[1]	50[1]	50[1]	50	1	1	1	1	1	1	1	1	1	1
Hindus	–	–	–	–	–	–	–	–	–	–	–	–	–	–	–
International Society for Krishna Consciousness	–	–	–	–	–	–	–	–	–	–	–	–	–	–	–
Jews	700	600[1]	500	470[1]	400	1	1	1	1	1	1	1	1	1	1
Muslims	100	150[1]	180	200[1]	250	2	2	4	4	5	2	2	4	4	5
Sikhs	50[1]	70[1]	90[1]	100[1]	110	1	1	1	1	1	1	1	1	1	1
Others	100[1]	100[1]	100[1]	100[1]	100	–	–	–	–	–	–	–	–	–	–
TOTAL	1,020	990	940	940	930	9	9	11	11	12	9	9	11	11	12

Table 15c: Total All Ireland 1980-1995

Religion	Active Members					Full-time Leaders					Buildings				
	1980	1985	1988	1990	1995E	1980	1985	1988	1990	1995E	1980	1985	1988	1990	1995E
Ahmadiyya Movement in Islam	100	100	100	100	100	1	1	1	1	1	2	2	2	2	2
Bahái World Faith	170	170	170	170	170	9	9	9	9	9	9	9	9	9	9
Buddhists	100	100	100	100	100	1	1	1	1	1	1	1	1	1	1
Hindus	500	550	580	600	650	5	5	5	5	5	1	1	1	1	1
International Society for Krishna Consciousness	0	0	50	150	250	0	0	5	15	25	0	0	1	2	4
Jews	1,100	1,000	900	870	800	2	2	2	2	2	2	2	2	2	2
Muslims	350	650	780	950	1,250	3	4	7	9	11	3	4	7	8	10
Sikhs	100	145	180	200	235	4	6	6	6	7	4	6	6	6	7
Others	300	300	300	300	300	–	–	–	–	–	–	–	–	–	–
TOTAL	2,720	3,015	3,160	3,440	3,855	25	28	36	48	61	22	25	29	31	36

[1] Estimate   [2] The 1981 Census gave community figures of: [3] 608 for Ahmadiyas and Muslims   [4] 192 for Baha'is
[5] 131 for Buddhists   [6] 830 for Hindus   [7] 517 for Jews and   [8] 144 for Sikhs

For diagrams illustrating these tables please see Page 42.

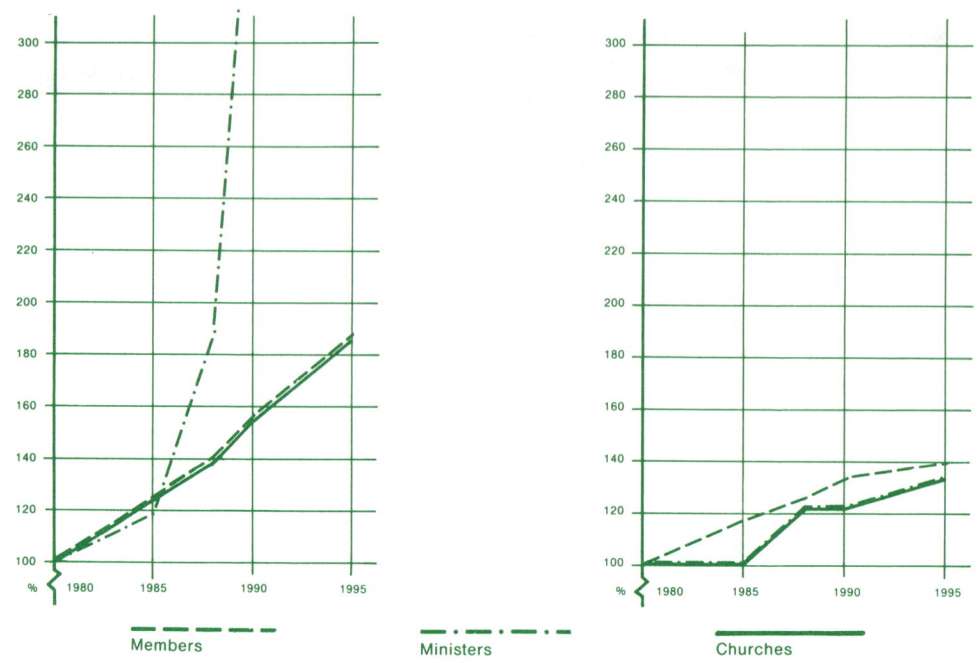

Fig 25: Proportional changes in Other Religions, Northern Ireland 1980-1995

Fig 26: Proportional changes in Other Religions, Republic of Ireland 1980-1995

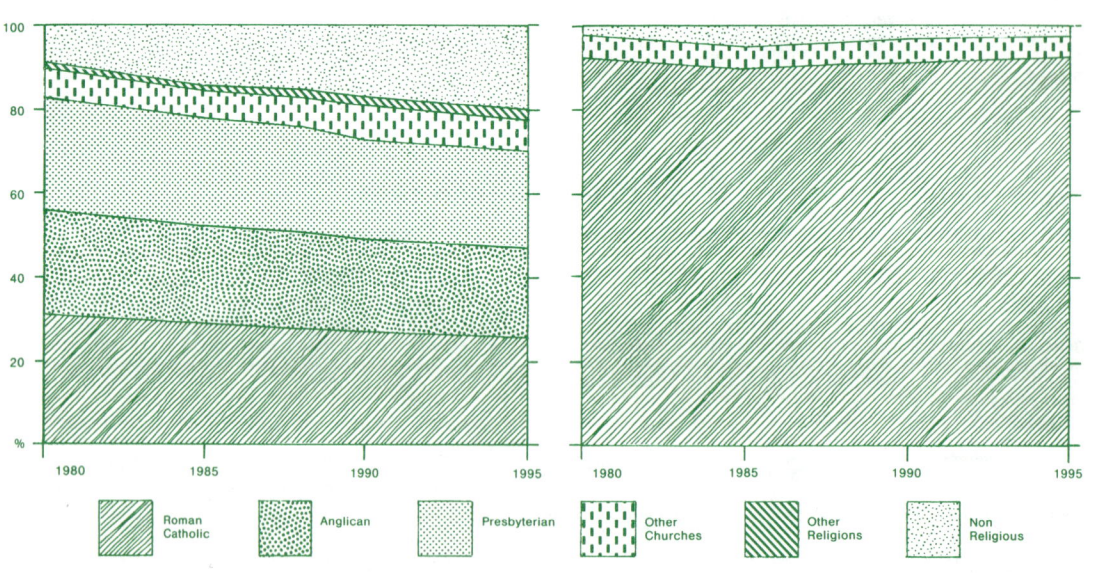

Fig 27: Changes in the Religious Community, Northern Ireland 1980-1995

Fig 28: Proportional changes in Religious Community, Republic of Ireland 1980-1995

COMMUNITY AND HISTORICAL TABLES
Religious Community

Table 16a: Northern Ireland 1980-1995

Church/Group	1980	1985	1988	1990	1995E
Anglican	377,000	365,000	355,000	351,000	345,000
Baptist[1]	11,000	12,000	13,000	13,000	13,000
Roman Catholic	419,000	401,000	394,000	379,000	361,000
Independent[1]	20,000	23,000	26,000	29,000	33,000
Methodist[1]	65,000	64,000	65,000	65,000	65,000
Presbyterian	484,000	455,000	442,000	432,000	411,000
Other Trinitarian Churches and Orthodox[1]	14,000	18,000	20,000	21,000	25,000
TOTAL Trinitarian	1,390,000	1,338,000	1,315,000	1,290,000	1,253,000
Non-Trinitarian	12,000	13,000	16,000	19,000	21,000
Other Religions	3,000	3,000	4,000	4,000	5,000
TOTAL all Religions	1,405,000	1,354,000	1,335,000	1,313,000	1,279,000
Percentage total Christian Churches of population	90%	85%	83%	81%	78%
Percentage total all religions of population	91%	86%	85%	83%	80%

Table 16b: Republic of Ireland 1980-1995

Church/Group	1980	1985	1988	1990	1995E
Anglican	136,000	129,000	125,000	121,000	112,000
Baptist[1]	1,000	1,000	1,000	1,000	1,000
Roman Catholic	3,202,000	3,205,000	3,218,000	3,244,000	3,247,000
Independent[1]	6,000	7,000	8,000	8,000	9,000
Methodist[1]	7,000	7,000	7,000	7,000	7,000
Presbyterian	21,000	20,000	19,000	18,000	17,000
Other Trinitarian Churches and Orthodox[1]	3,000	3,000	3,000	3,000	3,000
TOTAL Trinitarian	3,376,000	3,372,000	3,381,000	3,402,000	3,396,000
Non-Trinitarian	2,000	3,000	3,000	4,000	5,000
Other Religions	2,000	2,000	2,000	2,000	2,000
TOTAL all Religions	3,380,000	3,377,000	3,386,000	3,408,000	3,403,000
Percentage total Christian Churches of population	98%	95%	96%	97%	97%
Percentage total all religions of population	98%	95%	96%	97%	97%

Table 16c: Total All Ireland 1980-1995

Church/Group	1980	1985	1988	1990	1995E
Anglican	513,000	494,000	480,000	472,000	457,000
Baptist[1]	12,000	13,000	14,000	14,000	14,000
Roman Catholic	3,621,000	3,606,000	3,612,000	3,623,000	3,608,000
Independent[1]	26,000	30,000	34,000	37,000	42,000
Methodist[1]	72,000	71,000	72,000	72,000	72,000
Presbyterian	505,000	475,000	461,000	450,000	428,000
Other Trinitarian Churches and Orthodox[1]	17,000	21,000	23,000	24,000	28,000
TOTAL Trinitarian	4,766,000	4,710,000	4,696,000	4,692,000	4,649,000
Non-Trinitarian	14,000	16,000	19,000	23,000	26,000
Other Religions	5,000	5,000	6,000	6,000	7,000
TOTAL all Religions	4,785,000	4,731,000	4,721,000	4,721,000	4,682,000
Percentage total Christian Churches of population	96%	92%	92%	92%	91%
Percentage total all religions of population	96%	93%	92%	92%	92%

[1] Taken as membership plus 50%

Table 17: Church membership by selected denominations in Northern Ireland 1900-2000

	Church of Ireland Community	Ratio	Methodists	Ratio	Baptists	Ratio	Congregational Union of Ireland	Ratio
1900	317,000	100	28,000	100	2,700	100	2,200	100
1905	323,000[1]	102	29,000	104	3,000	111	2,300	105
1910	327,000	103	29,000	104	2,900	107	2,400	109
1915	330,000[1]	104	28,000	100	2,600	96	2,100	95
1920	333,000[1]	105	27,000	96	2,800	104	2,200[1]	100
1925	339,000	107	29,000	104	3,400	126	2,200[1]	100
1930	340,000[1]	107	30,000	107	3,600	133	2,300	105
1935	344,000[1]	109	31,000	111	3,900	144	2,200	100
1940	347,000[1]	109	31,000	111	3,700	137	2,100	95
1945	351,000[1]	111	31,000	111	3,800[1]	141	1,900	86
1950	353,000	111	32,000	114	4,500	167	1,700	77
1955	351,000[1]	111	33,000	118	5,000	185	1,900	86
1960	345,000	109	32,000	114	5,600	207	2,100[1]	95
1965	339,000[1]	107	31,000	111	6,400	237	2,300[1]	105
1970	338,000	107	28,000	100	7,200	267	2,500[1]	114
1975	307,000[1]	97	26,000	93	7,300	270	2,600[1]	118
1980	281,000	89	24,000	86	7,500	278	3,000	136
1985	280,000[1]	88	21,000	75	8,300	307	3,000	136
1990[1]	274,000	86	19,000	68	8,600	319	3,200	145
1995[1]	262,000	83	17,000	61	8,800	326	3,300	150
2000[1]	251,000	79	15,000	54	9,000	333	3,500	159

Table 18: Church membership of Roman Catholics 1900-2000

	Northern Ireland	Ratio	Percentage of Total Northern Population	Republic of Ireland[2]	Ratio	Percentage of Total Republic Population
			%			%
1900	430,000	100	35	2,878,000	100	89
1905	430,000[1]	100	35	2,847,000[1]	99	90
1910	430,000	100	34	2,813,000	98	90
1915	431,000[1]	100	34	2,797,000[1]	97	91
1920	420,000[1]	98	33	2,772,000[1]	96	92
1925	420,000	98	34	2,751,000	96	93
1930	430,000[1]	100	34	2,762,000[1]	96	92
1935	440,000[1]	102	34	2,774,000	96	92
1940	450,000[1]	105	34	2,779,000[1]	97	91
1945	460,000[1]	107	34	2,786,000	97	90
1950	471,000	110	34	2,748,000[1]	95	87
1955	484,000[1]	113	34	2,710,000[1]	94	85
1960	498,000	116	35	2,673,000	93	82
1965	488,000[1]	113	33	2,734,000[1]	95	84
1970	478,000	111	31	2,796,000	97	85
1975	442,000[1]	103	29	2,798,000[1]	97	88
1980	419,000[1]	97	27	2,850,000[1]	99	82
1985	401,000[1]	93	26	2,820,000[1]	98	80
1990[1]	379,000[1]	88	24	2,800,000	97	79
1995[1]	361,000[1]	84	22	2,790,000	97	80
2000[1]	334,000	78	21	2,760,000	96	79

[1] Estimate   [2] Based on Census accounts early in the year following that given

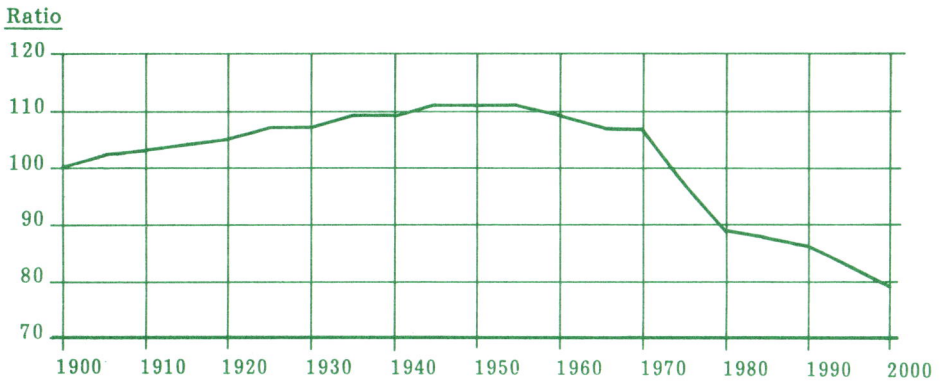

Fig 29: Church of Ireland Community in Northern Ireland

Fig 30: Roman Catholic membership

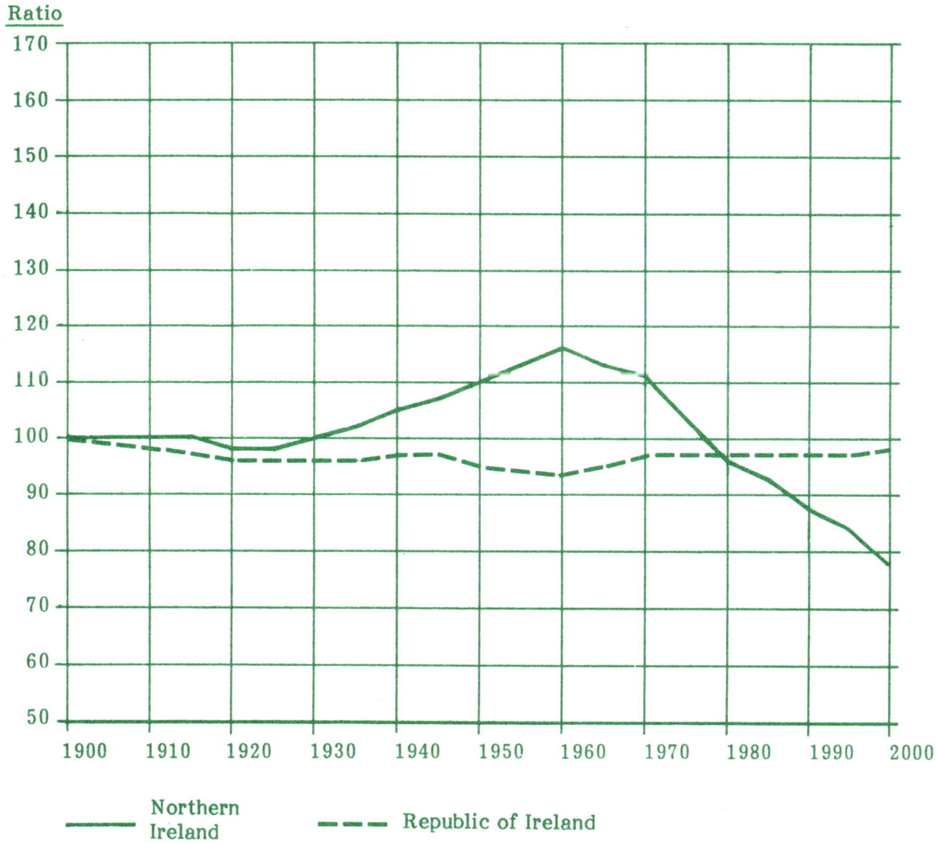

——— Northern Ireland   - - - Republic of Ireland

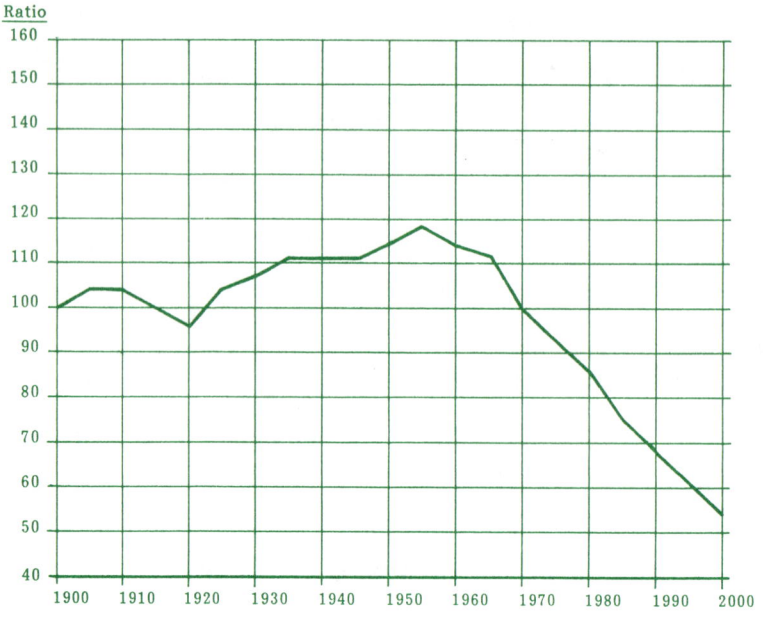

Fig 31: Methodist membership (all Ireland)

— Membership of Methodist churches in Ireland.

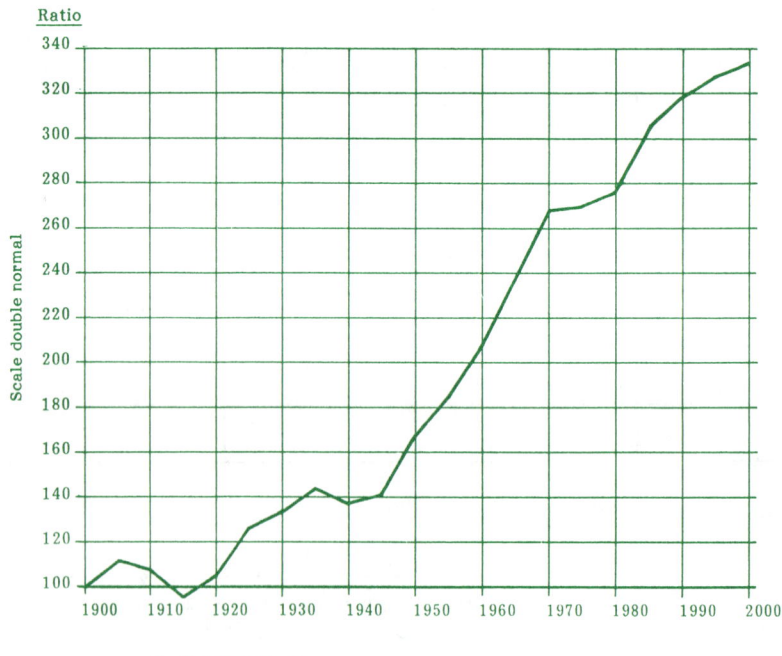

Fig 32: Baptist membership (all Ireland)

— Baptists in Ireland

Table 19: **Presbyterian Church Communicants 1900-2000**

	Presbyterian Church in Ireland					Reformed Presbyterian Church in Ireland	
	Total	Ratio	Active Number	Ratio	Active as percentage of Total Communicants	Total	Ratio
					%		
1900	107,000	100	68,000[1]	100	64	3,700	100
1905	106,000	99	70,000	103	66	3,900	105
1910	106,000	99	68,000	100	64	4,000	108
1915	104,000	97	68,000	100	64	3,600	97
1920	105,000	98	66,000	97	63	3,600	97
1925	109,000	102	69,000	101	63	3,400	92
1930	109,000	102	68,000	100	62	3,500	95
1935	114,000	107	80,000	118	70	3,500	95
1940	118,000	110	83,000	122	70	3,500	95
1945	119,000	111	81,000	119	68	3,500	95
1950	126,000	118	86,000	126	68	3,300	89
1955	133,000	124	94,000	138	70	3,400	92
1960	137,000	128	99,000	146	73	3,300	89
1965	144,000	135	103,000	151	72	3,300	89
1970	141,000	132	99,000	146	70	3,300	89
1975	139,000	130	100,000[1]	147	72[1]	3,100	84
1980	133,000	124	97,000[1]	143	73[1]	2,900	78
1985	131,000	123	98,000[1]	144	74[1]	2,800	76
1990	128,000	120	95,000[1]	140	74	2,600	70
1995[1]	125,000	117	95,000	140	76	2,700	73
2000[1]	121,000	114	92,000	135	76	2,700	73

[1] Estimate

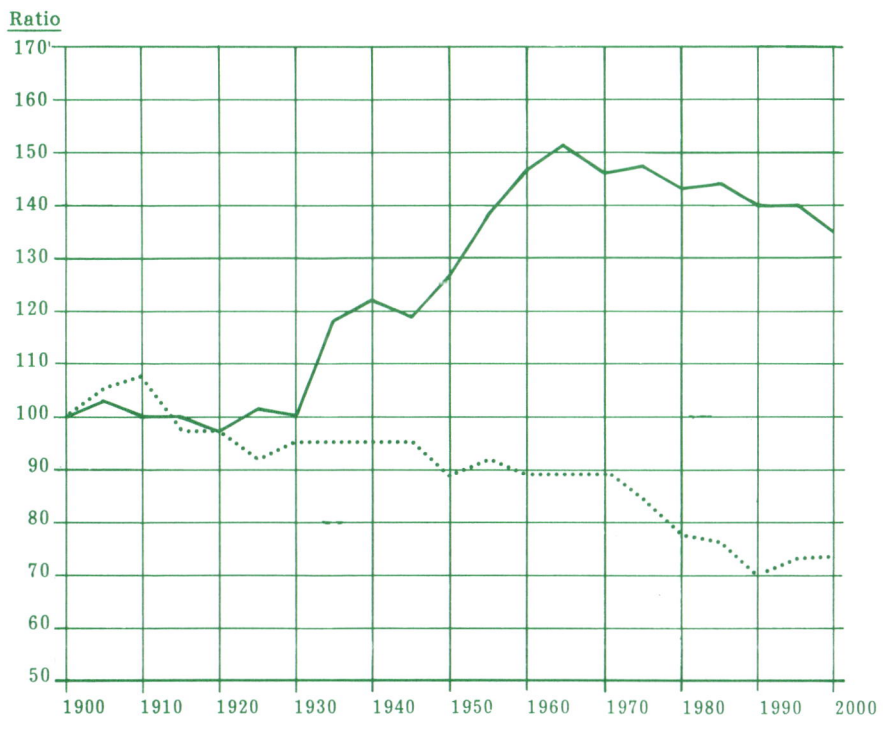

Fig 33: Presbyterian Church in Ireland Communicants

—— Presbyterian Church in Ireland   ·········· Reformed Presbyterian Church in Ireland

MARRIAGE TABLES

Table 20: Marriages in Northern Ireland

Numbers	Total	Percentage Religious	Percentage of Religious marriages which were:				
			Roman Catholic	Presbyterian	Church of Ireland	Methodist	Other Protestant Denominations
1900							
1905							
1910		Included indistinguishably with the figures for the Republic of Ireland in Table 18					
1915							
1920[2]	9,550	95%	30%	32%	31%	3%	4%
1925	7,682	95%	31%	31%	31%	3%	4%
1930	7,547	93%	30%	31%	33%	3%	4%
1935	8,844	93%	29%	30%	32%	3%	6%
1940	9,795	94%	28%	33%	30%	5%	4%
1945	10,452	92%	31%	33%	27%	6%	3%
1950	9,084	93%	31%	33%	27%	6%	3%
1955	9,153	97%	34%	33%	25%	5%	3%
1960	9,881	95%	35%	31%	25%	5%	4%
1965	10,452	95%	36%	32%	23%	5%	4%
1970	12,297	93%	41%	28%	22%	5%	4%
1975	11,757	92%	44%	27%	19%	5%	5%
1980	11,034	89%	45%	25%	19%	5%	6%
1985	11,743	86%	45%	26%	18%	5%	6%
1990	9,588[4]	86%	45%	25%	18%	5%	7%
1995[1]	10,180	84%	45%	25%	17%	5%	7%
2000[1]	9,930	82%	47%	24%	16%	5%	8%

Ratios[3]	Total	Religious	Roman Catholic	Presbyterian	Church of Ireland	Methodist	Other
1920	100	100	100	100	100	100	100
1925	80	80	83	78	80	80	80
1930	79	77	77	75	80	77	77
1935	93	91	88	85	94	91	136
1940	103	101	95	105	98	169	101
1945	109	106	110	109	92	212	79
1950	95	93	96	96	81	186	70
1955	96	98	111	101	79	163	73
1960	103	103	121	100	83	172	103
1965	109	109	131	109	81	182	109
1970	129	126	172	110	89	210	126
1975	123	119	175	101	73	199	149
1980	116	108	162	85	66	180	162
1985	123	111	167	90	65	186	167
1990[1]	100	91	136	71	53	152	159
1995[1]	107	94	141	74	52	157	165
2000[1]	104	90	141	71	49	157	188

[1] Estimate

[2] This line may be interpreted as follows. In 1920 there were 9,550 marriages altogether in Northern Ireland. Of these, 95% or 9,073 took place in a church, Of this 9,073, 31% or 2,813 took place in a Church of Ireland church, 32% or 2,903 took place in a Presbyterian church, 3% or 272 in a Methodist church, 4% or 363 in other Protestant churches, and the remaining 30% or 2,722 in Roman Catholic churches.

[3] The columns in this table were calculated as follows. The 1920 figure in each case is taken as the baseline. Thus in 1920 the total 9,550 marriages are treated as 100% or 100. In 1925 the number of marriages was 7,682 or 80% of the 1920 figure of 9,550. This is written simply as 80. In 1930 the number 7,547 was 79% of the 1920 figure. In 1920 the number of religious marriages was 9,073, taken as 100. In 1925, 80% of this number were recorded (5,838), and by 1930 the proportion had fallen to 77%. In 1920 the 2,813 Church of Ireland marriages are taken as 100% or 100. In 1925 80% of this number (2,250) were recorded, and so on.

[4] 1989 figure was 10,019, with 87% religious, 45% Roman Catholic, 25% Presbyterian, 18% Church of Ireland, 5% Methodist and 7% others.

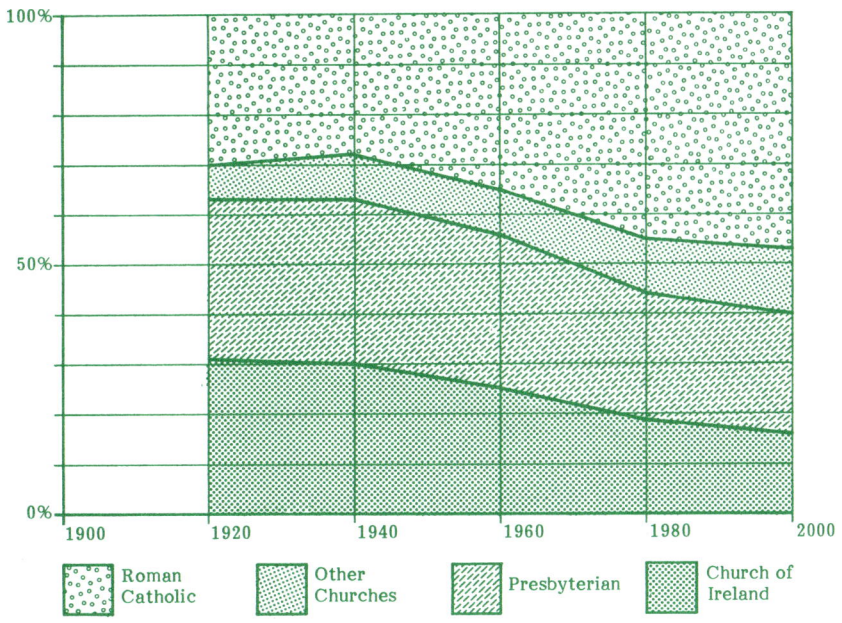

Fig 34: Trends in Religious Marriages in Northern Ireland

Fig 35: Religious Marriages in Northern Ireland by Church

Table 21: **Marriages in the Republic of Ireland**

Numbers	Total	Percentage Religious	Percentage of Religious marriages which were:			
			Church of Ireland	Presbyterian	Other Religious[5]	Roman Catholic
1900	21,330	98%	16%	11%	2%	71%
1905	23,078	98%	16%	11%	2%	71%
1910	22,112	98%	16%	10%	2%	72%
1915	24,154	98%	15%	10%	2%	73%
1920[4,5]	17,276	99%	7%	1%	1%	91%
1925	13,820	100%[2]	5%	1%	0%	94%
1930	13,631	99%	5%	1%	0%	94%
1935	14,336	99%	5%	1%	0%	94%
1940	15,212	100%[3]	5%	1%	0%	94%
1945	17,301	100%[3]	4%	1%	0%	95%
1950	16,018	100%[2]	4%	1%	0%	95%
1955	16,443	100%[2]	4%	1%	0%	95%
1960	15,465	100%[2]	3%	1%	0%	96%
1965	16,946	100%[3]	2½%	½%	0%	97%
1970	20,778	99%	2½%	½%	0%	97%
1975	21,504	99%	2%	½%	0%	97½%
1980	22,180	98%	2%	½%	0%	97½%
1985	18,791	97%	2%	½%	0%	97½%
1990[1]	17,490	96%	2½%	½%	0%	97%
1995[1]	17,360[1]	95%	2½%	½%	0%	97%
2000[1]	16,430[1]	94%	3%	½%	½%	96%

[1] Estimate   [2] More exactly 99.6%   [3] More exactly 99.7%   [4] For an explanation of this line, please see Footnote 2 of Table 20
[5] Methodist, Jewish and others
[6] From 1920 onwards the figures relate solely to the present Republic of Ireland; earlier figures relate to All Ireland

Ratios[2]	Total	Religious	All Protestants	Roman Catholic
1920	100	100	100	100
1925	80	80	54	76
1930	79	79	53	74
1935	83	83	55	78
1940	88	89	59	83
1945	100	101	56	96
1950	93	93	52	89
1955	95	96	53	91
1960	90	90	40	86
1965	98	99	33	96
1970	120	120	40	117
1975	124	124	55	119
1980	128	127	56	122
1985	112	110	73	103
1990[1]	116	113	88	105
1995[1]	121	116	103	107
2000[1]	125	119	132	107

[1] Estimate   [2] For an explanation of these columns, please see Footnote 3 of Table 20

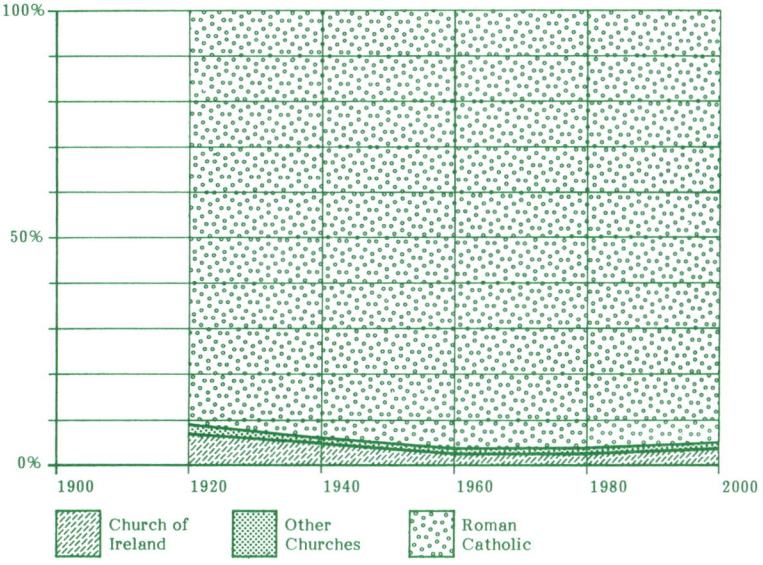

Fig 36: Trends in Religious Marriages in the Republic of Ireland

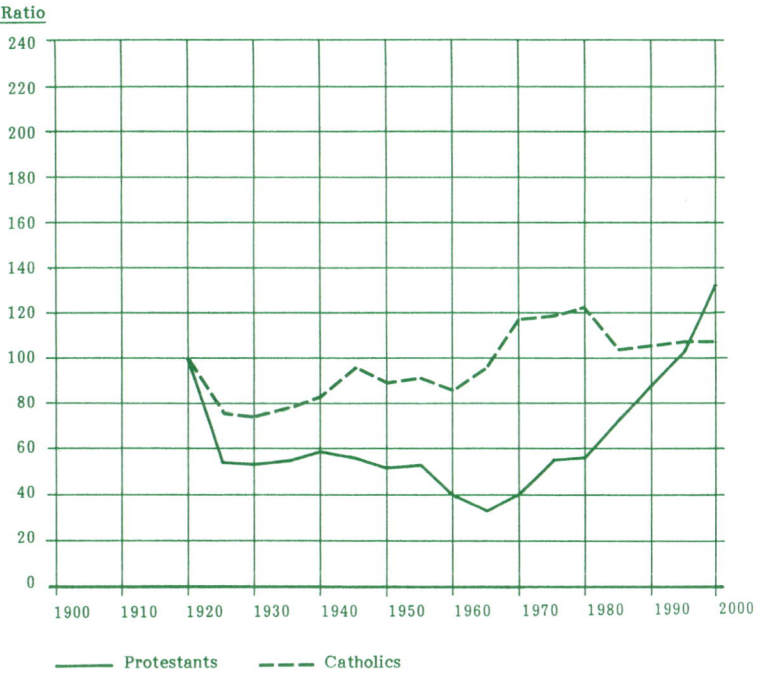

Fig 37: Religious Marriages in the Republic of Ireland by Church

NOTES AND DEFINITIONS

See also Notes and Definitions for Churches on Page 24 and for Missionary Societies on Page 87.

Criteria for Inclusion

Organisations are normally only listed in this volume if they are:

1 *Trinitarian,* that is, they accept the historic formulary of the Godhead as the three eternal persons, God the Father, God the Son and God the Holy Spirit, in one unchanging Essence. A fuller statement is available on request.
2 *Offering a definitive Christian product, service or function,* that is, the nature of their output or work reflects their belief, and could not be adequately performed without it.
3 *Not operating or trading under their own individual name* (musical artistes, evangelists and similar occupations apart), so that their listing represents an identifiable organisation (however small) rather than the work of one or a few persons.

Organisations with less than three full-time staff are generally not included unless they are registered charities.

Organisations working in a small geographical area are not normally included in this national Handbook.

Specific ministries within organisations listed are only listed separately upon payment of a fee.

Notwithstanding the above, the Editors reserve the right to make the final decision as to the inclusion of any organisation.

Name

The name of the organisation is given in **bold** type followed sometimes by a previous name if it has been changed recently.

The letters **CC** following a society's name indicates that they are registered with the Charity Commission.

The year of foundation of the present or originating organisation in Ireland is given in brackets after the name.

The type of society is also given in brackets after the name. The type is one of three — denominational (with denomination given), interdenominational/ecumenical/evangelical or non-denominational. No definition was deliberately given on the questionnaire for these last categories, which may therefore overlap slightly.

Magazine

The title of the magazine is given in *italics* (***bold italics*** in the Missionary Societies sections) followed by the number printed or circulated and the frequency of issue.

Similar details are given in the second or fourth column of some categories.

Location of Office

The telephone number is given on the first line in the second column, preceded by ☎ and the national code in brackets. A second number shown, preceded by ✆ is a Fax number.

To access Northern Ireland numbers from the Republic the (08) code is necessary preceded by international access code 00; to access the Republic from the North the (353) code is required preceded by international access code 010.

The address and postcode follows.

Similar details are given in the first column of the two Missionary Societies sections.

Chief Officer

The name is that of the chief executive officer with his actual designation given in *italics*. No title is shown for those belonging to the Society of Friends.

No academic degrees or other qualifications are shown, except for Principals of Theological Colleges and Bible Schools.

If two names are shown one is usually the international chief executive (for missionary societies) whose usual country of residence is other than Ireland, this country being stated, or the President or Chairman (for other societies), to whom correspondence should *not* normally be addressed.

Irish Staff

Numbers relate to the year 1992 as at 1st January. Figures were requested relating to full-time personnel only, but some organisations indicated part-time personnel as well, and these have been counted as half. If there are no full-time staff, any part-time staff are indicated as such.

Executive or administrative staff are usually those staff who are in management positions. Other staff were not defined, but will generally include clerical and/or manual staff as appropriate.

Field Staff are usually those serving outside the headquarters location or in non-administrative functions.

The absence of a particular category of personnel for a society either indicates the absence of any in that category for that society or none shown on the form. Categories not explicitly mentioned above are self-explanatory.

Numbers given in brackets indicate honorary and unpaid personnel, who are not included in the Summary Tables.

Income/Turnover

This relates to the (published) Income and Expenditure Account for the latest financial year. The month and year to which this relates is indicated. The year invariably ended on the last day of the month shown.

Work

A brief description of the work of each society is usually given, with a broad indication of the location of its activities where relevant.

Accommodation

	Page
Conference and Other Centres in Northern Ireland	55
Conference and Other Centres in the Republic of Ireland	56
Retreat Houses in Northern Ireland	59
Retreat Houses in the Republic of Ireland	59

CONFERENCE AND OTHER CENTRES IN NORTHERN IRELAND

Name	Location & Station	Chief Officer & Staff	Total person-spaces in residential rooms/Turnover
Benburb Conference & Retreat Centre (n/a; Roman Catholic)	☎ Benburb (08) 0861 548170 16 Main Street Benburb, Dungannon Co Tyrone BT71 7GZ	Sr Loretta Kennedy *Superior* Other staff 2	42 double n/a
"Castle Erin" Christian Hotel & Conference Centre (1926; interdenominational)	☎ Portrush (08) 0265 822744 Castle Erin Road, Portrush Co Antrim BT56 8DH *Rail:* Portrush	Miss Ann Doherty *Manageress* Admin staff 3	1 single 48 double 27 large 350 day room n/a – Dec 90
Castlewellan Castle Christian Conference Centre (*CC*; 1975; interdenominational)	☎ Castlewellan (08) 03967 78733 Castlewellan Co Down BT31 9BU *Rail:* Belfast	Mrs Netta Halyburton *Manageress* Admin staff 1 Other staff 3	2 single 10 double 100 large n/a – Sept 90
Christian Renewal Centre (1974; interdenominational)	☎ Rostrevor (08) 06937 38492 44 Shore Road. Rostrevor Newry, Co Down BT34 3ET *Rail:* Newry *Bus:* Rostrevor	Rev Cecil Kerr *Leader of Community* Executive staff 17	5 single 12 double n/a
Corrymeela Centre (*CC*; 1965; interdenominational)	☎ Ballycastle (08) 02657 62626 Ballycastle Co Antrim BT53 6QU *Bus:* Ballycastle **Also at:** (08) 0232 325008 8 Upper Crescent Belfast BT7 1NT *Rail:* Botanie	Mr Michael Earle *Centre Director* Executive staff 9 Other staff 26	50 double 4 large IR£350,000 – Dec 89
Glen River YMCA National Centre (*CC*; 1974; non-denominational)	☎ Newcastle (08) 03967 23172 143 Central Promenade Newcastle Co Down BT33 0EU *Rail:* Newry *Bus:* Newcastle	Mr Tim Hodnett *Centre Director* Admin staff 4 Other staff 21	3 single 6 double 33 large 80 tents 70 day room £200,000 – Mar 90
Glenada YWCA (*CC*; n/a; non-denominational)	☎ Newcastle (08) 03967 22402 29 South Promenade Newcastle Co Down BT33 0EX	To be appointed *General Manager* Other staff 12	106 maximum n/a

Conference and Other Centres in Northern Ireland

Name	Location & Station	Chief Officer & Staff	Total person-spaces in residential rooms/Turnover
Kilbroney Conservation Centre (n/a; Church of Ireland but ecumenical)	☎Rostrevor (08) 06937 38293 ☎Rostrevor (08) 06937 38401 15 Kilbroney Road Rostrevor, Newry Co Down BT34 3BH	Rev Canon D Jameson *Director* Mr Mark Jeffreys *Development Officer* n/a	65 large n/a

CONFERENCE AND OTHER CENTRES IN THE REPUBLIC OF IRELAND

Name	Location & Station	Chief Officer & Staff	Total person-spaces in residential rooms/Turnover
Arklow Rock (n/a; Roman Catholic)	☎Dublin (353) 01 725055 Arklow, Co Wicklow *Rail:* Arklow Town **Also at:** Ballycreen Centre Aughrim, Arklow, Co Wicklow *Bus:* Aughrim **And:** Oakwood Centre Wicklow Gap, Wicklow *Bus:* Laragh **And:** Brittas Bay Centre Brittas Bay, Wicklow *Bus:* Brittas Bay **And:** Teach Chaoimhin Glendasan, Glendalough Bray, Co Wicklow *Bus:* Laragh **Bookings:** Catholic Youth Council 20/23 Arran Quay, Dublin 7	Rev Martin Clarke *Director* n/a	20 large 14 large 32 large 24 large 25 large
Bellinter Adult Education Centre (n/a; Roman Catholic)	☎Navan (353) 046 29126 Navan, Co Meath *Rail:* Navan	Sr Maura Clune *Superior* Other staff 4	25 single 18 double n/a
Blowick Conference Centre (n/a; Roman Catholic)	☎Navan (353) 046 21407 Dowdstown House Navan, Co Meath *Rail:* Navan	Sr Elma Peppard *Director* n/a	25 single 60 double n/a
Brú Na Móna (1940; interdenominational)	☎Naas (353) 045 24366 "The Camp", Woodland Rathangan, Kildare *Rail:* Rathangan **Bookings:** Br A Lynch St Theresa, Parnell Road Dublin 12	Br Anthony Lynch *Manager* Executive staff 2 Other staff 4	4 single 86 large n/a – Dec 89
Carrig Eden (1936; interdenominational)	☎Dublin (353) 01 287 4012 Marine Road Greystones, Co Wicklow *Rail:* Greystones	Mr Ian Beere *Managing Director* Executive staff 2 Other staff 6	4 single 60 double 20 large n/a – Mar 89

Conference and Other Centres in the Republic of Ireland

Name	Location & Station	Chief Officer & Staff	Total person-spaces in residential rooms/Turnover
Chrysalis (n/a; interdenominational)	☎Naas (353) 045 54713 Donoughmore, Donard Dunlavin, Co Wicklow *Bus:* Baltinglass	Ms Ann Maria Dunne *Director* n/a	2 single 20 large n/a
Clar Ellagh (1940; non-denominational)	☎Ennis (353) 065 56016 West End, Kilkee Kilrush, Co Clare *Bus:* Kilkee **Bookings:** ☎(353) 01 984856 92 Landscape Park Churchtown, Dublin 14	Mrs Sheila McDougald *Manageress* Executive staff 2 Other staff 6	15 single 30 double 35 large IR£35,000 – Sept 89
Dominican Pastoral Centre (n/a; Roman Catholic)	☎Cork (353) 021 502267 St Mary's Pope Quay, Cork	Very Rev Dermot Brennan *Prior* n/a	Non-residential 6 Conference rooms 1 Hall
Holy Family Convent (n/a; Roman Catholic)	☎Dublin (353) 01 286 2064 or 282 9462 Ravenswell Bray, Co Wicklow *Rail:* Bray	Sr M Brid Honan *Superior* Other staff 12	36 single n/a
Irish Bible School (*CC*; 1982; interdenominational)	☎Clonmel (353) 052 54306 Coalbrook Thurles, Co Tipperary *Rail:* Thurles	Mr Warren Nelson *Registrar* Executive staff 2 Other staff 1	6 single 6 double
Irish Missionary Union Institute (n/a; Roman Catholic)	☎Navan (353) 046 21525 St Columban's Navan, Co Meath *Rail:* Navan	Rev John O'Connell *Director* n/a	54 people
Lucan Youth Centre (*CC*; 1977; Presbyterian) (Previously Mount Zion)	☎Dublin (353) 01 628 0393 ✉Fax (353) 01 628 0770 Primrose Lane Lucan, Co Dublin *Rail:* Dublin Heuston	Mr Morris Kennedy *Director* Executive staff 1 Other staff 3	Self-catering except weekends 50 large IR£30,000 – Jan 90
Marinella Pastoral Centre (n/a; Roman Catholic)	☎Dublin (353) 01 961688 75 Orwell Road Rathgar, Dublin 6 *Rail:* Dublin *Bus:* Orwell Road	Very Rev Eamon Breslin *Director* n/a	35 single n/a
Mount St Joseph Guest House (1878; Roman Catholic)	☎Roscrea (353) 0505 21711 The Guest House Mount St Joseph Abbey Roscrea, Co Tipperary *Rail:* Roscrea	Fr Gabriel McCarthy *Guestmaster* Executive staff 4 Other staff 6	15 single 20 double 3 large IR£60,000 – Dec 89
Our Lady of Sion Adult Education Centre (*CC*; 1966; Ecumenical)	☎Navan (353) 046 21241/29126 Bellinter Navan, Co Meath *Bus:* Navan	Miss Vanessa Clarke *Administrator* Executive staff 1 Other staff 8	23 single 40 double n/a – Aug 89

Conference and Other Centres in the Republic of Ireland

Name	Location & Station	Chief Officer & Staff		Total person-spaces in residential rooms/Turnover
St Patrick's Purgatory (*CC*; n/a; Roman Catholic)	☎Bundoran (353) 072 61518/61550 Lough Derg Pettigo, Donegal *Bus:* Ballyshannon	Rev Gerard McSorley *Prior* Executive staff	6	An ancient pilgrimage centre of a penitential nature Open 1 June-15 August only 1,000 persons IR£436,000 — Dec 90
Scripture Union Adventure Centre (*CC*; 1984; interdenominational)	☎Arklow (353) 0402 5369 Ovoca Manor Avoca, Arklow, Co Wicklow *Rail:* Arklow	Mr Herbert Harper *Warden* Executive staff	1	20 double 60 large IR£50,000 — Dec 89
YWCA, Waterford (*CC*; 1890; interdenominational)	☎Waterford (353) 051 81363 The Cliff, Church Road Tramore, Waterford *Rail:* Waterford	Mr Brendan & Mrs Barbara Payne *Managers* Admin staff Other staff	2 8	12 single 22 double 6 large 55 day room n/a

---

OUR LADY OF SION
ADULT EDUCATION CENTRE
BELLINTER HOUSE
Bellinter, Navan, Co Meath, Ireland

BELLINTER HOUSE is a splendid Georgian House set in 13 acres of grounds in the peace and quiet of the Boyne Valley. It is a centre of hospitality and reconciliation where people of all denominations, race and creed are welcomed.

The house offers:

★ Accommodation for up to 63 people
★ Conference/Training facilities for groups of 10-150
★ Full programme of courses including retreats (private and directed)
★ Spiritual direction available on request
★ Five week residential course (an experience of renewal) for religious over 55+
★ Facilities for General and Provincial Chapters
★ Facilities for reconciliation groups North and South

Further details, programme and brochure available from:

Vanessa Clark, Administrator — Above address
Tel: (046) 21241/29126/27910

★ Training in church based outreach Evangelism
★ Easter and Summer Projects
★ Open Airs, One to One, Street Evangelism
★ Music, Drama, Sketch Board Evangelism
★ Children's and Teenage meetings
★ Sports and Bible Studies
★ Short term Bible School, day and evening classes
★ Residential provision for the unemployed

Project House, 38 Mark Street Portrush, Co Antrim BT56 8BT

Tel: Portrush 822775

RETREAT HOUSES IN NORTHERN IRELAND

Name	Location & Station	Warden & Staff	Total person-spaces in rooms/Turnover
Columbanus Community of Reconciliation (*CC*; 1983; interdenominational)	☎ Belfast (08) 0232 778009 683 Antrim Road Belfast BT15 4EG *Rail:* Belfast Central or York Road	Rev Michael Hurley *Leader* Full-time staff 2	3 single 4 double 12 large 30 day room £35,000 – Dec 90
Dromantine (n/a; Roman Catholic)	☎ Newry (08) 0693 82224 Newry, Co Down BT34 1RY *Rail:* Newry	Rev William Foley *Superior* n/a	200 people n/a
Iona Carmelite Retreat Centre (n/a; Roman Catholic)	☎ Londonderry (08) 0504 262512 Termonbacca Londonderry BT48 9XE *Rail:* Londonderry	Very Rev Stephen McKeogh *Prior* n/a	26 single 22 double n/a
Our Lady of Apostles Guest & Retreat House (n/a; interdenominational)	☎ Rostrevor (08) 06937 38333 11 Greenpark Road Rostrevor, Newry Co Down BT34 1RY *Bus:* Rostrevor	Sr Eileen O'Driscoll *Sister-in-Charge* n/a	33 single 30 double
St Clements Retreat House (n/a; Roman Catholic)	☎ Antrim (08) 0232 776500/771799 722 Antrim Road Belfast BT36 7PH *Rail:* Belfast	Sr Eileen McElhone *Superior* Other staff 5	54 single 32 double n/a
St Patrick's Retreat (n/a; Roman Catholic)	☎ Downpatrick (08) 0396 830242 Tobar Mhuire, Crossgar Downpatrick Co Down BT30 9EA *Bus:* Downpatrick	Very Rev Salvian Maguire *Superior* n/a	10 single 10 double n/a

RETREAT HOUSES IN THE REPUBLIC OF IRELAND

Name	Location & Station	Warden & Staff	Total person-spaces in rooms/Turnover
Ardfert Diocesan Retreat Centre (*CC*; 1981; Roman Catholic)	☎ Tralee (353) 066 34276 Ardfert, Tralee, Co Kerry *Rail:* Tralee	Rev Tom Looney *Director* Admin staff 1	62 double 60 day room n/a – Dec 90
Ard Mhuire, Capuchin Franciscan Friary (n/a; Roman Catholic)	☎ Letterkenny (353) 074 38005/38031 Creeslough, Letterkenny Co Donegal *Rail:* Letterkenny	Rev Sylvester O'Flynn *Vicar & Director of* *Retreats* Executive staff 2 Other staff 5	25 single 25 double n/a
Carmelite Conference & Retreat Centre (n/a; Roman Catholic)	☎ Dublin (353) 01 298 4014 or 9811 Gort Mhuire Ballinteer, Dublin 16 *Rail:* Dublin *Bus:* Ballinteer Road	Very Rev Paul Graham *Superior* n/a	23 single 34 double
Cenacle Retreat House (n/a; Roman Catholic)	☎ Dublin (353) 01 823411 Military Road, Killiney Dunlaoghaire, Co Dublin *Rail:* Killiney	Sr Mary Toner *Superioress* Other staff 9	20 single 10 double n/a

LA RETRAITE HOSTEL

College Road, Cork   Tel: 021-546311

La Retraite Congregation:

The Sisters have communities in Cork, Dublin, Galway. The Congregation began in France just over three hundred years ago and works for spiritual and human growth mainly through retreats and education in the faith.

La Retraite Hostel

(100 bedrooms h/c) for University students (women) offers excellent facilities for Christian conferences, Chapters, Retreats, etc. It has a chapel, conference rooms, smaller group rooms, spacious grounds and parking space.

Catering on request and as required.

Retreat Houses in the Republic of Ireland

Name	Location & Station	Warden & Staff	Total person-spaces in rooms/Turnover
Cluain Mhuire Retreat Centre (n/a; Roman Catholic)	☎ Galway (353) 091 51523/53993 Wellpark, Galway *Rail:* Galway	Rev Thomas Byrne *Director of Retreats* n/a	4 single 70 double n/a
Dominican Retreat & Pastoral Centre (1928; Roman Catholic) (Previously St Joseph's Retreat House)	☎ Dublin (353) 01 515002 St Mary's Tallaght, Dublin 24 *Rail:* Dublin *Bus:* Tallaght	Dr Adrian Farrelly *Director* n/a	35 single 10 double n/a
Emmanuel House of Providence (n/a; non-denominational)	☎ Athlone (353) 0902 51501 Clonfert, Ballinasloe Co Galway *Rail:* Ballinasloe	Mr Michael Cullen Mrs Annette Cullen *Directors* n/a	25 large n/a
Emmaus Retreat Centre (n/a; Roman Catholic)	☎ Dublin (353) 01 840 1399 or 2450 Lissenhall, Swords Co Dublin *Bus:* Swords	Br M P MacThomais *Superior* n/a	78 single 5 double n/a
Grace Dieu Retreat House (n/a; Roman Catholic)	☎ Waterford (353) 051 74417 Waterford *Rail:* Waterford	Very Rev Michael Screene *Superior* n/a	30 double n/a
La Retraite (n/a; Roman Catholic)	☎ Cork (353) 021 546311 College Road, Cork *Rail:* Cork	Miss Kate O'Cleirigh *Director* n/a	100 single n/a

Retreat Houses in the Republic of Ireland

Name	Location & Station	Warden & Staff	Total person-spaces in rooms/Turnover
Manresa House (n/a; Roman Catholic)	☎Dublin (353) 01 331352 Dollymount, Dublin 3 *Bus:* Dollymount	Rev William Reynolds *Director* n/a	40 single n/a
Marie Reparatrice Retreat House (n/a; Roman Catholic)	☎Limerick (353) 061 312561 Laurel Hill Avenue South Circular Road Limerick	Sr Catherine Corry *Superior* n/a	27 single n/a
Mercy Conference & Retreat Centre (n/a; Roman Catholic)	☎Borrisoleigh (353) 0504 51109 Borrisoleigh, Thurles Co Tipperary	Sr Mary Coyle *Directoress* n/a	12 single 36 large n/a
Montfort House (n/a; Roman Catholic)	☎Monaghan (353) 047 81709 Monaghan *Rail:* Monaghan	Very Rev J Murray *Rector* n/a	25 persons n/a
Mount St Anne's (n/a; Roman Catholic)	☎Portarlington (353) 0502 26153 Killenard, Portarlington Co Laois *Rail:* Portarlington	Sister Elizabeth Maxwell *Director of Retreat House* Other staff 5	30 single 10 double 40 day room n/a – July 90
Mount St Joseph Retreat & Conference Centre (n/a; interdenominational)	☎Cork (353) 021 392160 Blarney Street, Cork *Rail:* Cork City	Br Matthew Feheny *Director* Other staff 6	35 single n/a
Myross Wood House (n/a; Roman Catholic)	☎Skibbereen (353) 028 33118 Skibbereen, Co Cork *Bus:* Skibbereen	Rev Eugene Clarkson *Director & Superior* n/a	31 single 14 double n/a
Our Lady's Retreat House (n/a; Roman Catholic)	☎Dublin (353) 01 341325/342550 Wellmount Road Finglas, Dublin 11 *Bus:* Finglas	Sr Eileen O'Neill *Superior* Other staff 13	54 large n/a
St Dominic's Retreat & Conference Centre (*CC*; 1953; Roman Catholic)	☎Cork (353) 021 502520 Ennismore, Montenotte Cork *Rail:* Cork	Rev Louis Hughes *Director* Admin staff 3 Other staff 4	40 single 12 double 40 large 80 day room n/a
St John of God Holiday & Retreat House (n/a; Roman Catholic)	☎Wexford (353) 053 37160 Ballyvaloo, Blackwater Enniscorthy, Co Wexford	Sr Assumption McCormack *Superior* Other staff 4	47 persons n/a
Stella Maris (n/a; Roman Catholic)	☎Dublin (353) 01 322228 Baily, Howth, Co Dublin *Rail:* Howth Village	Sr A Patricia Tyrell *Superior* Other staff 5	17 single n/a
Tabor House (n/a; Roman Catholic)	☎Dublin (353) 01 269 8335 Milltown Park, Dublin 6 *Bus:* Milltown Road	Rev John Callanan *Director* n/a	22 single 82 double

Retreat Houses in the Republic of Ireland

Name	Location & Station	Warden & Staff	Total person-spaces in rooms/Turnover
Teach Bridge House of Welcome for Young People (n/a; Roman Catholic)	☎Tullow (353) 0503 51374/51577 Tullow, Carlow	Very Rev Brendan Byrne *Parish Priest, Tullow* n/a	75 in sleeping bag accommodation n/a
Wesley House (1977; Methodist)	☎Dublin (353) 01 605367 Leeson Park, Dublin 6	Mr Frank D Whisker *Warden* Executive staff 3 Other staff 3	Student accommodation on yearly basis 10 double n/a

Books

	Page
Bookshops in Northern Ireland	63
Bookshops in the Republic of Ireland	66
Libraries	68
Publishers and Other Literature Producers and Distributors	68

Table 22: Irish Bookshops by Size and Number of Titles

Total titles: Size in sq ft	Under 1,000	1,000- 2,999	3,000- 9,999	10,000 or over	Not Stated	Total
Under 500	2	6	1	1	0	10
500-699	2	2	3	2	0	9
700-799	0	0	2	4	0	6
1,000-1,499	0	2	1	3	0	6
1,500 or over	0	2	1	4	1	8
Not Stated	2	0	1	2	7	12
Total	6	12	9	16[1]	8	51

[1] Eight of these are the chain of Faith Mission Bookshops with a potential of 10,000 titles in each shop

Table 23: Average Turnover, Titles and Size of Irish Religious Bookshops

	1991
Average turnover of Bookshops listed in this volume	£93,000
Average number of total titles stocked	5,300
Average number of Christian titles stocked	5,200
Average size of Bookshop in square feet	1,050
Total number of Bookshops listed	51

BOOKSHOPS IN NORTHERN IRELAND

Name	Location	Chief Officer & Staff	Turnover/Titles/Footage
Christian Book Centre (1982; non-denominational)	☎Ballyclare (08) 09603 52170 18 Rashee Road **Ballyclare** Co Antrim BT39 9HJ	Mrs Mary Campbell *Manageress* Other staff 2	n/a — Aug 90 800 titles 2 000 Christian titles 500 sq. ft.
Christian Literature Distributors (Wholesale) (1963; non-denominational)	☎Ballymena (08) 0266 652609 2 Mill Street **Ballymena** Co Antrim BT43 5AE	Mr Roy Semple *General Manager* Executive staff 2 Other staff 4	£279,893 — Mar 87 n/a titles n/a Christian titles 4,500 sq. ft.
Faith Mission Bookshop (*CC*; 1981; interdenominational)	☎Ballymena (08) 0266 49443 57 High Street, **Ballymena** Co Antrim BT43 6DT	Mr Edward Douglas *Manager* Other staff 1	n/a — Jan 91 10,000 titles 10,000 Christian titles 1,000 sq. ft.
Faith Mission Bookshop (*CC*; 1982; interdenominational)	☎Bangor (08) 0247 53222 1 Bingham Street, **Bangor** Co Down BT20 5DW	Mr Edward Douglas *Manager* Other staff 1	n/a 10,000 titles 10,000 Christian titles 750 sq. ft.
†**Belfast Cathedral** **Book Centre** **(APCK Book Centre)** (1978; Church of Ireland)	☎Belfast (08) 0232 244825 St Anne's Cathedral Donegall Street **Belfast** BT1 2HB	Mr James McAdam *General Manager* Executive staff 1 Other staff 3	n/a — May 90 1,000 titles 1,000 Christian titles 300 sq. ft.

Bookshops in Northern Ireland

Name	Location	Chief Officer & Staff	Turnover/Titles/Footage
Bethel (n/a; non-denominational)	☎Belfast (08) 0232 439525 ✆Fax (08) 0232 659518 3 Donegall Square East **Belfast** BT1 5HB	Mr Philip Lewis *Manager* Executive staff 1 Other staff 4	n/a n/a titles n/a Christian titles n/a
Covenanter Bookshop (1961; Reformed Presbyterian Church of Ireland)	☎Belfast (08) 0232 660689 98 Lisburn Road **Belfast** BT9 6AG	Rev H G Cunningham *Supervisor* Executive staff 2 Other staff 2	n/a – June 90 2,000 titles 2,000 Christian titles 400 sq. ft.
J & M Dowds Bible & Bookshop (1973; non-denominational)	☎Belfast (08) 0232 457048 183 Albertbridge Road **Belfast** BT5 4PS	Mr Stanley McDermott *Owner* Executive staff 2	n/a – Oct 90 3,000 titles 3,000 Christian titles 600 sq. ft.
Evangelical Book Shop (*CC*; 1926; interrelated trust with the Evangelical Presbyterian Church)	☎Belfast (08) 0232 320529 15 College Square East **Belfast** BT1 6DD	Mr John Grier *Manager* Executive staff 1 Other staff 3	£175,000 – Jan 90 20,000 titles 20,000 Christian titles 10,000 second-hand titles 1,000 sq. ft.
Faith Mission Bookshop (*CC*; 1889; interdenominational)	☎Belfast (08) 0232 233733 5 Queen Street **Belfast** BT1 6EA	Mr Edward Douglas *Manager* Other staff 7	n/a 10,000 titles 10,000 Christian titles 6,000 sq. ft.
Familybooks (1985; Presbyterian Church in Ireland)	☎Belfast (08) 0232 321323 The Spires Fisherwick Place **Belfast** BT1 6DX	Mrs Betty Bell *Manager* Executive staff 1 Other staff 6	£303,000 – July 90 14,000 titles 12,000 Christian titles 850 sq. ft.
Methodist Bookroom (1974; Methodist)	☎Belfast (08) 0232 320078 Aldersgate House 13 University Road **Belfast** BT7 1NA	Mr Richard Mairs *Manager* Executive staff 1 Other staff 1	n/a – Dec 90 3,000 titles 3,000 Christian titles 1,000 sq. ft.
Northern Publishing Belfast (1882; non-denominational)	☎Belfast (08) 0232 230064 64 Ann Street **Belfast** BT1 4EG	Mr Michael J Penfold *Proprietor* Executive staff 1 Other staff 3	n/a – Sept 90 10,000 titles 10,000 Christian titles 1,000 sq. ft.
Scripture Union Resource Centre (*CC*; 1954; interdenominational)	☎Belfast (08) 0232 454806 157 Albertbridge Road **Belfast** BT5 4PS	Rev David H S Armstrong *General Secretary* Executive staff 4 Other staff 3	n/a – Mar 91 1,200 titles 1,200 Christian titles 500 sq. ft.
Bookends (1978; non-denominational)	☎Coleraine (08) 0265 43300 1 Society Street **Coleraine** Co Londonderry BT52 1LA	Mr Frank Hunter *Manager* Executive staff 1	n/a 10,000 titles 2,000 Christian titles 720 sq. ft.
Mizpah Bible & Bookshop (1965; interdenominational)	☎Coleraine (08) 0265 43857 41 Kingsgate Street **Coleraine** Co Londonderry BT52 1LD	Mrs Ann Harrison *Manageress* Executive staff 1 Other staff 2	n/a – Mar 91 6,500 titles 6,500 Christian titles n/a
Faith Mission Bookshop (*CC*; 1974; interdenominational)	☎Cookstown (08) 06487 66569 48 Oldtown Street **Cookstown** Co Tyrone BT80 8EF	Mr Edward Douglas *Manager* Other staff 1	n/a 10,000 titles 10,000 Christian titles 300 sq. ft.

Bookshops in Northern Ireland

Name	Location	Chief Officer & Staff	Turnover/Titles/Footage
Christian Bookshop (1963; Elim Pentecostal) (Previously Christian Book Centre)	☎Portadown (08) 0762 334257 58 Bridge Street Portadown, **Craigavon** Co Armagh BT63 5AE	Miss Gwen Carrick *Manageress* Executive staff　1	£32,000 – Dec 90 7,000 titles 7,000 Christian titles 250 sq. ft.
Faith Mission Bookshop (*CC*; 1977; interdenominational)	☎Lurgan (08) 07622 325404 17 High Street, Lurgan **Craigavon** Co Armagh BT66 8AA	Mr Edward Douglas *Manager* Other staff　1	n/a 10,000 titles 10,000 Christian titles 500 sq. ft.
Faith Mission Bookshop (*CC*; 1972; interdenominational)	☎Portadown (08) 0762 334123 20 Thomas Street Portadown, **Craigavon** Co Armagh BT62 3NP	Mr Edward Douglas *Manager* Other staff　1	n/a 10,000 titles 10,000 Christian titles 500 sq. ft.
Evangelical Bookshop (*CC*; 1936; interdenominational)	☎Enniskillen (08) 0365 322400 8 Dublin Road, **Enniskillen** Co Fermanagh BT74 6HH	Ms Angela Jones *Manageress* Executive staff　1	£55,000 – Jan 91 2,000 titles 2,000 Christian titles 500 sq. ft.
North-West Books (1978; non-denominational)	☎Limavady (08) 05047 22835 23 Main Street, **Limavady** Co Londonderry BT49 0EP	Mr Ronald Witherow *Manager* Executive staff　1 Other staff　5	n/a – Apr 91 10,000 titles 2,000 Christian titles 700 sq. ft.
Faith Mission Bookshop (*CC*; 1986; interdenominational)	☎Lisburn (08) 0846 665888 26 Railway Street, **Lisburn** Co Antrim BT28 1XG	Mr Edward Douglas *Manager* Other staff　2	n/a 10,000 titles 10,000 Christian titles n/a
The Lisburn Bookshop **(APCK Book Centre)** (1981; Church of Ireland)	☎Lisburn (08) 0846 679680 58 Bow Street, **Lisburn** Co Antrim BT28 1BN	Mr James McAdam *General Manager* Executive staff　1 Other staff　4	n/a – May 91 20,000 titles 4,000 Christian titles 200 second-hand titles 3,000 sq. ft.
Faith Mission Bookshop (*CC*; 1986; interdenominational)	☎Londonderry (08) 0504 45137 94 Spencer Road **Londonderry** BT47 1AG	Mr Edward Douglas *Manager* Other staff　1	n/a 10,000 titles 10,000 Christian titles n/a
†**Beulah Bookshop** (1966; Free Presbyterian)	☎Newcastle (08) 03967 22629 67 Central Promenade **Newcastle** Co Down BT33 0HH	Mr G McConnell *Manager* No full-time staff	£16,300 – Dec 87 2,000 titles 2,000 Christian titles 300 second-hand titles 300 sq. ft.
Ards Evangelical Bookshop (1965; non-denominational)	☎Newtownards (08) 0247 817530 7 High Street **Newtownards** Co Down BT23 4JN	Mr Richard 　M'Coubrey *Owner & Manager* Executive staff　3 Other staff　3	n/a 20,000 titles 20,000 Christian titles 1,600 sq. ft.
Christian Book Centre (1982; non-denominational)	☎Randalstown (08) 08494 73195 14 New Street **Randalstown** Antrim BT41 3AF	Mrs Mary Campbell *Manageress* Other staff　2	n/a – Aug 90 800 titles 800 Christian titles 400 sq. ft.

BOOKSHOPS IN THE REPUBLIC OF IRELAND

Name	Location	Chief Officer & Staff	Turnover/Titles/Footage
St Paul Book Centre (1981; non-denominational)	☎ Athlone (353) 902 92882 Castle Street, **Athlone** Co Westmeath	Rev Pio Rizzo *Senior Assistant* n/a	n/a 1,000 titles 700 Christian titles 1,600 sq. ft.
Columba (1985; non-denominational)	☎ Dublin (353) 01 283 2954 93 The Rise, Mount Merrion **Blackrock,** Co Dublin	Mr Sean O'Boyle *Managing Director* Executive staff 2	n/a 950 titles 950 Christian titles n/a
Veritas Bookshop (n/a; Roman Catholic)	☎ Dublin (353) 01 889231 4 Dublin Road Stillorgan, **Blackrock** Co Dublin	Mr Chris Cunningham *Manager* Executive staff 2 Other staff 1	n/a 12,000 titles 12,000 Christian titles 400 second-hand titles 2,016 sq. ft.
APCK Book Centre (*CC*; 1982; Church of Ireland)	☎ No telephone St Finn Barres Cathedral Bishop Street **Cork**	Mrs Eva Deane *Senior Assistant* Other staff 2	n/a — May 91 500 titles 500 Christian titles n/a
†**Veritas Bookshop** (n/a; Roman Catholic)	☎ Cork (353) 074 24814 14 Bridge Street **Cork**	Mr Thomas W Egan *Manager* Executive staff 4 Other staff 1	n/a — Dec 90 2,500 titles 1,000 Christian titles 100 second-hand titles 2,100 sq. ft.
Bestseller – NBSI Bookshop (*CC*; 1806; interdenominational)	☎ Dublin (353) 01 773272 41 Dawson Street **Dublin** 2	Dr Fergus O'Ferrall *Director* Executive staff 4	n/a 5,000 titles 5,000 Christian titles 600 sq. ft.
Carmelite Book Service (1975 UK; 1981 Ireland; Roman Catholic)	☎ Dublin (353) 01 683155 Avila, Carmelite Centre of Spirituality Morehampton Road **Dublin** 4	Rev Louis Gallagher *Administrator* Executive staff 2	£12,000 — Apr 90 200 titles 200 Christian titles 600 sq. ft.
Cathedral Books Ltd (1988; non-denominational)	☎ Dublin (353) 01 787372 Fax (010 353) 01 787704 4 Sackville Place, **Dublin** 1	Mr Aidan Tarbett *Manager* Executive staff 5 Other staff 1	n/a — Jan 91 6,000 titles 6,000 Christian titles 2,000 sq. ft.
Charismatic Renewal Services (*CC*; n/a; Roman Catholic)	☎ Dublin (353) 01 685551 3 Pembroke Park Donnybrook **Dublin** 4	Ms Barbara Byrne *Shop Administrator* n/a	n/a n/a titles n/a Christian titles n/a
Christian Publication Centre (*CC*; 1965; interdenominational)	☎ Dublin (353) 01 726754 Fax 01 726754 110 Middle Abbey Street **Dublin** 1	Miss Esther Mawhinney *General Director* Executive staff 1 Other staff 2	£90,000 — Jan 91 3,000 titles 3,000 Christian titles 600 sq. ft.
St Ann's Book Centre (APCK) (1982; Church of Ireland)	☎ Dublin (353) 01 616400 St Ann's Church Dawson Street **Dublin** 2	Mr Fergus McCullough *Manager* Executive staff 1 Other staff 2	n/a — May 90 2,000 titles 2,000 Christian titles 50 second-hand titles 400 sq. ft.
Sunday School Society for Ireland Religious Education Resource Centre (n/a; Church of Ireland)	☎ Dublin (353) 01 972821 Holy Trinity Church Church Avenue Rathmines **Dublin**	Mrs Norah Bedlow *Secretary* Rev Canon R S J H McKelvey *N Ireland Representative*	n/a n/a titles n/a Christian titles n/a

Bookshops in the Republic of Ireland

Name	Location	Chief Officer & Staff	Turnover/Titles/Footage
Veritas Bookshop (n/a; Roman Catholic)	☎ Dublin (353) 01 788177 7/8 Lower Abbey Street **Dublin** 1	Ms Amanda Hughes *Manager* n/a	n/a n/a titles n/a Christian titles n/a
Scripture Union Book Centre (*CC*; 1981; interdenominational)	☎ Dublin (353) 01 280 2300 87 Lower George Street **Dun Laoghaire,** Co Dublin **Also at:** Dublin (353) 01 363764 40 Talbot Street, **Dublin** 1	Mr Kingsley Prescott *General Secretary* Executive staff 5 Other staff 1	£90,000 — Dec 90 3,000 titles 3,000 Christian titles 900 sq. ft.
Veritas Bookshop (n/a; Roman Catholic)	☎ Ennis (353) 065 28696 83 O'Connell Street **Ennis,** Co Clare	Mrs Helen O'Connor *Manager* n/a	n/a n/a titles n/a Christian titles n/a
The Upper Room (1983; non-denominational)	☎ Letterkenny (353) 074 21054 56 Upper Main Street **Letterkenny,** Co Donegal	Mr Alan Speer *Owner* No full-time staff	n/a 2,000 titles 1,000 Christian titles 1,000 sq. ft.
Veritas Bookshop (n/a; Roman Catholic)	☎ Letterkenny (353) 074 24814 13 Main Street Lower **Letterkenny,** Co Donegal	Mr Frank Greave *Manager* n/a	n/a n/a titles n/a Christian titles n/a
Limerick Christian Bookshop (1987; non-denominational)	☎ Limerick (353) 061 49730 7a Upper William Street **Limerick**	Mr Timothy O'Connell *Manager* Executive staff 1	£13,000 — Dec 87 700 titles 100 Christian titles 78 sq. ft.

LEARN NEW SKILLS!

Skills that will enable you to give positive Christian leadership amid the pressures of today's world.

Based on Biblical principles, these one-day seminars give you practical guidelines on:

- Personal communication skills • Effective use of time • Making the most of your team • Conflict & Reconciliation • Managing change • Vision building • Leadership & Motivation • Towards excellence in the ministry

"It's sharpened my thinking, renewed my vision and strengthened my skills" (Liverpool seminar)

"Wonderful biblical integration of management" (London Seminar)

Thousands have benefitted. Will you join them?

Send for details to: **MARC Europe,**
Vision Building,
4 Footscray Road,
Eltham, London SE9 2TZ.
Tel: 081-294 1989

A ministry of World Vision

MARC EUROPE

Limerick Christian Bookshop

MUSIC
CARDS
BOOKS
etc.

Supplying the entire Christian Community in the Mid Western Region

Bookshops in the Republic of Ireland

Name	Location	Chief Officer & Staff	Turnover/Titles/Footage
The Maynooth University Bookshop (1979; Roman Catholic)	☎ Dublin (353) 01 628 5222 ✆Fax (353) 01 628 9063 St Patrick's College **Maynooth,** Co Kildare	Mr John Bryne *Manager* Executive staff 3 Other staff 1	£150,000 — July 90 2,000 titles 2,000 Christian titles 900 sq. ft.
Christian Book Centre (*CC*; 1973; interdenominational)	☎ No telephone 2 Lower Market Street **Monaghan**	Mrs Elsie Moynan *Manager* No full-time staff	£30,000 — Dec 90 n/a titles n/a Christian titles n/a
Veritas Bookshop (n/a; Roman Catholic)	☎ Sligo (353) 071 61800 Adelaide House John Street, **Sligo**	Mrs Anne Hurley *Manager* n/a	n/a n/a titles n/a Christian titles n/a
The Cenacle Christian Bookshop (1984; Roman Catholic)	☎ Wexford (353) 053 44365 25 Henrietta Street **Wexford**	Mrs C Fitzgerald Mrs A Breen *Managing Partners* Other staff 1	n/a 2,500 titles 2,500 Christian titles 400 sq. ft.

LIBRARIES

Name & Magazine	Location	Chief Officer & Staff	Work & Income
Central Catholic Library (*CC*; 1922; Roman Catholic) *Biblio* 500 half-yearly	☎ Dublin (353) 01 761264 74 Merrion Square Dublin 2	Miss Nicole Arnould *Assistant Librarian* Executive staff 1 Other staff 1	Providing information regarding the Roman Catholic Church IR£20,000 — Dec 88
Community Lending Library (*CC*; 1986; Independent) No magazine	☎ Dublin (353) 01 316912 Mask Road Artane, Dublin 5	Mr Dale Taylor *Librarian* Executive staff 1 Other staff 2	Christian books covering a wide variety of topics; music and video tapes
Representative Church Body Library (1932; Church of Ireland) No magazine	☎ Dublin (353) 01 979979 Braemor Park Dublin 14	Dr Raymond Refausse *Librarian* Executive staff 2	Theological and reference library, with archives and and manuscripts IR£42,000 — Dec 88

PUBLISHERS AND OTHER LITERATURE PRODUCERS AND DISTRIBUTORS

Name & Magazine	Location	Chief Officer & Staff	Work & Income/Turnover
Ambassador Productions Ltd (1980; evangelical)	☎ Belfast (08) 0232 658462 ✆Fax (08) 0232 659518 16 Hillview Avenue Belfast BT5 6JR	Mr Samuel Lowry *Managing Director* Executive staff 2 Other staff 4	New Christian books published 1990: 14
Association for Promoting Christian Knowledge (n/a; Church of Ireland)	☎ Dublin (353) 01 555462 35 Kimmage Road West Dublin 12	Mr H R Roberts *Hon Secretary* No full-time staff	New Christian books published 1990: n/a
Berean Books (1988; non-denominational) No magazine	☎ No telephone 32 Queen's Park Coleraine Co Londonderry BT51 3JU	Mr W R Haine *Secretary* No full-time staff	Free distribution of Berean Publishing Trust tapes and literature to 32 countries n/a
Bible Society (*CC*; 1804; interdenominational) *Word of Action* Every four months	☎ Belfast (08) 0232 226577 27 Howard Street Belfast BT1 6NB *Also at:* ☎ Dublin (353) 01 773272 41 Dawson Street, Dublin 2	North Office: Mr J Dennison South Office: Dr Fergus O'Ferrall	Enabling the Word of God to reach the hearts of people everywhere n/a

Publishers and Other Literature Producers and Distributors

Name & Magazine	Location	Chief Officer & Staff	Work & Income/Turnover
Centre for Parish Development (1988; non-denominational) *In Service* Monthly	☎ Belfast (08) 0232 301130 238 Kingsway, Dunmurry Belfast BT17 9BR	Rev Canon R S J H McKelvey *Director* No full-time staff	Publications to support clergy and parish leaders n/a
Columba Press (1985; Roman Catholic) No magazine	☎ Dublin (353) 01 283 2954 ℻ Fax (353) 01 288 3770 93 The Rise, Mount Merrion Blackrock, Co Dublin	Mr Seán O'Boyle *Managing Director* Executive staff 2 Other staff 2	New Christian books published 1990: 2
Every Home Crusade (*CC*; 1960; interdenominational)	☎ Belfast (08) 0232 455026 ℻ Fax (08) 0232 455026 52 Redcar Street Belfast BT6 9BP	Mr William E Allen *Founder & Secretary* Executive staff 3 Other staff 11	Publishing Gospel tracts and booklets in 21 languages sent to over 50 countries £260,000 – Dec 89
Gill and Macmillan (1968; non-denominational)	☎ Dublin (353) 01 531005 ℻ Fax (353) 01 541688 Goldenbridge, Inchicore Dublin 8	Mr Michael Gill *Managing Director* Executive staff 35	New Christian books published 1990: 10
Mourne Missionary Trust (1976; Free Presbyterian) No magazine	☎ Kilkeel (08) 069 37 62248 Hor-Kesel, 4 Church Road Carginagh, Kilkeel Newry, Co Down BT34 4QB	Mr George McConnell *Director* Executive staff 1	Bookseller, publisher and literature distributor at markets and fairs in Ulster £33,000 – n/a
National Bible Society of Ireland (*CC*; 1806; interdenominational) *Briathar Dé Newsletter*	☎ Dublin (353) 773272 ℻ Fax (353) 710040 41 Dawson Street Dublin 2	Dr Fergus O'Ferrall *Director* Executive staff 3 Other staff 1	The widest possible effective distribution of the Bible £110,000 – Dec 89
Renewal Publications (1975; non-denominational)	☎ Belfast (08) 0232 301130 238 Kingsway, Dunmurry Belfast BT17 9AE	Rev Canon R S J H McKelvey *Director* n/a	New Christian books published 1990: 2
Scripture Gift Mission Inc (*CC*; 1888; non-denominational) *SGM News* 20,000 quarterly	☎ Belfast (08) 0232 321923 1st Floor Scottish Provident Building 7 Donegall Square West Belfast BT1 6JB	Mr John McIlvenna *Secretary for Ireland* Executive staff 1 Other staff 2	Publishing Scripture booklets and leaflets in 400 languages for use in personal evangelism. Produce Bibles and Scripture posters £71,000 – Dec 89
Sunday School Society for Ireland (*CC*; 1809; Anglican) No magazine	☎ Dublin (353) 01 972821 Holy Trinity Church Church Avenue Rathmines, Dublin	Mrs Norah Bedlow *Secretary* Full-time staff 3	Supplying Sunday School materials for teachers and pupils £11,331 – Dec 90
Veritas Publications (*CC*; 1969; Roman Catholic)	☎ Dublin (353) 01 788177 ℻ Fax (353) 01 786507 7 Lower Abbey Street Dublin 1	Mr Tom Griffin *Commercial Manager* Executive staff 3 Other staff 16	New Christian books published 1990: 20

Fig 38: Counties of Ireland

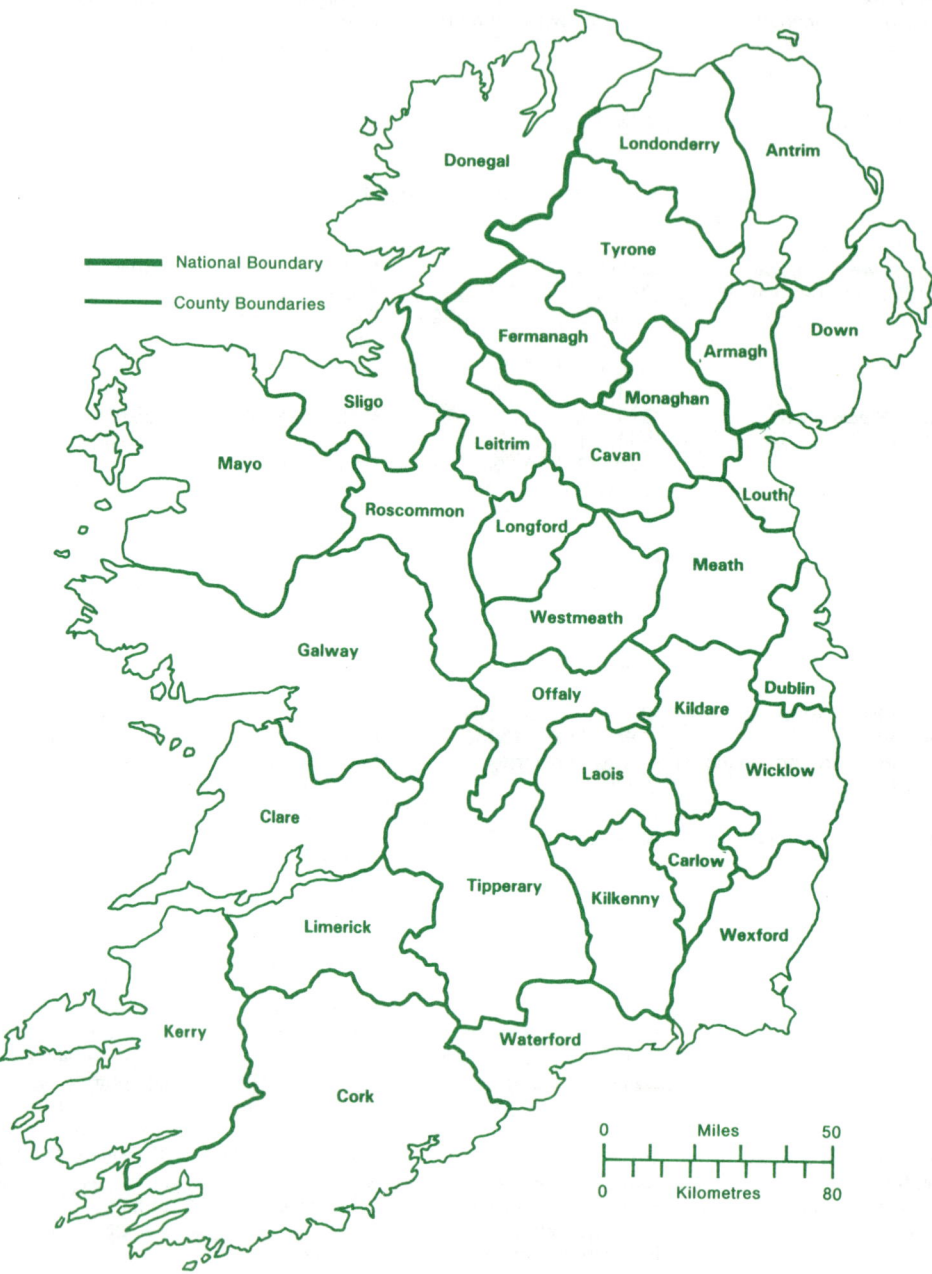

Churches & Evangelism

	Page
Church Headquarters	71
Church and Other Organisations	82
City and Town Missions	82
Evangelistic Agencies	83

CHURCH HEADQUARTERS

Name	Location	Chief Officer & Staff	Magazine
Baptist Union of Ireland (1650)	☎ Belfast (08) 0232 663108 Fax (08) 0232 663616 117 Lisburn Road Belfast BT9 7AF	Rev J R Grant *Secretary* Executive staff 4 Other staff 4	*The Irish Baptist* 3,200 monthly
Southern Association of Irish Baptist Churches	☎ Limerick (353) 061 327124 60 Blackthorn Drive Caherdavin, Limerick	Mr P O'Driscoll *Secretary*	*The Irish Baptist* 3,200 monthly
Catholic Press and Information Office (1975; Roman Catholic) No magazine	☎ Dublin (353) 01 288 5043 Fax (353) 01 283 4161 169 Booterstown Road Blackrock, Co Dublin	Mr Jim Cantwell *Director* Executive staff 5	Liaison between the Roman Catholic Church in Ireland and the media n/a
Roman Catholic Archdiocese of Armagh (444)	☎ Armagh (08) 0861 522045 Fax (08) 0861 526182 Ara Coeli Armagh BT61 7QY	Most Rev Cahal B Daly *Archbishop of Armagh & Primate of All Ireland* Executive staff 2 Diocesan clergy 246	No magazine
Diocese of Ardagh and Clonmacnois	☎ Longford (353) 043 46432 Bishops House St Michael's, Longford	Most Rev Colm O'Reilly *Bishop of Ardagh and Clonmacnois* Diocesan clergy 95	
Diocese of Clogher	☎ Monaghan (353) 047 81019 Bishops House, Monaghan	Most Rev Joseph Duffy *Bishop of Clogher* Diocesan clergy 112	
Diocese of Derry	☎ Derry (08) 0504 262302 Bishops House St Eugene's Cathedral Londonderry BT48 9AP	Most Rev Edward Daly *Bishop of Derry* Diocesan clergy 147	
Diocese of Down and Connor	☎ Belfast (08) 0232 776185 Lisbreen 73 Somerton Road Belfast BT15 4DE	Most Rev Patrick J Walsh *Bishop of Down and Connor* Diocesan clergy 308	

Fig 39: Roman Catholic Diocesan boundaries

Provinces and their Dioceses:

Province of Armagh
1. Armagh Archdiocese
2. Ardagh & Clonmacnois
3. Clogher
4. Derry
5. Down & Connor
6. Dromore
7. Kilmore
8. Meath
9. Raphoe

Province of Dublin
10. Dublin Archdiocese
11. Ferns
12. Kildare & Leighlin
13. Ossory

Province of Cashel
14. Cashel & Emly Archdiocese
15. Cloyne
16. Cork & Ross
17. Kerry
18. Killaloe
19. Limerick
20. Waterford & Lismore

Province of Tuam
21. Tuam Archdiocese
22. Achonry
23. Clonfert
24. Elphin
25. Galway
26. Killala

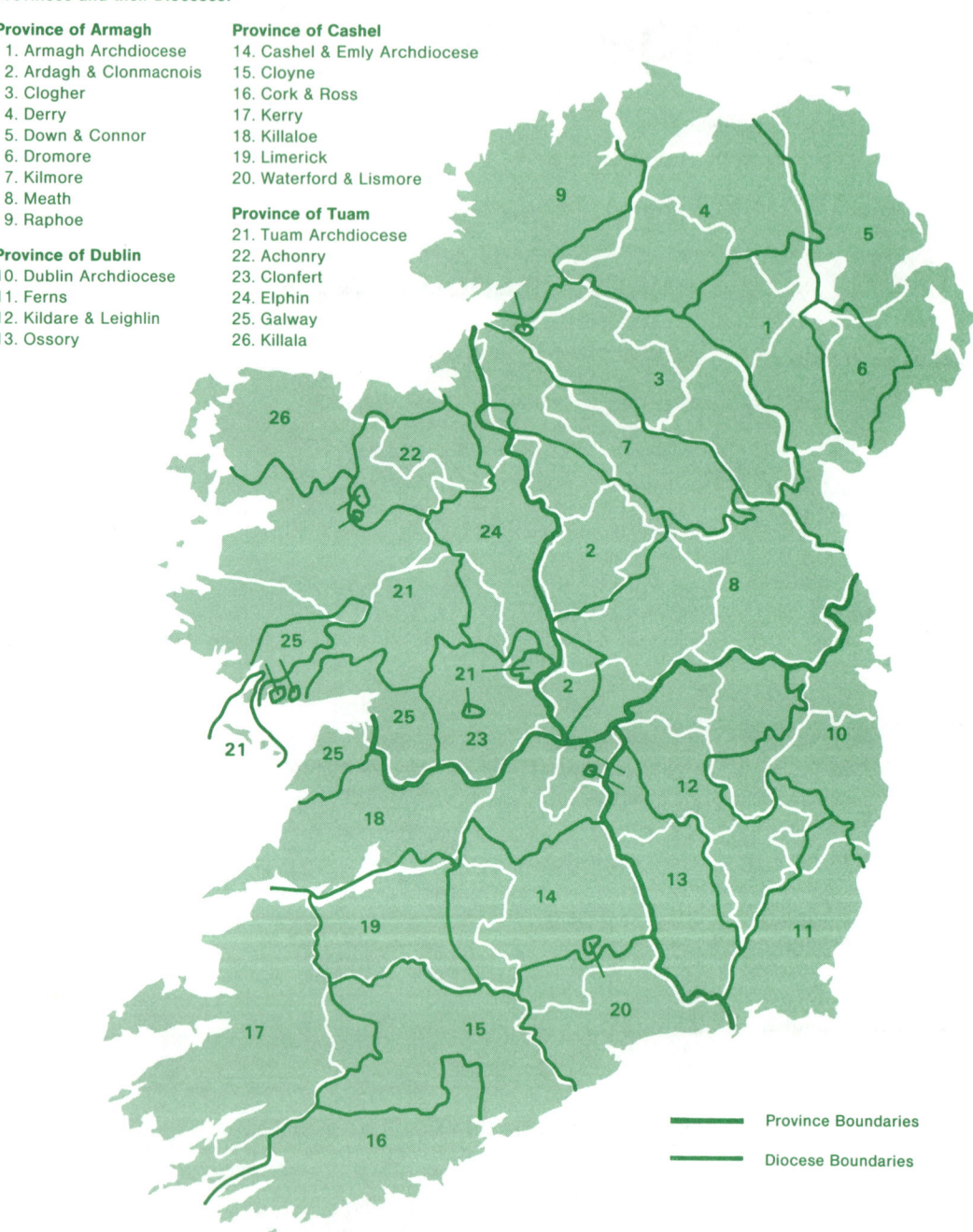

Province Boundaries
Diocese Boundaries

© John Whitehorn

Name	Location	Chief Officer & Staff	Church Headquarters Magazine
Diocese of Dromore	☎Newry (08) 0693 62444 Bishops House Violet Hill, Newry Co Down BT35 6PN	Most Rev Francis Brooks *Bishop of Dromore* Diocesan clergy 75	
Diocese of Kilmore	☎Cavan (353) 049 31496 Bishops House Cullies, Cavan	Most Rev Francis McKiernan *Bishop of Kilmore* Diocesan clergy 106	
Diocese of Meath	☎Mullingar (353) 044 48841 Bishops House Dublin Road, Mullingar Co Westmeath	Most Rev Michael Smith *Bishop of Meath* Diocesan clergy 252	
Diocese of Raphoe	☎Letterkenny (353) 074 21208 Ard Adhamhnain Letterkenny, Co Donegal	Most Rev Seamus Heaney *Bishop of Raphoe* Diocesan clergy 72	

Roman Catholic Archdiocese of Cashel
(n/a)
	☎Thurles (353)
	0504 21512
	Bishop's House, Thurles
	Co Tipperary
		Most Rev Dermot
		  Clifford
		Archbishop of Cashel
		Diocesan
		  clergy 121
			No magazine

Diocese of Cloyne	☎Cork (353) 021 811430 Bishops House Cobh, Co Cork	Most Rev John Magee *Bishop of Cloyne* Diocesan clergy 159	
Diocese of Cork and Ross	☎Cork (353) 021 501717 Bishops House Redemption Road, Cork	Most Rev Michael Murphy *Bishop of Cork and Ross* Diocesan clergy 341	
Diocese of Kerry	☎Killarney (353) 064 31168 Bishops House Killarney, Co Kerry	Most Rev Dermot O'Sullivan *Bishop of Kerry* Diocesan clergy 134	
Diocese of Killaloe	☎Ennis (353) 065 28638 Westbourne Ennis, Co Clare	Most Rev Michael Harty *Bishop of Killaloe* Diocesan clergy 339	
Diocese of Limerick	☎Limerick (353) 061 315856 Diocesan Offices 66 O'Connell Street Limerick	Most Rev Jeremiah Newton *Bishop of Limerick* Diocesan clergy 220	

Diocese of Waterford and Lismore	☎Waterford (353)
	051 81531
	Bishops House
	John's Hill, Waterford
		Most Rev Michael Russell
		*Bishop of Waterford and
		  Lismore*
		Diocesan
		  clergy 109	

Roman Catholic Archdiocese of Dublin
(n/a)
	☎Dublin
	(353) 01 373732
	Archbishop's House
	Dublin 9
		Most Rev Desmond
		  Connell
		Archbishop of Dublin
		Diocesan
		  clergy 790
			No magazine

Diocese of Ferns	☎Wexford (353) 053 23706 Bishops House Summerhill, Co Wexford	Most Rev Brendan Comiskey *Bishop of Ferns* Diocesan clergy 143	

Church Headquarters

Name	Location	Chief Officer & Staff	Magazine
Diocese of Kildare and Leighlin	☎Carlow (353) 0503 31102 Bishops House Carlow	Most Rev Laurence Ryan *Bishop of Kildare and Leighlin* Diocesan clergy 195	
Diocese of Ossory	☎Kilkenny (353) 056 21060 Sion House, Kilkenny	Most Rev Laurence Forristal *Bishop of Ossory* Diocesan clergy 118	
Roman Catholic Archdiocese of Tuam (n/a)	☎Galway (353) 0912 4166 Archbishop's House Tuam, Co Galway	Most Rev Joseph Cassidy *Archbishop of Tuam* Diocesan clergy 176	No magazine
Diocese of Achonry	☎Roscommon (353) 0907 60021 Bishops House Ballaghaderreen Co Roscommon	Most Rev Thomas Flynn *Bishop of Achonry* Diocesan clergy 50	
Diocese of Clonfert	☎Galway (353) 091 41560 Bishops House St Brendans, Corrheen Loughrea, Co Galway	Most Rev John Kirby *Bishop of Clonfert* Diocesan clergy 77	
Diocese of Elphin	☎Sligo (353) 071 62670 St Mary's, Sligo	Most Rev Dominic Conway *Bishop of Elphin* Diocesan clergy 99	
Diocese of Galway Kilmacduagh and Kilfenora	☎Galway (353) 091 63566 Mount St Mary's Galway	To be appointed *Bishop of Galway, Kilmacduagh and Kilfenora* Diocesan clergy 133	
Diocese of Killala	☎Ballina (353) 096 22177 Diocesan Office Cathedral Close Ballina, Co Mayo	Most Rev Thomas Finnegan *Bishop of Killala* Diocesan clergy 49	
Church of Ireland (Disestablished 1869)	☎Dublin (353) 01 978422 Fax (353) 01 978821 Church of Ireland House Church Avenue Rathmines, Dublin 6	Mr R H Sherwood *Chief Officer & Secretary* Admin staff 23	*Church of Ireland Gazette* 6,000 weekly
Church of Ireland Archdiocese of Armagh	☎Armagh (08) 0861 522851 The See House Cathedral Close Armagh BT61 7EE	Most Rev Robin Eames *Archbishop of Armagh, Primate of All Ireland and Metropolitan*	*Church of Ireland Gazette* 6,000 weekly
Diocese of Clogher (493)	☎Fivemiletown (08) 0365 521265 The See House 150 Ballagh Road Fivemiletown Co Tyrone BT75 0QP	Rt Rev Brian D A Hannon *Bishop of Clogher*	*Clogher Diocesan Magazine* 2,000 monthly

(continued on Page 76)

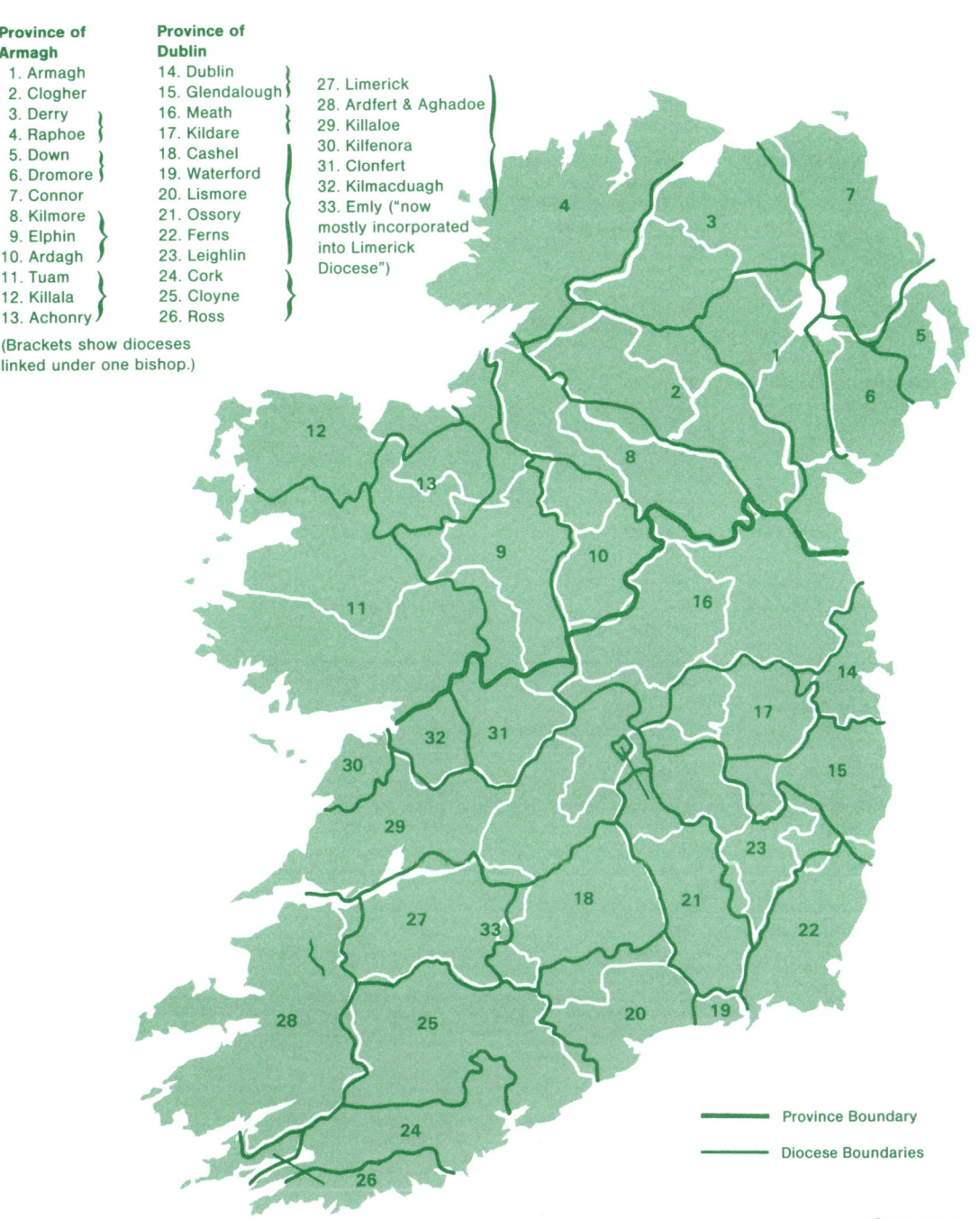

Fig 40: Church of Ireland Diocesan boundaries

Province of Armagh
1. Armagh
2. Clogher
3. Derry
4. Raphoe }
5. Down
6. Dromore }
7. Connor
8. Kilmore
9. Elphin
10. Ardagh }
11. Tuam
12. Killala
13. Achonry }

Province of Dublin
14. Dublin
15. Glendalough }
16. Meath
17. Kildare
18. Cashel
19. Waterford
20. Lismore }
21. Ossory
22. Ferns
23. Leighlin }
24. Cork
25. Cloyne
26. Ross }
27. Limerick
28. Ardfert & Aghadoe
29. Killaloe
30. Kilfenora
31. Clonfert
32. Kilmacduagh
33. Emly ("now mostly incorporated into Limerick Diocese")

(Brackets show dioceses linked under one bishop.)

— Province Boundary
— Diocese Boundaries

© John Whitehorn

Church Headquarters

Name	Location	Chief Officer & Staff	Magazine
Diocese of Clogher (493) (continued)	☎Ballinamallard (08) 0365 81 477 St Michael's Rectory Rossfad, Ballinamallard Enniskillen Co Fermanagh BT94 2LS	Canon T R Moore *Diocesan Secretary*	
Diocese of Connor	☎Belfast (08) 0232 668422 Bishops House 22 Deramore Park Belfast BT9 5JU	Rt Rev Samuel Poyntz *Bishop of Connor*	
Diocese of Derry and Raphoe	☎Londonderry (08) 0504 351206 The See House 112 Culmore Road Londonderry BT48 8JF	Rt Rev James Mehaffey *Bishop of Derry and Raphoe*	
Diocese of Down and Dromore	☎Belfast (08) 0232 471973 The See House 32 Knockdene Park South Belfast BT5 7AB	Rt Rev Gordon McMullan *Bishop of Down and Dromore*	
Diocese of Kilmore, Elphin and Ardagh (1692)	☎Cavan (353) 049 31336 The See House Kilmore, Cavan	Rt Rev William G Wilson *Bishop of Kilmore, Elphin and Ardagh*	
Diocese of Tuam, Killala and Achonry (1622)	☎Ballina (353) 096 31317 Bishops House Crossmolina, Co Mayo	Rt Rev John R W Neill *Bishop of Tuam, Killala and Achonry*	
Church of Ireland Archdiocese of Dublin	☎Dublin (353) 01 977849 The See House 17 Temple Road Milltown, Dublin 6	Most Rev Donald Caird *Archbishop of Dublin and Glendalough*	*Church of Ireland Gazette* 6,000 weekly
Diocese of Cashel and Ossory	☎Kilkenny (353) 056 21560 The Palace, Kilkenny	Rt Rev Noel V Willoughby *Bishop of Cashel, Waterford, Lismore, Ossory, Ferns and Leighlin*	
Diocese of Cork, Cloyne and Ross (606)	☎Cork (353) 021 271214 The Palace Bishop Street, Cork ☎Cork (353) 021 968467 Fax (353) 021 968467 The Diocesan Office Cove Street, Cork	Rt Rev Robert A Warke *Bishop of Cork, Cloyne and Ross* Mr Wilfred Baker *Diocesan Secretary* Executive staff 2	*Diocesan Magazine* 1,400 monthly
Diocese of Limerick and Killaloe (1661)	☎Limerick (353) 061 51532 Bishops House North Circular Road Limerick	Rt Rev Edward Darling *Bishop of Limerick and Killaloe*	
Diocese of Meath and Kildare	☎Dublin (353) 01 628 9354 Bishops House Moyglare, Maynooth Co Kildare	Most Rev Walton N F Empey *Bishop of Meath and Kildare*	

Church Headquarters

Name	Location	Chief Officer & Staff	Magazine
Congregational Union of Ireland (1829)	☎ Belfast (08) 0232 653140 38 Edgecumbe Gardens Belfast BT4 2EH	Rev Malcolm Coles *Secretary* n/a	*The Congregationalist* 1,400 quarterly
Elim Pentecostal Church (n/a)	☎ Belfast (08) 0232 657744 20 Kings Road Belfast BT5 6JJ	Rev E McComb *Irish Superintendent*	No magazine
Evangelical Presbyterian Church (1927)	☎ Belfast (08) 0232 320529 15 College Square East Belfast BT1 6DD	Rev Samuel Watson *Clerk of Presbytery* Executive staff 11	*Evangelical Presbyterian* 1,000 ten times a year
Free Presbyterian Church of Ulster (1951)	☎ Belfast (08) 0232 457106 Church House 356 Ravenhill Road Belfast BT6 8GL ***Correspondence:*** ☎ Lisburn (08) 0846 674664 40 Lombard Avenue, Lisburn Co Antrim BT28 2UP	Dr John Douglas *Clerk of Presbytery* n/a	*The Revivalist* 4,000 monthly *Truth for Youth* 3,200 every two months
Methodist Church in Ireland (1738)	☎ Belfast (08) 0232 324554 1 Fountainville Avenue Belfast BT9 6AN	Rev Edmund T I Mawhinney *Secretary of Conference* Executive staff 1	*Methodist Newsletter* 4,750 monthly
Belfast District	☎ Belfast (08) 0232 241917 Grosvenor Hall 5 Glengall Street Belfast BT12 5AD	Rev David J Kerr *District Chairman*	
Down District	☎ Bangor (08) 0247 472551 1 Brooklyn Avenue, Bangor Co Down BT20 5RB	Rev Richard H Taylor *District Chairman*	
Dublin District	☎ Dublin (353) 01 906998 Mayo House Rathdown Park Rathfarnam, Dublin	Rev Paul Kingston *District Chairman*	
Enniskillen and Sligo District	☎ Lisnaskea (08) 036 57 22144 Aldersgate, Lisnaskea Co Fermanagh BT92 0DX	Rev Christopher G Walpole *District Chairman* Serving ministers 12	
Londonderry District	☎ Londonderry (08) 0504 42644 11 Clearwater Clooney Hall Londonderry BT47 1BE	Rev Kenneth Best *District Chairman*	
Midlands and Southern District	☎ Cork (353) 021 292503 Epworth, Woolhara Park Cork	Rev Robert Roddie *District Chairman*	
North East District	☎ Belfast (08) 0232 851144 103 Station Road Greenisland, Carrickfergus Co Antrim BT38 8UW	Rev Duncan Alderdice *District Chairman*	

Fig 41: Methodist Church in Ireland District boundaries

Districts:
1. Dublin
2. Midlands and Southern
3. Enniskillen and Sligo
4. Londonderry
5. North East
6. Belfast
7. Down
8. Portadown

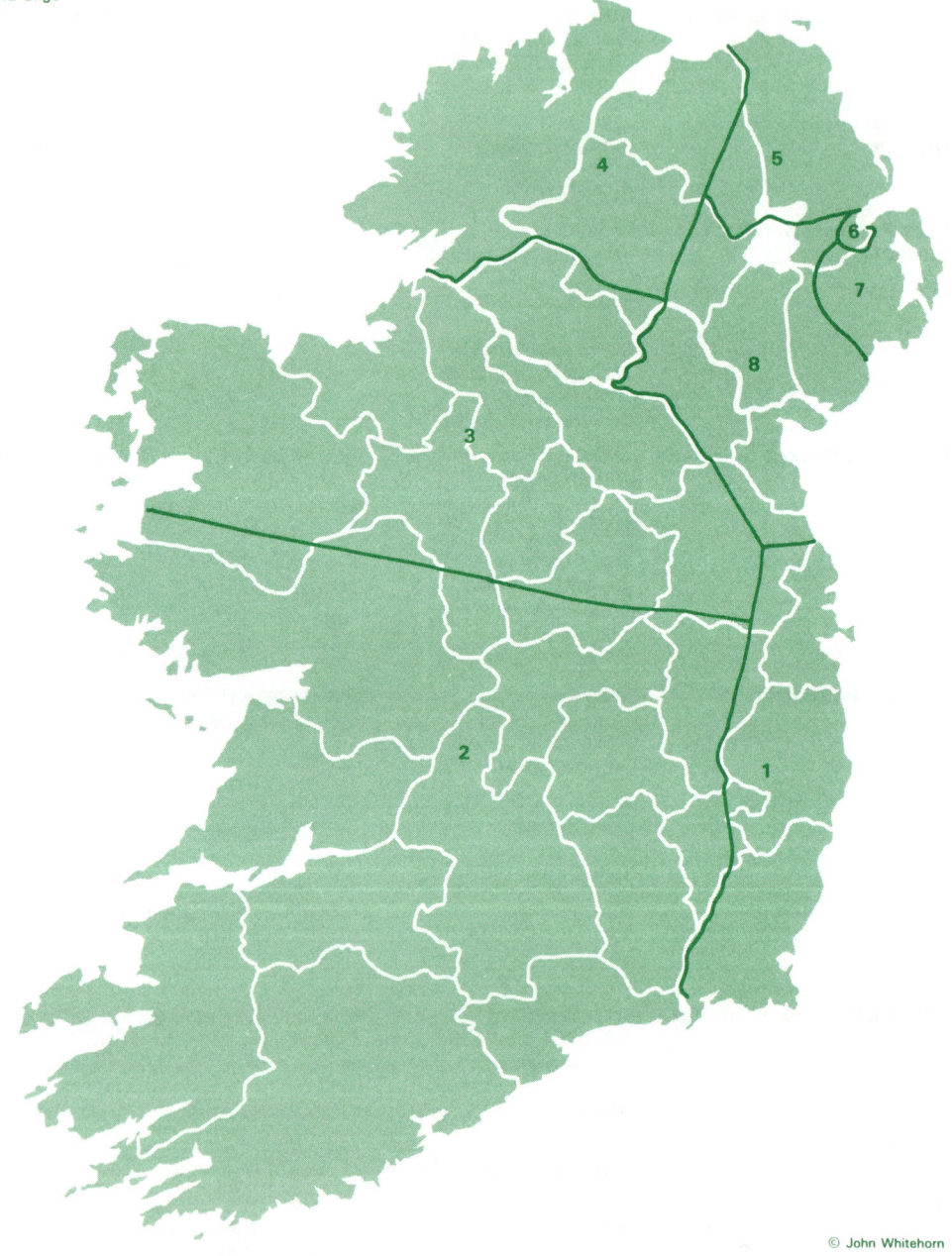

© John Whitehorn

Church Headquarters

Name	Location	Chief Officer & Staff	Magazine
Portadown District	☎ Craigavon (08) 9762 223367 1 Corby Drive Lurgan, Craigavon Co Armagh BT66 7AF	Rev S Kenneth Todd *District Chairman*	
Non-subscribing Presbyterian Church of Ireland (1910)	☎ Larne (08) 0574 72600 102 Carrickfergus Road Larne Co Antrim BT40 3JX	Rev Dr J W Nelson *Clerk of the General Synod* No full-time staff	*The Non-subscribing Presbyterian* 1,100 monthly
The Presbyterian Church in Ireland (1642; synods united 1840)	☎ Belfast (08) 0232 322284 ✉ Fax (08) 0232 248377 Church House Fisherwick Place Belfast BT1 6DW	Rev Samuel Hutchinson *Clerk of Assembly & General Secretary* Executive staff 10 Other staff 32	*The Presbyterian Herald* 20,000 monthly
Ards Presbytery	☎ Bangor (08) 0247 450141 3 Second Avenue Baylands, Bangor Co Down BT20 5JZ	Rev Dr Donald Watts *Clerk of Presbytery*	
Armagh Presbytery	☎ Lurgan (08) 0762 881276 23 Mill Hill Waringstown, Lurgan Co Armagh BT66 7QL	Rev T W D Johnston *Clerk of Presbytery*	
Ballymena Presbytery	☎ Ballymena (08) 0266 83221 The Manse, 120 Church Road Glenwherry, Ballymena Co Antrim BT42 3EJ	Rev James Gordon *Clerk of Presbytery*	
Belfast East Presbytery	☎ Belfast (08) 0232 622626 20 Glendun Park, Dunmurry Belfast BT17 9AY	Rev Herbert Courtney *Clerk of Presbytery*	
Belfast North Presbytery	☎ Belfast (08) 0232 778565 11 Waterloo Gardens Belfast BT15 4EX	Rev J R Dickinson *Clerk of Presbytery*	
Belfast South Presbytery	☎ Belfast (08) 0232 667247 3 Shrewsbury Gardens Belfast BT9 6PJ	Rev R T Anderson *Clerk of Presbytery*	
Carrickfergus Presbytery	☎ Larne (08) 0574 583643 19 Wheatfield Heights Ballygally, Larne Co Antrim BT40 2RT	Very Rev Dr R V A Lynas *Clerk of Presbytery*	
Coleraine Presbytery	☎ Coleraine (08) 0265 731310 8 Ballywatt Road Cloughfin, Coleraine Co Londonderry BT52 2LT	Rev W I Hunter *Clerk of Presbytery*	
Derry and Strabane Presbytery	☎ Londonderry (08) 0504 42478 59 Limavady Road Londonderry BT47 1LR	Rev R C Graham *Clerk of Presbytery*	

Fig 42: Presbyterian Church in Ireland Presbytery boundaries

Presbyteries:
1. Ards
2. Armagh
3. Ballymena
4. Belfast North
5. Belfast South
6. Belfast East
7. Carrickfergus
8. Coleraine
9. Derry
9. Strabane*
10. Donegal
11. Down
12. Dromore
13. Dublin & Munster
14. Foyle
15. Iveagh
16. Monaghan
17. Newry
18. Omagh
19. Route
20. Templepatrick
21. Tyrone

* Now united with Derry

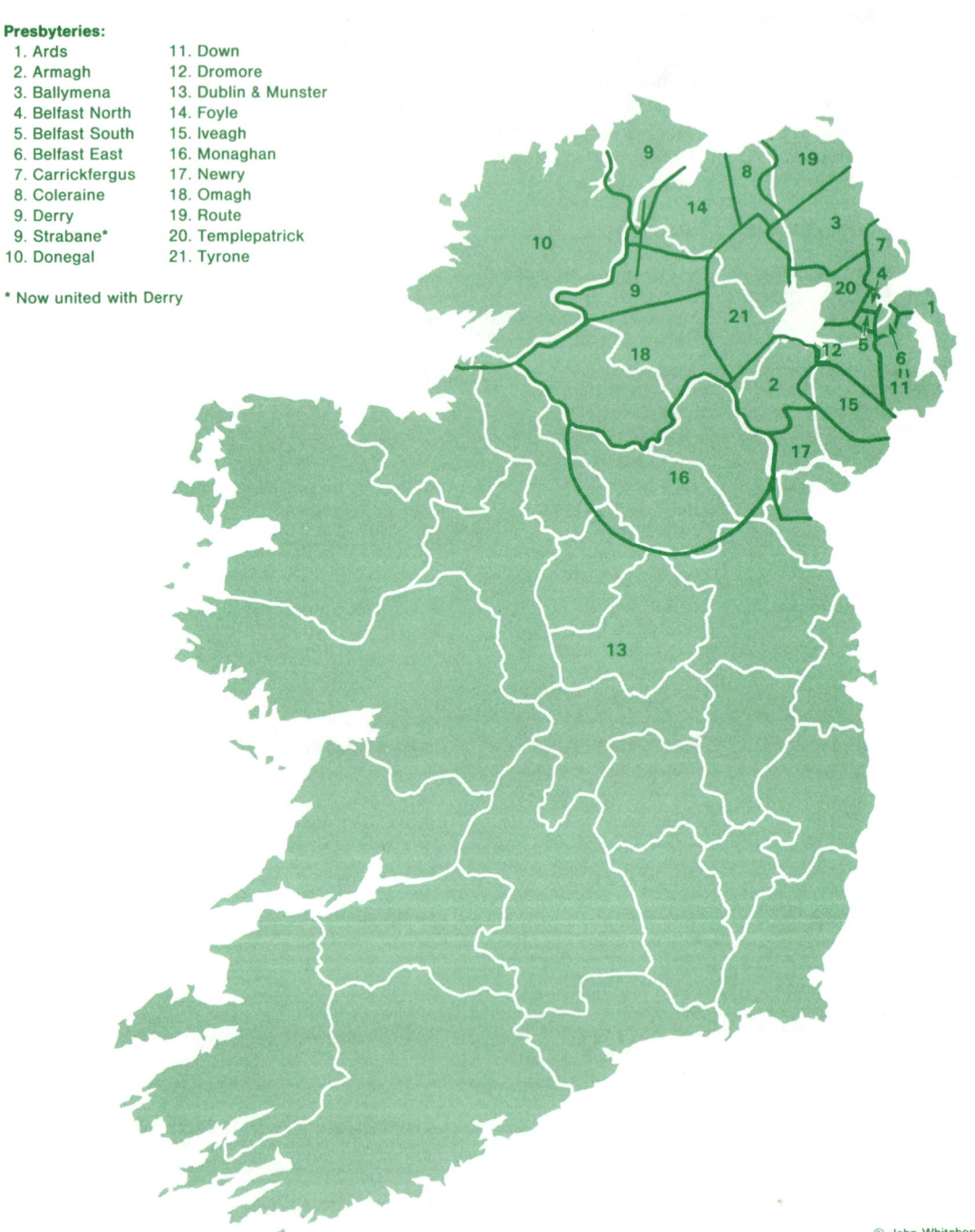

© John Whitehorn

Church Headquarters

Name	Location	Chief Officer & Staff	Magazine
Donegal Presbytery	☏Letterkenny (353) 074 45220 Lisnoble Manse, Raphoe Lifford, Co Donegal	Rev Brian Brown *Clerk of Presbytery*	
Down Presbytery	☏Downpatrick (08) 0396 830041 17 Downpatrick Road Crossgar, Downpatrick Co Down BT30 9EQ	Rev Samuel Armstrong *Clerk of Presbytery*	
Dromore Presbytery	☏Dromore (08) 0846 683696 2 Lisburn Road Hillsborough Co Down BT26 6AE	Rev J I Davey *Clerk of Presbytery*	
Dublin Presbytery	☏Dublin (353) 01 378600 523 Griffith Avenue Dublin 11	Rev A V Martin *Clerk of Presbytery*	
Foyle Presbytery	☏Limavady (08) 050 47 22617 48 Scroggy Road Limavady Co Londonderry BT49 0NB	Mr R W Alcorn *Clerk of Presbytery*	
Iveagh Presbytery	☏Craigavon (08) 0762 831265 28 Manse Road Ballynagarrick, Craigavon Co Armagh BT63 5NW	Rev D C Porter *Clerk of Presbytery*	
Monaghan Presbytery	☏Monaghan (353) 047 57023 15 Sperrin Park Armagh BT61 9EP	Rev Walter Herron *Clerk of Presbytery*	
Newry Presbytery	☏Newcastle (08) 039 67 68232 156 Glasdrumman Road Annalong, Newry Co Down BT34 4QL	Rev S A Finlay *Clerk of Presbytery*	
Omagh Presbytery	☏Omagh (08) 0662 242239 28 Dublin Road, Omagh Co Tyrone BT78 1HE	Rev J F Murdoch *Clerk of Presbytery*	
Route Presbytery	☏Bushmills (08) 026 57 31305 211 Straid Road, Bushmills Co Antrim BT57 8XB	Rev H B Wallace *Clerk of Presbytery*	
Templepatrick Presbytery	☏Templepatrick (08) 084 94 22436 50 Killead Road, Crumlin Co Antrim BT29 4EN	Rev W D Weir *Clerk of Presbytery*	
Tyrone Presbytery	☏Moneymore (08) 064 87 48012 10 Ministers Walk Moneymore, Magherafelt Co Londonderry BT45 7QE	Rev J B McCormick *Clerk of Presbytery*	

Church Headquarters

Name	Location	Chief Officer & Staff	Magazine
Reformed Presbyterian Church of Ireland (1763)	☎ Newtownards (08) 0247 813506 Cameron House 98 Lisburn Road Belfast BT9 6AG	Rev C Knox Hyndman *Clerk of Synod* n/a	*Covenanter Witness* 500 monthly *The Messenger* (youth) 500 every two months
*****Salvation Army: Northern Ireland Division** (n/a)	☎ Belfast (08) 0232 324730 4 Curtis Street Belfast BT1 2ND	Major Alan Hart *Divisional Commander* Executive staff 4 Other staff 3 Serving officers 42	No magazine
Seventh-day Adventist Church	☎ Banbridge (08) 08206 26361 Irish Mission Office 9 Newry Road, Banbridge Co Down BT32 3NB	Mr Alan Hodges *President of Irish Mission*	

CHURCH AND OTHER ORGANISATIONS

Name & Magazine	Location	Chief Officer & Staff	Work & Income
*****Evangelical Alliance** (*CC*; 1846; interdenominational) *IDEA* 38,000 every two months	☎ Belfast (08) 0232 247920 3 Fitzwilliam Street Belfast BT9 6AW	Rev Howard Lewis *General Secretary* Other staff 1	Promoting unity and co-operation among evangelical churches and organisations and providing services to them n/a
Inter-Church Relations Board (n/a; Presbyterian Church in Ireland) No magazine	☎ Ballybay (353) 42 41051 Clones Road Ballybay, Co Monaghan	Rev David Nesbitt *Convener* No full-time staff	Encouraging relations with other churches, councils of churches and ecumenical organisations n/a
Irish Council of Churches (*CC*; 1920; interdenominational) *Irish Ecumenical News* 5,000 quarterly	☎ Belfast (08) 0232 663145 ☎Fax (08) 0232 381737 Inter-Church Centre 48 Elmwood Avenue Belfast BT9 6AZ	Rt Hon David W Bleakley *General Secretary* Executive staff 6 Other staff 6	Partnership of the main Protestant churches, working in co-operation with the Roman Catholic Church £75,000 – Dec 90
Pontifical Missionary Union of Priests and Religious (n/a; Roman Catholic) No magazine	☎ Dublin (353) 01 972035/ 972 422 64 Lower Rathmines Road Dublin 6	Rev Seamus Galvin *National Director* n/a	To unite clergy and religious into an organisation for assisting the missions n/a
Religious Press Association (n/a; non-denominational)	☎ Dublin (353) 01 749464 27 Upper Sherrard Street Dublin 1	Miss Maureen Manning *Secretary* n/a	Support and resource service for the religious press n/a

CITY AND TOWN MISSIONS

Name	Location	Chief Officer & Staff	Work & Income
Belfast Central Mission (n/a; Methodist)	☎ Belfast (08) 0232 241917 Grosvenor Hall 5 Glengall Street Belfast BT12 5AD	Rev David J Kerr *Superintendent* n/a	Chaplaincy, social work and counselling, open-air witness n/a

City and Town Missions

Name	Location	Chief Officer & Staff	Work & Income
Belfast City Mission (*CC*; 1827; Presbyterian) *Annual Report* 2,750 annually	☎ Belfast (08) 0232 320557 Church House Fisherwick Place Belfast BT1 6DW	Mr William H Cooke *General Secretary* Executive staff 2 Mission and office staff 23	Evangelism through home visitation, personal work, gospel meetings and youth activities £220,000 – Feb 88
Dublin Central Mission (1893; Methodist) No magazine	☎ Dublin (353) 01 742123 7 Marlborough Place Dublin 1	Rev Desmond C Bain *Superintendent* Executive staff 5 Other staff 21	Incorporates a worshipping community; ministry to alcoholics; sheltered housing for elderly; half-way house for ex-prisoners; emergency relief £325,000 – Dec 89
†Dublin Christian Mission (*Irish CC*; 1966; non-denominational) *Spotlight* 1,500 every two months	☎ Dublin (353) 01 775548 5 Chancery Place, Dublin 7 *Also at:* ☎ Lisburn (08) 023 82 3595 2 Ruskin Heights, Lisburn Co Antrim BT27 5QN *And:* 47 Sunningdale Park Ballymena Co Antrim BT43 5NQ *And:* 93 Church Street Cookstown Co Tyrone BT80 8HT	Mr Gordon Lewis *Secretary* Executive staff 2 Other staff 1	Preaching the Gospel and meeting social and material needs as they arise £27,000 – Dec 87
East Belfast Mission (n/a; Methodist)	☎ Belfast (08) 0232 458560 239 Newtownards Road Belfast BT4 1AF	Rev W James Rea *Superintendent* n/a	Christian caring for the needy, day centre, ministry to alcoholics n/a
Irish Church Missions (1849; Church of Ireland) No magazine	☎ Dublin (353) 01 730829 28 Bachelor's Walk Dublin 1	Rev W J Bridcut *Superintendent* Other staff 3	Involved in evangelistic mission in the city and other areas n/a
Londonderry City Mission (n/a; Methodist)	☎ Londonderry (08) 0504 48531 11 Clearwater Clooney Road Londonderry BT47 1BE	Rev Kenneth Best *Superintendent* n/a	Evangelism, social and pastoral care, Christian education n/a
North Belfast Mission (1898; Methodist)	☎ Belfast (08) 0232 852546 Rathcoole Drive Newtownabbey Co Antrim BT37 9AQ	Rev William T Buchanan *Superintendent* n/a	Evangelistic outreach, worship and training, community services n/a
†Shankill Road Mission (*CC*; 1898; Presbyterian Church in Ireland) No magazine	☎ Belfast (08) 0232 324345 116 Shankill Road Belfast BT13 2BD	Rev W M Campbell *Superintendent* Executive staff 4 Other staff 5	Promoting the welfare of local people through evangelism and social witness £70,000 – Dec 87

EVANGELISTIC AGENCIES

Name & Magazine	Location	Chief Officer & Staff	Work & Income
26.3 Trust (*CC*; 1989; non-denominational) No magazine	☎ Belfast (08) 0232 669833 12 Derryvolgie Avenue Belfast BT9 6FL	Mr Eric Lennon *Secretary* No full-time staff	Evangelism; setting up homes for care and respite of addicts and single homeless

Evangelistic Agencies

Name & Magazine	Location	Chief Officer & Staff	Work & Income
Agapé (Ireland) (1973; interdenominational) (Previously Campus Crusade for Christ (Ireland)) *Together* 1,000 quarterly	☎ Dublin (353) 01 2695611 264 Merrion Road Dublin 4	Mr Joe Carey *Co-ordinator* Executive staff 5	Presenting the challenge of the Christian faith to Irish society £116,311 – June 87
Agape Fellowship (*CC*; 1969; non-denominational) *Prayer letter* 400 quarterly	☎ Belfast (08) 0232 796368 22 Everton Drive Belfast BT6 0LJ	Mr Robert Hunsdale *Director & Pastor* Executive staff 1 Other staff 7	Evangelising the unchurched, establishing and developing various ministries, assisting other churches £40,000 – June 90
***Ian Bothwell** (Crossfire Trust) (1980; Independent) *Crossfire Trust News* 1,500 quarterly	☎ Keady (08) 0861 531636 95 Darkley Road Keady Armagh BT60 3AY	Mr Ian Bothwell *Director* Other staff 2	Reaching out to society with God's love n/a
Christian Businessmen's Committee of Great Britain and Ireland (*CC*; 1967; interdenominational) No magazine	☎ Belfast (08) 0232 667187 9 Newforge Grange Belfast BT9 5BQ **Also at:** No telephone PO Box 129 Belfast BT9 5QQ	Mr James Whitley *Executive Director* Executive staff 1	Reaching businessmen with the Gospel £10,000 – Dec 90
Church Army (*CC*; 1882; Anglican) No separate magazine	☎ Perth (0738) 86386 The Rectory, Glencarse Perth PH2 7LX	Captain K J Cavanagh *Co-ordinator for Ireland*	Direct evangelism and social responsibility n/a
County Antrim Reformation Movement	See either **North Antrim Reformation Movement** or **South East Antrim Reformation Movement**		
Rodney Cordner (1976; Church of Ireland) No magazine	☎ Portadown (08) 0762 337668 21 Tandragee Road Portadown, Craigavon Co Armagh BT62 3BG	Mr Rodney Cordner *Singer/Evangelist* No full-time staff	International evangelist and teacher using Irish music as vehicle for Gospel n/a
EYM Ministries (1965; interdenominational) (Previously Evangelical Youth Movement) *In Contact* 2,000 quarterly	☎ (08) 0232 455158 285 Newtownards Road Belfast BT4 1AG	Mr David Millen *Director* Executive staff 5 Other staff 2	Equipping believers by training in evangelism and discipleship. Consultancy for church and youth leaders. Evangelistic outreaches
Evangelical Protestant Society (1948; non-denominational) *Ulster Bulwark* 2,800 every two months	☎ Belfast (08) 0232 325608 26 Howard Street Belfast BT1 6PD	Mr Seamus Milligan *Secretary* Executive staff 1	Maintaining the Reformed faith and Protestant heritage £28,000 – May 88
***The Faith Mission** (*CC*; 1886; non-denominational) *Life Indeed* 9,500 every two months	☎ Belfast (08) 0232 613316 43a Upper Lisburn Road Belfast BT10 0GX **And:** ☎ Portlaoise (353) 0502 25288 Oakvale, Stradbally Portlaoise, Co Laois	Mr W J Porter *Director* n/a Mr David Stevenson *District Superintendent*	An evangelistic movement geared to reach all ages in rural areas of the UK and Republic of Ireland
The Festivals of Male Voice Praise (1934; non-denominational) *Interlink* 3,000 quarterly	☎ Ahoghill (08) 0266 871643 82 Lismurn Park Ahoghill, Ballymena Co Antrim BT42 1JW	Mr Walter W Leech *Chairman* No full-time staff	Gospel witness through the medium of male voice song and related music publication £5,000 – May 85

Evangelistic Agencies

Name & Magazine	Location	Chief Officer & Staff	Work & Income
International Gospel Outreach (*CC*; 1967; interdenominational) *Christian Vision* 2,000 quarterly	☎ Portadown (08) 0762 339739 47 Bleary Road Portadown, Craigavon Co Armagh BT63 5NE	Rev D J Greenow *President* Rev Bob Searle *General Secretary* Executive staff 7 Field staff* 240 Office staff 3 * ministers linked with the Fellowship	Fellowship of ministers, worldwide team ministries, conferences, holiday conventions, cassette and video ministries, youth missions n/a
Ireland Outreach (1972; Christian Brethren) *Outlook on Ireland Outreach* 4,000 periodically	☎ Ballyclare (08) 09603 52470 11 Old Ballybracken Road Doagh, Ballyclare Co Antrim BT39 0SF	Mr James W Gillett *International Co-ordinator* Part-time staff 5	Co-ordinating short-term evangelism teams and distributing Christian literature £49,800 — Mar 87
Irish Evangelistic Band (*CC*; 1936; interdenominational) *Prayer and Praise* Circular 500 quarterly	☎ Enniskillen (08) 0365 322400 39 Belmore Street Enniskillen Co Fermanagh BT74 6HH	Mr Charles Wesley Bell *General Secretary* Executive staff 2 Other staff 6	Evangelising Ireland; colportage ministry, youth work, summer teams, bookshops, Missionary emphasis £55,000 — Jan 91
Irish Gospel Outreach (1961; interdenominational) No magazine	☎ Calverhall (0044) 094 876688 Cloverley Hall Conference Centre, Whitchurch Shropshire SY13 4PH	Rev John C W Rosser *Director* No full-time staff	Financial assistance to Christian causes in the Republic of Ireland n/a — Sept 90
***Irish Mission** (1710; Presbyterian) *The Christian Irishman Magazine* 10,500 monthly	☎ Belfast (08) 0232 320598 ℻ Fax (08) 0232 248377 Church House Fisherwick Place Belfast BT1 6DW	Rev David J Temple *Superintendent* Office staff 5 Other staff 10	Literature, visitation and video evangelism in schools, markets, homes and churches with all age groups £300,000 — Dec 90
Irish Missionary Fellowship (*CC*; 1966; non-denominational) *Insight* 1,500 quarterly	☎ Dublin (353) 01 298 7184 95 Meadow Grove Dundrum, Dublin 16	Mr Stanley Mawhinney *Founder/Director* Executive staff 5	Missionary society operating in the Republic of Ireland; bookshops £100,000 — Jan 92
Knights of St Columbanus (n/a; Roman Catholic)	☎ Dublin (353) 01 761835 ℻ Fax (353) 01 762839 Ely House 8 Ely Place, Dublin 2	Mr Niall Kennedy *Supreme Secretary* n/a	Engages in adult religious formation by the study of the gospels, pastorals and papal encyclicals. Seeking to evangelise Irish society n/a
Lausanne Committee for Evangelism in Ireland (1989; interdenominational) No magazine	☎ Naas (353) 045 83629 The Manse Brannockstown, Naas Co Kildare *Also at:* ☎ Belfast (08) 0232 710606 3 Kylemore Park Belfast BT14 6SA	Rev Robert Dunlop *Chairman* No full-time staff Mrs Heather Boland *Secretary* No full-time staff	Fostering and facilitating countrywide evangelistic initiative in every part of Ireland n/a
Legion of Mary (n/a; Roman Catholic) *Maria Legionis* Quarterly	☎ Dublin (353) 01 723153 De Montfort House Brunswick Street Dublin 7	Mr Patrick Fay *President* Executive staff 2	Catholic lay organisation for men and women, engaged in charitable and apostolic work n/a

Evangelistic Agencies

Name & Magazine	Location	Chief Officer & Staff	Work & Income
Lord's Day Observance Society (*CC*; 1831; interdenominational) *Joy and Light* 18,000 every four months	☎ Belfast (08) 0232 238224 29 Howard Street Belfast BT1 6ND	Mr Nelson McCausland *General Secretary* n/a	Evangelism; show exhibitions, children's missions; Sunday observance; book publishing, selling; religious, social, political meetings, prison ministry n/a
North Antrim Reformation Movement (1986; Reformed and Calvinistic)	☎ Cloughmills (08) 026 563 3 Omerbane Road Cloughmills, Ballymena Co Antrim BT44 9PD	Mr James Peden *Secretary* No full-time staff	To call churches and individuals back to the simplicity of Puritan theology and practice n/a
Project Evangelism (*CC*; 1969; interdenominational) *News letter* 11,000 quarterly	☎ Portrush (08) 0265 822775 Project House 38 Mark Street, Portrush Co Antrim BT56 8BT	Mr John Moxen *Director* Executive staff 2 Other staff 5	Training in church based outreach evangelism, street evangelism, children's and teenage meetings, short term Bible school £25,000 – Dec 91
Sandes Soldiers' and Airmen's Centres (*CC*; 1869; non-denominational) *Forward* 2,700 every four months	☎ Belfast (08) 0232 652592 30a Belmont Road Belfast BT4 2AN	Miss Hazel M Knox *General Secretary* Executive staff 2 Other staff 34	Christian ministry to HM Forces, offering love and care to Army and RAF personnel £460,000 – Dec 89
Seamen's Christian Friend Society (n/a; interdenominational) *Helmsman* 8,000 quarterly	☎ (08) 0232 654272 58 Orangefield Road Belfast 5 *Also at:* ☎ (353) 01 295 6969 21 Dun Emer Drive Dundrum, Dublin 16 *And:* ☎ (353) 021 354032 "Sunny Heights" Annmount Glounthane, Cork	Mr David Knox *Port missionary* Mr Billy & Mrs Martha Jones *Port missionaries* Mr Walter & Mrs Mary Burrell *Port missionaries*	Evangelism at the dock-side and on ships n/a
South East Antrim Reformation Movement (1986; Reformed and Calvinistic) *Contend for the Faith* 200 half-yearly	☎ Belfast (08) 0232 866174 1 Laral Gardens Monkstown Newtownabbey Co Antrim BT37 0LJ	Mr Raymond Stewart *Secretary* No full-time staff	To call churches and individuals back to the simplicity of Puritan theology and practice n/a
United Beach Missions (1970; non-denominational) Associated with Young Life Campaign *Prayer Letters* Regularly	☎ Belfast (08) 0232 231133 Room 511 Scottish Provident Buildings 7 Donegall Square West Belfast BT1 6JG	Mr Bertie Coffey *Executive Officer* Staff 2	Reaching families for Christ on the beaches of UK, Republic of Ireland, France and Belgium n/a

Overseas

	Page
Missionary Societies (Protestant)	88
Missionary Societies (Roman Catholic)	91
Index: Irish Missionaries by Country	101
Missionary Support Organisations	106

NOTES AND DEFINITIONS FOR MISSIONARY SOCIETIES (PROTESTANT AND ROMAN CATHOLIC)

These notes particularly relate to the sections which begin on Pages 88 and 91.

See also the General Notes and Definitions on Page 54.

Chief Officer
The name is that of the chief executive officer with his actual designation given in *italics*.

If two names are shown one is usually the international chief executive whose usual country of residence is other than Ireland (this country being stated) or the President or Chairman. Correspondence should not normally be addressed to the second person named.

Irish Personnel
Although numbers were requested as at 1/1/92, some societies could only give numbers near that date.

Figures were requested relating to Irish personnel only, but as many societies have non-Irish members the size of a particular society should not be judged by the total shown of serving Irish members. An approximate total of the missionary personnel of all nationalities is included as the last item given for the majority of societies.

The number abroad includes those working in United Missions.

Main Countries of Activity
Two groups of countries are listed:
(1) Countries given before the semi-colon (;) are countries in which Irish missionaries are specifically working.
(2) Other countries in which the organisation or church is involved but where no Irish missionary personnel are currently serving with that society.

Table 24: Irish Missionaries by Continent 1992

	Protestant	Roman Catholic	Total
	%	%	%
Africa	30	64	61
Americas	18	14	14
Asia (South, East, Australasia)	11	16	16
Europe	21	–	2
Indian Subcontinent and Middle East	20	6	7
TOTAL (= 100%)	418	3,886	4,304

Based on total number abroad by the 89% of Societies giving the necessary detail.

Table 25: Missionaries from Ireland 1992

		Number of Missionaries			Percentage	Average missionaries
Society type	Number	Male	Female	Total	male	per Society
Protestant	22	248	362	610	41%	28
Roman Catholic	93	2,142	2,102	4,244	50%	46
Total	115	2,390	2,464	4,854	49%	42

Fig 43: Proportions of Irish Missionaries by Continent 1992

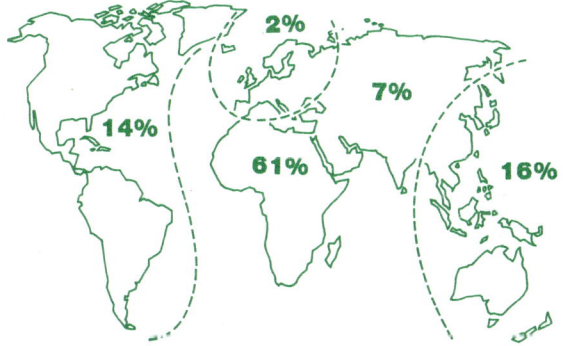

MISSIONARY SOCIETIES (PROTESTANT)

Name & Location	Chief Officer/Magazine	Main Countries of Activity			
Acre Gospel Mission (*CC*; 1937; interdenominational) ☎ Belfast (08) 0232 642638 33 Ravensdene Park Belfast BT6 0DA	Dr T H Geddis *President* ***Missionary News*** 600 quarterly	Total number abroad . . **21** **11M** **10W** Brazil (15), Canary Islands (2), Portugal (4) *Missionaries of all nationalities: 21*			
Africa Inland Mission International (*CC*; 1895; interdenominational) ☎ Belfast (08) 0232 453497 279 Woodstock Road Belfast BT6 8PR	Rev Timothy G Alford *General Secretary for UK* Mr Laurence Ferguson *Irish Secretary* ***AIM International*** 6,400 quarterly	Total number abroad . . **16** **7M** **9W** Comoro Islands (1), Kenya (6), Namibia (2) Tanzania (5), Zaire (2) *Missionaries of all nationalities: 944*			
Baptist Missions (*CC*; 1888; Baptist) ☎ Belfast (08) 0232 663108 📠 Fax (08) 0232 663616 117 Lisburn Road Belfast BT9 7AF	Rev Derek Baxter *Mission Secretary* ***Info-Mission*** (incorporated in *The Irish Baptist*) 3,000 monthly	Total number abroad . . **32** **15M** **17W** France (5), Irish Republic (14), Peru (13) *Missionaries of all nationalities: 32*			
BCMS Crosslinks (*CC*; 1922; Anglican) ☎ Dublin (353) 01 976103 Overseas House 3 Belgrave Road, Dublin 6 *Also at:* ☎ Belfast (08) 0232 326077 15 College Square East Belfast BT1 6DD	Rev Canon John M Ball *General Secretary for UK* Miss Olive Williams *Co-ordinator for the Republic of Ireland* Dr Ron Elsdon *Co-ordinator for Northern Ireland* ***Mission*** Distributed every two months	Total number abroad . . **11** **4M**[1] **7W**[1] India (1), Kenya (2), Peru (3), Tanzania (4) Zimbabwe (1) *Missionaries of all nationalities: 88*			
The Church's Ministry among the Jews — Ireland **(Incorporating Church of Ireland Jews Society)** (*CC*; n/a; Church of Ireland) ☎ Portadown (08) 0762 337466 67 Abercorn Park Killycolnain, Portadown Co Armagh BT63 5JW	Mr A Stracey *General Secretary* n/a	Total number abroad . . **49** **21M** **28W** Argentina (3), Israel (41), South Africa (2) USA (3) *Missionaries of all nationalities: 50*			
Church Missionary Society Ireland (*CC*; 1814; Anglican) ☎ Belfast (08) 0232 324581 📠 Fax (08) 0232 231666 Overseas House 12 Talbot Street, Belfast BT1 2LE *Also at:* ☎ Dublin (353) 970931 📠 Fax (353) 970939 Overseas House 3 Belgrave Road, Dublin 6	Rev Cecil Wilson *General Secretary* Rev Declan Smith *Overseas Secretary* ***Transmission*** 5,000 every four months	Total number abroad . . **42** **20M** **22W** Egypt (5), Israel (2), Kenya (3), Nepal (4) North Africa (1), Singapore (1), Tanzania (9) Uganda (12), Zaire (2) *Missionaries of all nationalities: 45*			
European Christian Mission (*CC*; 1904; interdenominational) ☎ Belfast (08) 0232 620526 Glenburn House Glenburn Road South Dunmurry, Belfast BT17 9JP	Mr Gordon Scobie *British Director* ***Europe's Millions*** 6,700 quarterly	(Irish & UK missionaries) Total number abroad . . **46** **23M** **23W** Austria (4), Eastern Europe (11), France (7) Irish Republic (4), Italy (10), Spain (10) *Missionaries of all nationalities: 100*			

[1] Estimate

Missionary Societies (Protestant)

Name & Location	Chief Officer/Magazine	Main Countries of Activity			
European Missionary Fellowship (*CC*; 1944; interdenominational) ☎ Belfast (08) 0232 324240 12 Portview, Bangor Co Down BT20 5QB	Rev Daniel Webber *Director for UK* Mr Jonathan Watson *Irish Representative* **Vision of Europe** 10,000 quarterly	Total number abroad . . **5** **2M** **3W** Irish Republic (2), Italy (1), Norway (1), Spain (1) *Missionaries of all nationalities: 100*			
FEBA Radio (Far East Broadcasting Association) (*CC*; 1968; interdenominational) ☎ Newtownards (08) 0247 814793 22 Ballyhurry Park Newtownards, Co Down BT23 3QX	Mr L John Wheatley *General Director for UK* **FEBA Radio News** 20,000 quarterly	Total number abroad . . **3** **2M** **1W** Seychelles (3) *Missionaries of all nationalities: 35*			
Free Presbyterian Church of Ulster Mission Board (1978; Free Presbyterian Church of Ulster) ☎ Belfast (08) 0232 797757 23 Briarwood Park Belfast BT5 7HZ	Rev David McIlven *Chairman* **Missionary Newsletter** 6,500 quarterly	Total number abroad . . **27** **13M** **14W** Australia (6), Cameroon (3), Canada (8) Kenya (1), Spain (5), USA (4) *Missionaries of all nationalities: 00*			
INTERSERVE (*CC*; 1852; interdenominational) ☎ Belfast (08) 0232 40221 14 Glencregagh Court Belfast BT6 0PA *Also at:* ☎ Dublin (353) 01 863311 Comer, Glencormac Bray, Co Wicklow	Mr Tony McGall *NI Director* Miss Elaine Graham *Secretary for Ireland* **GO** 800 quarterly	Total number abroad . . **8** **2M** **6W** Bhutan (1), International HQ (2), Nepal (1), Middle East (2), Pakistan (2) *Missionaries of all nationalities: 400*			
The Leprosy Mission International (*CC*; 1874; interdenominational) ☎ Belfast (08) 0232 381937 Fax (08) 0232 381842 Northern Ireland Office 44 Ulsterville Avenue Belfast BT9 7AQ *Also at:* ☎ Dublin (353) 01 269 8804 Republic of Ireland Office 5 St James Terrace Clonskeagh Road, Dublin 6	Mr A C Ferguson *Director (N Ireland)* Mr Jack Teggin *National Director (Eire)* **New Day** 4,500 half-yearly	Total number abroad . . **4** **1M** **3W** Ethiopia (1), Indonesia (1), Tanzania (2) *Missionaries of all nationalities: 75*			
Methodist Missionary Society (Ireland) (*CC*; 1785; Methodist) ☎ Belfast (08) 0232 320078 Aldergate House 13 University Road, Belfast BT7 1NA	Rev S Leslie Wallace *General Secretary* n/a	Total number abroad . . **17** **7M**[1] **10W**[1] Gambia (2), Haiti (3), India (3), Ivory Coast (1) Nepal (2), Sri Lanka (2), Zimbabwe (4) *Missionaries of all nationalities: 00*			
Overseas Missionary Fellowship (*CC*; 1865; interdenominational) ☎ Belfast (08) 0232 381995 13 Windsor Avenue Belfast BT9 6EE	Mr David Pickard *General Director,* *Singapore* **East Asia Millions** 10,000 every two months	Total number abroad . . **28** **11M**[1] **17W**[1] Hong Kong (1), Indonesia (2) Japan (2), Korea (1), Malaysia (1) Philippines (12), Singapore (4), Taiwan (3) Thailand (2) *Missionaries of all nationalities: 1,000*			

[1] Estimate

Missionary Societies (Protestant)

Name & Location	Chief Officer/Magazine	Main Countries of Activity			
Presbyterian Church in Ireland Overseas Board (*CC*; 1840; Presbyterian) ☎Belfast (08) 0232 323556 Fax (08) 0232 236605 Church House Fisherwick Place Belfast BT1 6DW	Rev R J T McMullen *Executive Officer & Secretary of Overseas Board* **Wider World** 30,000 quarterly	Total number abroad . . Brazil (3), China (2), India (3), Indonesia (2) Israel (2), Jamaica (6), Kenya (8), Malawi (13) Nepal (9), Singapore (2), Spain (2) UK (Gujarati work) (4) *Missionaries of all nationalities: 60*	**52**	**20M**	**32W**
Qua Iboe Fellowship (*CC*; 1887; interdenominational) ☎Belfast (08) 0232 326150 Room 317 7 Donegall Square West Belfast BT1 6JE	Rev William E Leach *General Secretary* **Dispatch** 3,800 every four months	Total number abroad . . Nigeria (15) *Missionaries of all nationalities: 28*	**15**	**6M**	**9W**
SIM UK (Society for International Ministries) (*CC*; 1893; interdenominational) ☎Belfast (08) 0232 451451 285a Woodstock Road Belfast BT6 8PR	Rev John H Pickett *UK Director* Rev Dr Ian M Hay *General Director, USA* **SIM Now** 13,000 quarterly	Total number abroad . . Benin (1), Bolivia (5), Nigeria (2), Pakistan (2) *Missionaries of all nationalities: 1,700*	**10**	**6M**	**4W**
South American Missionary Society (*CC*; 1844; Anglican) ☎Lurgan (08) 0762 322044 33 Upper Toberhewny Lane Craigavon BT66 7AA *Also at:* ☎Dublin (353) 01 977429 Overseas House 3 Belgrave Road Rathmines, Dublin 6	Mr Denis Johnston *General Secretary All Ireland* **Share** 16,000 quarterly	Total number abroad . . Peru (2) *Missionaries of all nationalities: 90*	**2**	**1M¹**	**1W¹**
UFM Worldwide (*CC*; 1931; interdenominational) ☎Belfast (08) 0232 232404 Howards Buildings 26 Howard Street Belfast BT1 6PD *Also at:* ☎Cork (353) 021 932373 22 Waldin Grange Heights Douglas, Cork	Mr George P Rabey *General Secretary, UK* **Light and Life** 9,500 every four months	Total number abroad . . Brazil (4), Spain (1), Zaire (5) *Missionaries of all nationalities: 61*	**10**	**4M**	**6W**
United Society for the Propagation of the Gospel (*CC*; 1968; Anglican) ☎Belfast (08) 0232 693921 21 Rosetta Road Belfast BT6 0LQ ☎Dublin (353) 01 280 9537 Christ Church Vicarage 2 Park Road Dun Laoghaire, Co Dublin ☎Londonderry (08) 0504 44306 All Saints Rectory 20 Limavady Road Londonderry BT47 1JD	Rev A N Kelly *Belfast Area Secretary* Rev Canon R C Armstrong *Dublin Area Secretary* Rev J C D Mayes *Derry Area Secretary*	Total number abroad . . Malawi (1), Zimbabwe (2) *Missionaries of all nationalities: 173*	**3**	**3M**	

¹ Estimate

(continued on Page 91)

Missionary Societies (Protestant)

Name & Location	Chief Officer/Magazine	Main Countries of Activity
United Society for the Propagation of the Gospel ☎ Cork (353) 021 821098 The Rectory Glanmire, Cork	(continued) Ven M H G Mayes *Cork Area Secretary*	
Wycliffe Bible Translators (*CC*; 1955; interdenominational) ☎ Belfast (08) 0232 866649 5 Glenkeen Avenue Newtownabbey Co Antrim BT37 0PH	Mr Ian Gray *Regional Co-ordinator* Mr David Cummings *President, Australia* **Wycliffe News** 3,000 quarterly	Total number abroad . . **17 5M 12W** Brazil (1), Cameroon (1), Ghana (1), Ivory Coast (5) Kenya (4), Mali (1), Pakistan (2), Senegal (2) *Missionaries of all nationalities: 4,600*

MISSIONARY SOCIETIES (ROMAN CATHOLIC)

Name & Location	Chief Officer/Magazine	Main Countries of Activity
Alexian Brothers (CFA) (1348; Roman Catholic) ☎ Dublin (353) 01 375973 47 Upper Drumcondra Road Dublin 9	Brother Francis Spense *Vocations Director* No magazine	Total number abroad . . **2 2M** Ghana (2) *Missionaries of all nationalities: 10*
Augustinian Fathers (OSA) (n/a; Roman Catholic) ☎ Dublin (353) 01 944966 ✉ Fax (353) 01 944338 Taylors Lane, Ballyboden Dublin 16	Very Rev Thomas F Cooney *Provincial Superior* No magazine	Total number abroad . . **45 45M** Ecuador (10), Nigeria (35)
Benedictines (OSB) (n/a; Roman Catholic) ☎ Limerick (353) 061 386103 Glenstal Abbey, Murroe Limerick	Rt Rev Celestine Cullen *Abbot* No magazine	Total number abroad . . **5 5M** Nigeria (5)
Bon Secours Sisters of Paris (n/a; Roman Catholic) ☎ Cork (353) 021 542416 College Road, Cork	Sister M A Leamy *Provincial Superior* No magazine	Total number abroad . . **8 8W** Peru (8)
Brigidine Sisters (n/a; Roman Catholic) ☎ Portlaoise (353) 0502 32627 Castledown Road Mountrath, Co Laois	Sister Rita Minehan *Provincial Superior* No magazine	Total number abroad . . **6 6W** Kenya (3), Mexico (3)
Brothers of Charity (1807; Roman Catholic) ☎ Dublin (353) 01 970063 Triest House 52 Terenure Road East, Dublin 6	Brother Peter Sheehy *Provincial Superior* No magazine	Total number abroad . . **4 4M** South Africa (1), Sri Lanka (3)
Capuchin Franciscans (OFM Cap) (n/a; Roman Catholic) ☎ Dublin (353) 01 730250 Provincial Curia Church Street, Dublin 7	Very Rev Eustace McSweeney *Minister Provincial* No magazine	Total number abroad . . **45 45M** Korea (4), Namibia (2), South Africa (15) Zambia (24)
Carmelites (OCarm) (n/a; Roman Catholic) ☎ Dublin (353) 01 298 4014 or 9811 Gort Muire, Ballinteer, Dublin 16	Rev Martin Farragher *Vocations Director* No magazine	Total number abroad . . **26 26M** Kenya (1), Peru (1), South Africa (1) Zimbabwe (23)

Missionary Societies (Roman Catholic)

Name & Location	Chief Officer/Magazine	Main Countries of Activity		
Carmelites (Discaled OCD) (n/a; Roman Catholic) ☎Dublin (353) 01 718466/718127 St Teresa's, Clarendon Street Dublin 2	Very Rev Vincent O'Hara *Father Provincial* No magazine	Total number abroad . . **7** Nigeria (4), Philippines (3)		**7M**
Christian Brothers (CFC) (1802; Roman Catholic) ☎Dublin (353) 01 300247 274 North Circular Road Dublin 7	Brother J J Honeghan *Provincial Superior* Rev Brother J C Keating *Superior General, Italy* No magazine	Total number abroad . . **149** Argentina (16), Gambia (1), India (47), Liberia (6) Paraguay (3), Sierra Leone (6), South Africa (30) Uruguay (5), Zambia (31), Zimbabwe (4) *Missionaries of all nationalities: 2,293*		**149M**

Cistercian Order (OCSO)
(1098; Roman Catholic)
Waterford (353) 058
54404/54133
Mount Mellory Abbey
Cappoquin, Co Waterford
	Rt Rev Dom Justin
	    McCarthy
	Abbot
	Most Rev Dom Ambrose
	    Southey
	Abbot General, Rome
	No magazine
		Total number abroad . . **3**
		Kenya (1), Nigeria (1), Uganda (1)
		Missionaries of all nationalities: 3,500
				3M

Cistercian Sisters (n/a; Roman Catholic) ☎Waterford (353) 058 56168 St Mary's Abbey Glencairn, Co Waterford	Sister M Dominic Lee *Abbess* No magazine	Total number abroad . . **4** Nigeria (4)		**4W**
Comboni Missionaries (MCCJ) (Verona Fathers) (1867; Roman Catholic) ☎Dublin (353) 01 626 5951 29 Woodfarm Avenue Palmerstown, Dublin 20	Rev Rinaldo Ronzani *Superior* Rev David Glenday *Provincial Superior, London* **Comboni Missions** 12,000 quarterly	Total number abroad . . **4** Brazil (1), Malawi (1), Uganda (2) *Missionaries of all nationalities: 2,000*		**4M**
Daughters of Charity (DC) (n/a; Roman Catholic) ☎Dublin (353) 01 288 2669 St Catherines, Dunardagh Temple Hill, Blackrock Co Dublin	Sister Bernadette MacMahon *Provincial Superior* No magazine	Total number abroad . . **25** Nigeria (21), Sierra Leone (4)		**25W**
Daughters of Mary and Joseph (1869; Roman Catholic) ☎Naas (353) 045 31842 3/4 Connell Drive Newbridge, Co Kildare	Sister Margaret Moloney *Provincial Superior* No magazine	Total number abroad . . **24** Burundi (1), Cameroon (1), Ghana (6), Uganda (16)		**24W**
Daughters of Our Lady of the Sacred Heart (n/a; Roman Catholic) ☎Dublin (353) 01 512183 50 Maplewood Road, Springfield Tallaght, Dublin 24	n/a No magazine	Total number abroad . . **14** Brazil (1), Nauru (1), Papua New Guinea (3) South Africa (9)		**14W**
Daughters of the Holy Spirit (1902; Roman Catholic) ☎Dublin (353) 01 628 6010 Convent of the Holy Spirit Maynooth, Co Kildare	n/a *Superior* Sister Anne Marie Couloigner *Superior General, France* No magazine	Total number abroad . . **7** Nigeria (7) *Missionaries of all nationalities: 76*		**7W**

Missionary Societies (Roman Catholic)

Name & Location	Chief Officer/Magazine	Main Countries of Activity
De La Salle Brothers (FSC) (1680; Roman Catholic) ☎ Dublin (353) 01 331815 Provincialate 121 Howth Road, Dublin 3	Brother Felan Burns *Provincial Superior* No magazine	Total number abroad . . **56 56M** Hong Kong (12), Malaysia (13), Mauritius (2) Nigeria (6), Singapore (5), South Africa (17) Turkey (1) *Missionaries of all nationalities: 700*
Divine Word Missionaries (SUD) (1931; Roman Catholic) ☎ Roscommon (353) 0903 7222 Donamon Castle Donamon, Roscommon	Very Rev George Agger *Father Provincial* **The Word** Monthly **Kairos** Bi-monthly	Total number abroad . . **65 65M** Angola (1), Argentina (3), Benin (1), Botswana (1) Bolivia (2), Brazil (12), Colombia (1), Ecuador (5) Ghana (5), Hong Kong (3), India (2), Indonesia (2) Japan (2), Kenya (3), Mexico (5), Nicaragua (1) Papua New Guinea (7), Paraguay (5), Philippines (4) *Missionaries of all nationalities: 4,289*
Dominican Order (OP) (1216; Roman Catholic) ☎ Dublin (353) 01 515842 St Mary's, Tallaght, Co Dublin	Very Rev Thomas Jordan *Provincial Superior* **Doctrine and Life** Ten times a year	Total number abroad . . **39 39M** Argentina (5), Costa Rica (1), India (1), Israel (2) Trinidad & Tobago (30) *Missionaries of all nationalities: 7,275*
Dominican Sisters (OP) (n/a; Roman Catholic) ☎ Dublin (353) 972430 The Generalate 5 Westfield Road, Dublin 6	Sister Marian O'Sullivan *Prioress General* No magazine	Total number abroad . . **145 145W** Argentina (9), South Africa (132), Swaziland (4)
Faithful Companions of Jesus (1820; Roman Catholic) ☎ Dublin (353) 01 971803 St Joseph's Villa 54 Kenilworth Square Rathgar, Dublin 6	Sister Kathryn Lennon *Provincial Superior* No magazine	Total number abroad . . **5 5W** Sierra Leone (5) *Missionaries of all nationalities: 14*
Franciscan Brothers (OSF) (n/a; Roman Catholic) ☎ Galway (353) 0905 79295 Generalate House Mount Bellew, Co Galway	Brother Matthew McCormack *Superior General* No magazine	Total number abroad . . **11 11M** Kenya (9), Nigeria (1), Paraguay (1)
Franciscans (OFM) (n/a; Roman Catholic) ☎ Dublin (353) 01 771128 Adam and Eve's 4 Merchants' Quay, Dublin 8	Rev Fiachra O'Ceallaigh *Provincial Superior* **Troubador** Quarterly	Total number abroad . . **61 61M** El Salvador (10), South Africa (38), Zimbabwe (13)
Franciscan Missionaries of Mary (FMM) (1901; Roman Catholic) ☎ Dublin (353) 01 470591 "Assisi", 36 Grange Abbey Drive Donaghmede, Dublin 13	Sister Mona Considine *Regional Superior* Sister Maura O'Connor *Superior General, Italy* No magazine	Total number abroad . . **29 29W** Chile (1), Ghana (2), India (5), Kenya (1), Korea (1) Liberia (4), Macao (1), Malaysia (1), Pakistan (6) South Africa (7) *Missionaries of all nationalities: 8,000*
Franciscan Missionaries of Our Lady (FMOL) ☎ Dublin (353) 01 908678 St Francis, 21 Mayfield Road Terenure, Dublin 6	Sister Patricia Kenny *Superior* No magazine	Total number abroad . . **1 1W** Djibouti (1)
Franciscan Missionaries of the Divine Motherhood (FMDM) (1887; Roman Catholic) ☎ Dublin (353) 01 932537 St Francis, 3 Fonthill Abbey Ballyboden Road Rathfarnham, Dublin 14	Sister Brendon McGarry *Resident Irish Area Superior* **The Voice** 2,000 half-yearly	Total number abroad . . **43 43W** Jordan (4), Nigeria (5), Zambia (16), Zimbabwe (18) *Missionaries of all nationalities: 360*

Missionary Societies (Roman Catholic)

Name & Location	Chief Officer/Magazine	Main Countries of Activity
Franciscan Missionary Sisters for Africa (OSF) (1952; Roman Catholic) ☎Dundalk (353) 042 71123 Franciscan Convent Mount Oliver, Dundalk, Co Louth	Sister Marie O'Brien *Superior General* **Day Star in Africa** 2,000 every four months	Total number abroad . . 81 81W Ethiopia (8), Kenya (27), Malawi (1), South Africa (3) Uganda (24), Zambia (11), Zimbabwe (7) *Missionaries of all nationalities: 202*
Franciscan Missionary Sisters of St Joseph (1883; Roman Catholic) ☎Kilkenny (353) 056 31196 Wayside, Johnstown, Co Kilkenny	Sister Ursula McCarthy *Regional Superior* No magazine	Total number abroad . . 9 9W Ecuador (3), Kenya (6) *Missionaries of all nationalities: 221*
Good Shepherd Sisters (n/a; Roman Catholic) ☎Dublin (353) 01 269 3199 Good Shepherd Convent 55 Eglinton Road Donnybrook, Dublin 4	Sister Evelyn Fergus *Provincial Superior* No magazine	Total number abroad . . 63 63W Egypt (4), Ethiopia (5), India (13), Indonesia (7) Kenya (3), Madagascar (3), Philippines (1) Reunion (1), Senegal (1), Singapore (2) South Africa (12), Sri Lanka (10), Sudan (1)
Holy Ghost Fathers (CSSP) (1703; Roman Catholic) ☎Dublin (353) 01 975127/977230 ✆Fax (353) 01 975399 Holy Ghost Provincialate Temple Park Richmond Avenue South Dublin 6	Very Rev Michael F McCarthy *Provincial Superior* **Missionwide** 10,500 quarterly **Outlook** Bi-monthly	Total number abroad . . 217 217M Angola (7), Brazil (34), Ethiopia (7), Gambia (15) Ghana (16), Kenya (62), Liberia (1), Malawi (6) Mauritius (5), Mexico (2), Nigeria (7), Pakistan (9) Papua New Guinea (6), Sierra Leone (28) South Africa (2), Swaziland (1), Tanzania (3) Trinidad & Tobago (4), Uganda (1), Zambia (1) *Missionaries of all nationalities: 3,450*
Little Company of Mary (1877; Roman Catholic) ☎Dublin (353) 01 942324 14 Heather Lawn, Marley Wood Grange Road, Dublin 16	n/a *Superior* No magazine	Total number abroad . . 51 51W Haiti (3), South Africa (30), Zimbabwe (18)
Little Sisters of the Assumption (n/a; Roman Catholic) ☎Dublin (353) 01 909850 Provincial House 42 Rathfarnham Road, Dublin 6	Sister Nuala O'Brien *Provincial* No magazine	Total number abroad . . 4 4W Brazil (1), Ethiopia (3)
Little Sisters of the Poor (n/a; Roman Catholic) ☎Dublin (353) 01 332308 Sacred Heart Residence Sybil Hill Road, Raheny, Dublin 5	Sister Geraldine *Provincial Superior* No magazine	Total number abroad . . 23 23W Algeria (3), American Samoa (1), Hong Kong (6) India (4), Kenya (3), Malaysia (1), New Caledonia (1) Nigeria (1), Singapore (2), Zaire (1)
Marianists (n/a; Roman Catholic) ☎Dublin (353) 01 285 8301 Marianist Community St Columba's, Church Avenue Ballybrack, Dunlaoghaire Co Dublin	Rev Michael Reaume *Director* No magazine	Total number abroad . . 1 1M Malawi (1)
Marist Brothers (FMS) (1817; Roman Catholic) ☎Dublin (353) 01 269 7831 Farranboley House, Bird Avenue Clonskeagh, Dublin 14	Brother Colman Parker *Provincial Superior* No magazine	Total number abroad . . 7 7M Hong Kong (1), Kenya (1), Singapore (1) South Africa (4)

Missionary Societies (Roman Catholic)

Name & Location	Chief Officer/Magazine	Main Countries of Activity
Marists (SM) (1836; Roman Catholic) ☎Dublin (353) 01 269 8100 St Joseph's Lodge Milltown, Dublin 14	Very Rev James O'Connell *Provincial Superior* No magazine	Total number abroad . . **22 22M** Brazil (1), Fiji (11), Japan (2), Papua New Guinea (3) Philippines (1), Solomon Islands (3), Vanuatu (1) *Missionaries of all nationalities: 1,750*
Marist Sisters (n/a; Roman Catholic) ☎Dublin (353) 01 972196 Provincialate 51 Kenilworth Square Rathgar, Dublin 6	Sister Brendan Dodd *Provincial Superior* No magazine	Total number abroad . . **20 20W** Brazil (1), Colombia (3), Fiji (9), Gambia (2) Mexico (3), Senegal (2)
Medical Missionaries of Mary (1973; Roman Catholic) ☎Dublin (353) 01 288 2722 📠Fax (353) 01 283 4626 Rosemount Terrace Booterstown, Blackrock Co Dublin	Sister M Vincent Ryan *Regional Superior* Sister Catherine Dwyer *Superior General* **Medical Missionaries of Mary** 30,000 quarterly	Total number abroad . . **144 144W** Angola (6), Brazil (8), Ethiopia (4), Kenya (26) Liberia (2), Malawi (12), Nigeria (47), Sudan (3) Tanzania (26), Uganda (10) *Missionaries of all nationalities: 446*
Mill Hill Missionaries (n/a; Roman Catholic) ☎Dublin (353) 01 972033 St Joseph's Dartry House Rathgar, Dublin 6	Very Rev Maurice Crean *Regional Supervisor* **St Joseph's Advocate** Quarterly	Total number abroad . . **46 46M** Cameroon (6), Chile (1), China (1), Kenya (19) Malaysia (2), Pakistan (5), Philippines (2), Sudan (4) Uganda (6)
Missionaries of Africa (White Fathers) (1868; Roman Catholic) ☎Dublin (353) 01 902489 Cypress Grove Templeogue, Dublin 16	Very Rev Charles Timoney *Provincial Superior* Very Rev Etienne Renaud *Superior General, Italy* **White Fathers/ White Sisters** 30,000 every two months	Total number abroad . . **18 18M** Burkina Faso (1), Ethiopia (1), Ghana (4), Malawi (1) Nigeria (2), South Africa (1), Sudan (1), Tanzania (2) Uganda (2), Zambia (3) *Missionaries of all nationalities: 2,500*
Missionary Franciscan Sisters of the Immaculate Conception (n/a; Roman Catholic) ☎Portadown (08) 0762 332860 St Francis Convent Charles Street, Portadown Craigavon, Co Armagh BT62 4BD	n/a n/a No magazine	Total number abroad . . **23 23W** Bolivia (3), Egypt (11), Papua New Guinea (3) Peru (6)
Missionary Sisters of the Assumption (n/a; Roman Catholic) ☎Dromara (08) 0238 561765 Convent of the Assumption Ballynahinch, Co Down BT24 8EA	Sister Patricia Langan *Superioress* No magazine	Total number abroad . . **64 64W** South Africa (64)
Missionary Sisters of Our Lady of Apostles (n/a; Roman Catholic) ☎Cork (353) 021 291851 Provincialate, Ardfoyle Convent, Cork	Sister Catherine O'Farrell *Provincial* No magazine	Total number abroad . . **61 61W** Ghana (13), Israel (1), Nigeria (45), Sudan (2)
Missionary Sisters of the Holy Rosary (MSHR) (1924; Roman Catholic) ☎Dublin (353) 01 288 1708 23 Cross Avenue, Blackrock Co Dublin	Rev Sister Therese Dillon *Superior General* No magazine	Total number abroad . . **195 195W** Brazil (16), Cameroon (21), Ethiopia (10), Ghana (4) Kenya (22), Nigeria (37), Sierra Leone (25) South Africa (34), Zambia (26) *Missionaries of all nationalities: 420*

Missionary Societies (Roman Catholic)

Name & Location	Chief Officer/Magazine	Main Countries of Activity		
Missionary Sisters of St Columban (SSC) ☎Wicklow (353) 0404 67348 St Columban's Convent Magheramore, Co Wicklow	Sister Marie Galvin *Superior General* ***The Far East*** 67,000 nine times a year	Total number abroad . . **91** Chile (11), China (1), Hong Kong (19), Korea (28) Pakistan (3), Peru (10), Philippines (19) *Missionaries of all nationalities: 221*		**91W**
Missionary Society of St Columban (SSC) (1918; Roman Catholic) ☎Dublin (353) 01 847 6647 St Columban's, Grange Road Donaghmede, Dublin 5	Very Rev J Bernard Cleary *Superior General* ***The Far East*** 67,000 nine times a year	Total number abroad . . **415** Belize (7), Brazil (13), Chile (27), China (3) Fiji (25), Hong Kong (2), Jamaica (8), Japan (58) Korea (76), Pakistan (12), Peru (22) Philippines (150), Taiwan (12) *Missionaries of all nationalities: 890*		**415M**
Montfort Missionaries (SMM) (1712; Roman Catholic) ☎Monaghan (353) 047 81709 Montfort House, Monaghan	Rev Michael Rooney *Foreign Missions* Very Rev Samuel Erskine *Provincial Superior, UK* No magazine	Total number abroad . . **2** Malawi (2) *Missionaries of all nationalities: 1,400*		**2M**
Oblates of Mary Immaculate (OMI) (1816; Roman Catholic) ☎Dublin (353) 01 269 3658 Provincial Residence 170 Merrion Road Ballsbridge, Dublin 4	Very Rev William McGonagle *Provincial Superior* ***Oblate Lourdes Messenger*** Bi-monthly	Total number abroad . . **56** Brazil (14), Indonesia (1), Lesotho (1) Philippines (3), South Africa (37)		**56M**
Order of St Camillus (n/a; Roman Catholic) ☎Dublin (353) 01 288 2873 St Camillus, South Hill Avenue Blackrock, Co Dublin	Very Rev Patrick Murphy *Provincial* ***Recover*** Bi-monthly	Total number abroad . . **3** Kenya (2), Tanzania (1)		**3M**
Pallottines (SCA) (n/a; Roman Catholic) ☎Dublin (353) 01 295 6180 Provincial House Sandyford, Road, Dundrum Dublin 16	Very Rev William Hanly *Provincial* No magazine	Total number abroad . . **30** Argentina (13), Colombia (1), Kenya (3) Tanzania (13)		**30M**
Passionists (CP) (1720; Roman Catholic) ☎Dublin (353) 01 975154 St Paul's Retreat Mount Argus, Dublin 6	Rev Hilarion Cleary *Mission Secretary* Very Rev Ignatius Waters *Provincial Superior* No magazine	Total number abroad . . **20** Botswana (14), Kenya (1), Paraguay (1) South Africa (4)		**20M**
Patrician Brothers (FSP) (1808; Roman Catholic) ☎Carlow (353) 0503 51190 Patrician Brothers Generalate Tullow Hill, Tullow, Carlow	Brother Felim Ryan *Provincial Superior* Brother Aongus Kavanagh *Superior General* No magazine	Total number abroad . . **10** India (3), Kenya (6), Papua New Guinea (1)		**10M**
Poor Sisters of Nazareth (n/a; Roman Catholic) ☎Dublin (353) 01 338205/316809 Nazareth House Malahide Road, Dublin 3	Mother Joseph Gabriel *Superioress* Mother Paul of the Cross *Regional Superior* No magazine	Total number abroad . . **43** American Samoa (1), South Africa (37) Zimbabwe (5)		**43W**

Missionary Societies (Roman Catholic)

Name & Location	Chief Officer/Magazine	Main Countries of Activity		
Presentation Brothers (FPM) (1802; Roman Catholic) ☎Cork (353) 021 364752 Provincialate Coláiste Mhuire Douglas Road, Cork	Brother Stephen O'Gorman *Provincial Superior* Brother Matthew Foheney *Secretary General* No magazine	Total number abroad . . Ghana (8), Grenada (3), Peru (4), St Lucia (5) Trinidad & Tobago (5) *Missionaries of all nationalities: 170*	**25**	**25M**
Presentation Sisters (PBVM) (n/a; Roman Catholic) ☎Naas (353) 045 25335 Generalate Monasterevin, Co Kildare	Sister Elizabeth Starkon *Superior General* No magazine	Total number abroad . . Chile (3), Ecuador (8), India (13), Pakistan (36) Papua New Guinea (2), Philippines (7), Zambia (20) Zimbabwe (25)	**114**	**114W**
Redemptorists (CSSR) (1732; Roman Catholic) ☎Dublin (353) 01 961688 ✉Fax (353) 01 961654 Liguori House 75 Orwell Road, Dublin 6	Very Rev Raphael Gallagher *Provincial Superior* ***Reality*** 25,000 monthly	Total number abroad . . Brazil (38), India (7), Nigeria (3), Philippines (36) Virgin Islands (1) *Missionaries of all nationalities: 85*	**85**	**85M**
Religious of Jesus and Mary (n/a; Roman Catholic) ☎Dublin (353) 01 295 1609 Provincialate Goatstown Road, Dublin 14	Sister Sheila Dolly *Provincial* No magazine	Total number abroad . . India (3), Pakistan (15)	**18**	**18W**
Rosminian Fathers (IC) (n/a; Roman Catholic) ☎Cork (353) 021 775202 St Patrick's, Upton Innishannon, Cork	Very Rev James Flynn *Provincial* No magazine	Total number abroad . . Kenya (1), Tanzania (18), Venezuela (1) *Missionaries of all nationalities: 60*	**20**	**20M**
Sacred Heart Fathers (SCJ) (1936; Roman Catholic) ☎Dublin (353) 01 538655 Fairfield 66 Inchicore Road, Dublin 8	Rev Michael Walshe *Superior* Rev Antonio Pantoglini *General Superior, Italy* ***Contact*** 5,000 every four months	Total number abroad . . South Africa (1) *Missionaries of all nationalities: 600*	**1**	**1M**
Sacred Heart Missionaries (MSC) (n/a; Roman Catholic) ☎Cork (353) 021 543711 Western Road, Cork	Rev Tadgh O'Dalaigh *Vocations Director* Very Rev Timothy Gleeson *Provincial Superior* No magazine	Total number abroad . . Papua New Guinea (3), South Africa (34), Sudan (1) Venezuela (9)	**47**	**47M**
Sacred Hearts Community (SSCC) (1954; Roman Catholic) ☎Dublin (353) 01 604898 Coudrin House 27 Northbrook Road, Dublin 6	Very Rev Eamon Aylward *Provincial Superior* No magazine	Total number abroad . . Bahamas (1), Ecuador (2), Japan (5)	**8**	**8M**
St John of God Brothers (OH) (n/a; Roman Catholic) ☎Dublin (353) 01 288 2200 Provincial Curia, Granada Stillorgan, Blackrock, Co Dublin	Brother Laurence Kearns *Provincial Superior* ***Caritas*** Quarterly	Total number abroad . . Korea (6), Philippines (1)	**7**	**7M**
St John of God Sisters (n/a; Roman Catholic) ☎Kilkenny (353) 056 22870 Provincialate College Road, Kilkenny	Sister Monica Sinnott *Provincial Superior* No magazine	Total number abroad . . Cameroon (5), Pakistan (4)	**9**	**9W**

Missionary Societies (Roman Catholic)

Name & Location	Chief Officer/Magazine	Main Countries of Activity
St Patrick's Missionary Society (SPS) (1932; Roman Catholic) Kiltegan (353) 0508 73233 St Patrick's, Kiltegan Baltinglass, Co Wicklow	Rev Kieran Birmingham *Superior General* *Africa* 100,000 nine times a year	Total number abroad . . **239 239M** Brazil (21), Cameroon (4), Grenada (10), Kenya (86) Malawi (19), Nigeria (65), South Africa (8) Sudan (6), Zambia (16), Zimbabwe (4) *Missionaries of all nationalities: 378*
Salesians (SDB) (1859; Roman Catholic) ☎ Dublin (353) 01 555787/555605 Provincialate, Crumlin House St Teresa's Road, Crumlin Dublin 12	Very Rev Joseph Harrington *Provincial Superior* Very Rev Egidio Vigano *Rector Major, Italy* *Salesian Bulletin* Quarterly	Total number abroad . . **47 47M** Argentina (1), Bolivia (1), Brazil (4), Ecuador (1) Hong Kong (4), India (1), Japan (1), Lesotho (1) Liberia (2), Macao (1), Philippines (1) South Africa (18), Swaziland (11) *Missionaries of all nationalities: 7,600*
Salesian Sisters of St John Bosco (1872; Roman Catholic) ☎ Dublin (353) 01 298 5188 Provincial House 203 Lower Kilmacud Road Stillorgan, Co Dublin	Sister Mary Doran *Mother Provincial* No magazine	Total number abroad . . **10 10W** Hong Kong (1), Lesotho (3), South Africa (4) Syria (1), Thailand (1)
Servite Friars (OSM) (1233; Roman Catholic) ☎ Dublin (353) 01 932913 Servite Priory, Grange Wood Rathfarnham, Dublin 16	Very Rev Colum McDonnell *Provincial Superior* *Servite Missions* 2,500 annually	Total number abroad . . **8 8M** South Africa (8) *Missionaries of all nationalities: 1,200*
Sisters of Charity (n/a; Roman Catholic) ☎ Dublin (353) 01 269 7833 Mount St Anne's Milltown, Dublin 6	Mother Francis I Fahy *Superior General* No magazine	Total number abroad . . **47 47W** Ethiopia (2), Nigeria (12), Venezuela (4) Zambia (29)
Sisters of Charity of St Paul the Apostle (1847; Roman Catholic) ☎ Birmingham (0044) 021 472 2061 St Paul's Convent Greenhills, Dublin 12	Sister Maria Rosa O'Sullivan *Mother Superior, UK* No magazine	Total number abroad . . **13 13W** South Africa (13) *Missionaries of all nationalities: 21*
Sisters of Loreto (IBUM) (n/a; Roman Catholic) ☎ Dublin (353) 01 933827 Provincialate, Loreto House Beaufort, Dublin 14	Sister M Angela Higgins *Provincial* No magazine	Total number abroad . . **158 158W** India (51), Kenya (32), Mauritius (15) Peru (2), South Africa (58)
Sisters of Marie Reparatrice (n/a; Roman Catholic) ☎ Dublin (353) 01 902968 Provincial House 14 Rossmore Avenue Templeogue, Dublin 12	Sister Bernadette O'Driscoll *Provincial Superior* No magazine	Total number abroad . . **3 3W** Kenya (2), Uganda (1)
Sisters of Mercy (n/a; Roman Catholic) ☎ Dublin (353) 01 288 4495 Generalate Convent of the Mother of Mercy Carysfort Park, Blackrock Co Dublin	Sister Sebastian Cashen *Superior General* No magazine	Total number abroad . . **120 120W** Brazil (7), Ethiopia (1), Kenya (55), Nigeria (12) Pakistan (1), Peru (15), South Africa (6) Zambia (21), Zimbabwe (2)

Missionary Societies (Roman Catholic)

Name & Location	Chief Officer/Magazine	Main Countries of Activity		
Sisters of St Clare (n/a; Roman Catholic) ☎ Dublin (353) 01 269 5731 St Clare's Convent 131 Stillorgan Road, Dublin 4	Sister Margaret McGill *Abbess General* No magazine	Total number abroad El Salvador (2)	2	2W
Sisters of St Joseph of Annecy (1650; Roman Catholic) ☎ Cwmbran (0044) 0633 33232 St Joseph's Convent Killorglin, Killarney, Co Kerry	Sister M James Cleary *Provincial Superior, UK* No magazine	Total number abroad Gambia (4), India (3), Senegal (3)	10	10W
Sisters of St Joseph of Chambery (n/a; Roman Catholic) ☎ Dublin (353) 01 847 8351 Springdale Road, Raheny Dublin 5	Sister Nora Doyle *Superioress* No magazine	Total number abroad India (2), Liberia (1), Pakistan (1)	4	4W
Sisters of St Joseph of Cluny (n/a; Roman Catholic) ☎ Dublin (353) 01 621 3104 Mt Sackville Convent Chapelizod, Dublin 20	Sister Morag Collins *Provincial Superior* No magazine	Total number abroad Fiji (4), Gambia (5), Grenada (2), India (13) Peru (1), St Lucia (6), St Vincent (1) Seychelles (13), Sierra Leone (15) Trinidad & Tobago (15)	75	75W
Sisters of St Joseph of Peace (1884; Roman Catholic) ☎ Dublin (353) 01 971011 Peace House 43 Kenilworth Park Harold's Cross, Dublin 6	Sister Hilda Baxter *Provincial Superior, UK* No magazine	Total number abroad Liberia (1) *Missionaries of all nationalities: 15*	1	1W
Sisters of St Joseph of the Apparition (n/a; Roman Catholic) ☎ Alderley Edge (0044) 0625 585655 St Joseph's, Garden Hill, Sligo	n/a *Superior* No magazine	Total number abroad India (1), Israel (11), Jordan (3), Peru (2) Thailand (2)	19	19W
Sisters of St Louis (n/a; Roman Catholic) ☎ Dublin (353) 01 977974 Generalate, Louisville 5 Grosvenor Road, Rathgar Dublin 6	Sister Dorothy McCloskey *Superior General* No magazine	Total number abroad Brazil (10), Ghana (5), Nigeria (20)	35	35W
Sisters of the Holy Cross (n/a; Roman Catholic) ☎ Dublin (353) 01 961617 28 Orwell Park, Rathgar Dublin 6	Sister Ailbe Halpin *Superioress* No magazine	Total number abroad South Africa (72), Zambia (23), Zimbabwe (3)	98	98W
Sisters of the Holy Faith (n/a; Roman Catholic) ☎ Dublin (353) 01 371426 Generalate, Aylward House Glasnevin, Dublin 11	Sister Mary E Bergin *Superior General* No magazine	Total number abroad American Samoa (4), Peru (4) Trinidad & Tobago (8)	16	16W
Sisters of the Holy Family of Bordeaux (1820; Roman Catholic) ☎ London (0044) 071 624 7573 11 Arran Road, Dublin 9	Sister Margaret Muldoon *Provincial Superior, UK* No magazine	Total number abroad India (1), Lesotho (2), Pakistan (3), Paraguay (1) Peru (1), Philippines (1), South Africa (45) *Missionaries of all nationalities: 60*	54	54W

Missionary Societies (Roman Catholic)

Name & Location — *Chief Officer/Magazine* — *Main Countries of Activity*

Sisters of the Infant Jesus
(n/a; Roman Catholic)
☎ Dublin (353) 01 339577
Provincial House
56 St Laurence Road
Clontarf, Dublin 3

Sister Paula Kilbride
Provincial
No magazine

Total number abroad . . **23**   **23W**
Cameroon (3), Japan (5), Malaysia (7), Nigeria (3)
Peru (1), Singapore (4)

Sisters of the Sacred Heart of Mary
(1849; Roman Catholic)
☎ Dublin (353) 01 379898
70 Upper Drumcondra Road
Dublin 9

Sister Josepha O'Sullivan
Provincial Superior, UK
No magazine

Total number abroad . . **14**   **14W**
Brazil (5), Zambia (9)

Society of African Missions (SMA)
(1856; Roman Catholic)
☎ Cork (353) 021 292871
St Joseph's Provincial House
Blackrock Road, Cork

Very Rev Cornelius Murphy
Provincial Superior
Very Rev P Harrington
Superior General, Italy
African Missionary
5,000 quarterly

Total number abroad . . **164**   **164M**
Argentina (3), Benin (1), Ghana (8), India (1)
Liberia (16), Nigeria (106), Philippines (2)
South Africa (7), Tanzania (7), Zambia (13)
Missionaries of all nationalities: 1,100

Society of Jesus (SJ)
(1540; Roman Catholic)
☎ Dublin (353) 01 269 6577
Loyola
87 Eglinton Road, Dublin 4

Very Rev Philip Harnett
Provincial Superior
Very Rev Peter Kolvenbach
Superior General, Italy
Jesuits & Friends
12,000 every four months
Irish Messenger
n/a

Total number abroad . . **109**   **109M**
El Salvador (1), Hong Kong (39), India (1)
Japan (4), Kenya (4), Paraguay (1)
Seychelles (1), Singapore (5), Zambia (53)
Missionaries of all nationalities: 6,600

Society of the Holy Child Jesus (SHCJ)
(1846; Roman Catholic)
☎ Dublin (353) 01 823799
Military Road, Killiney
Dunlaoghaire, Co Dublin

n/a
Superior
Sister Madeleine Mulrennan
Provincial Superior, UK
No magazine

Total number abroad . . **5**   **5W**
Nigeria (4), Zimbabwe (1)

Society of the Sacred Heart
(1800; Roman Catholic)
☎ Dublin (353) 01 360866
Provincial House, 6 Achill Road
Drumcondra, Dublin 9

Sister Phil Kilroy
Provincial Superior
No magazine

Total number abroad . . **6**   **6W**
Japan (1), Kenya (1), Philippines (1), Uganda (3)

Ursulines (Irish Ursuline Union)
(1862; Roman Catholic)
☎ Dublin (353) 01 285 2117
Ursuline Generalate
Cabinteely, Dublin 18

Sister Ursula McDermott
Superior General
No magazine

Total number abroad . . **11**   **11W**
Kenya (11)

Viatores Christi
(1960; Roman Catholic)
☎ Dublin (353) 01 749346/ 728027
38/39 Upper Gardiner Street
Dublin 1

Miss Una Twomey
Secretary
Viatores Christi
300 quarterly

Total numbers abroad . . **46**   **46W**
Argentina (1), Bhutan (1), Bolivia (1), Brazil (2)
Chile (2), Haiti (2), India (3), Kenya (1), Liberia (1)
Nigeria (3), Mexico (2), Papua New Guinea (2)
Peru (2), Philippines (1), Sierra Leone (4)
South Africa (1), Tanzania (3), Thailand (1)
Venezuela (2), Zambia (3), Zimbabwe (8)
Missionaries of all nationalities: 46

Vincentians (CM)
(n/a; Roman Catholic)
☎ Dublin (353) 01 305068
Provincial House
4 Cabra Road, Dublin 7

Very Rev Mark Noonan
Provincial Superior
No magazine

Total number abroad . . **8**   **8M**
Nigeria (8)

Missionary Societies (Roman Catholic)

Name & Location	Chief Officer/Magazine	Main Countries of Activity
Volunteer Missionary Movement (1969; Roman Catholic) ☎Dublin (353) 01 376565 High Park, Grace Park Road Dublin 9	Ms Anne Reilly *Co-ordinator of VMM Ireland* **VMM Newsletter** 2,000 every four months	Total number abroad . . **13 5M 8W** Kenya (3), Papua New Guinea (2), Sierra Leone (1) South Africa (2), Uganda (1), Zambia (3) Zimbabwe (1) *Missionaries of all nationalities: 48*

IRISH MISSIONARIES BY COUNTRY

Only those countries where Irish missionaries are specifically known to be working are included in this list. The total number shown for each society corresponds to that shown in brackets in the "main countries of activity" line in the alphabetical list of societies.

P = Protestant   RC = Roman Catholic

Society Codes

Missionary Societies (Protestant)

AGM	Acre Gospel Mission
AIMI	Africa Inland Mission International
BCMS	BCMS Crosslinks
BM	Baptist Missions
CMJI	Church's Ministry among the Jews — Ireland
CMSI	Church's Missionary Society Ireland
ECM	European Christian Mission
EMF	European Missionary Fellowship
FEBA	FEBA Radio
FPC	Free Presbyterian Church of Ulster Mission Board
IS	INTERSERVE
LMI	Leprosy Mission International
MMS	Methodist Missionary Society (Ireland)
OMF	Overseas Missionary Fellowship
PCI	Presbyterian Church in Ireland Overseas Board
QIF	Qua Iboe Fellowship
SAMS	South American Missionary Society
SIM	SIM UK
UFM	UFM Worldwide
USPG	United Society for the Propagation of the Gospel
WBT	Wycliffe Bible Translators

Missionary Societies (Roman Catholic)

AB	Alexian Brothers
AF	Augustinian Fathers
B	Benedictines
BC	Brothers of Charity
BS	Brigidine Sisters
BSSP	Bon Secours Sisters of Paris
CB	Christian Brothers
CD	Carmelites (Discaled OCD)
CF	Capuchin Friars
CM	Comboni Missionaries
CO	Cistercian Order
COC	Carmelites (OCarm)
CS	Cistercian Sisters
DC	Daughters of Charity
DHS	Daughters of the Holy Spirit
DLSB	De La Salle Brothers
DLSH	Daughters of Our Lady of the Sacred Heart
DMJ	Daughters of Mary and Joseph
DO	Dominican Order
DS	Dominican Sisters
DWM	Divine Word Missionaries
F	Franciscans
FB	Franciscan Brothers
FCJ	Faithful Companions of Jesus
FMDM	Franciscan Missionaries of the Divine Motherhood
FMM	Franciscan Missionaries of Mary
FMOL	Franciscan Missionaries of Our Lady
FMSA	Franciscan Missionary Sisters for Africa
FMSJ	Franciscan Missionary Sisters of St Joseph
GSS	Good Shepherd Sisters
HGF	Holy Ghost Fathers
LCM	Little Company of Mary
LSA	Little Sisters of the Assumption
LSP	Little Sisters of the Poor
MA	Missionaries of Africa (White Fathers)
MB	Marist Brothers
MFSIC	Missionary Franciscan Sisters of the Immaculate Conception
MHM	Mill Hill Missionaries
MM	Montfort Missionaries
MMM	Medical Missionaries of Mary
MR	Marists
MRN	Marianists
MS	Marist Sisters
MSA	Missionary Sisters of the Assumption
MSC	Missionary Society of St Columban
MSHR	Missionary Sisters of the Holy Rosary
MSLA	Missionary Sisters of Our Lady of Apostles
MSSC	Missionary Sisters of St Columban
OMI	Oblates of Mary Immaculate
OSC	Order of St Camillus
P	Passionists
PB	Patrician Brothers
PL	Pallotines
PRB	Presentation Brothers
PS	Presentation Sisters
PSN	Poor Sisters of Nazareth
R	Redemptorists

Irish Missionaries by Country

RF	Rosminian Fathers		SJGB	St John of God Brothers
RJM	Religious of Jesus and Mary		SJGS	St John of God Sisters
S	Salesians		SJP	Sisters of St Joseph of Peace
SAM	Society of African Missions		SL	Sisters of Loreto
SC	Sisters of Charity		SM	Sisters of Mercy
SCPA	Sisters of Charity of St Paul the Apostle		SMR	Sisters of Marie Reparatrice
SF	Servite Friars		SPMS	St Patrick's Missionary Society
SHC	Sacred Hearts Community		SSC	Sisters of St Clare
SHCJ	Society of the Holy Child Jesus		SSH	Society of the Sacred Heart
SHF	Sacred Heart Fathers		SSHM	Sisters of the Sacred Heart of Mary
SHFB	Sisters of the Holy Family of Bordeaux		SSJB	Salesian Sisters of St John Bosco
SHM	Sacred Heart Missionaries		SSL	Sisters of St Louis
SIJ	Sisters of the Infant Jesus		STHC	Sisters of the Holy Cross
SJ	Society of Jesus		STHF	Sisters of the Holy Faith
SJA	Sisters of St Joseph of the Apparition		UIUU	Ursulines (Irish Ursuline Union)
SJAN	Sisters of St Joseph of Annecy		V	Vincentians
SJC	Sisters of St Joseph of Chambery		VC	Viatores Christi
SJCL	Sisters of St Joseph of Cluny		VMM	Volunteer Missionary Movement

Country		Societies working in country	Total personnel	Grand total
Algeria	RC	LSP(3)	3	**3**
American Samoa	RC	LSP(1), PSN(1), SHF(4)	6	**6**
Angola	RC	DWM(1), HGF(7), MMM(6)	14	**14**
Argentina	P	CMJI(3)	3	**54**
	RC	CB(16), DO(5), DS(9), PL(13), S(1), SAM(3), VC(1)	51	
Australia	P	FPC(6)	6	**6**
Austria	P	ECM(4)	4	**4**
Bahamas	RC	SHC(1)	1	**1**
Belize	RC	MSC(7)	7	**7**
Benin	P	SIM(1)	1	**3**
	RC	DWM(1), SAM(1)	2	
Bhutan	P	IS(1)	1	**2**
	RC	VC(1)	1	
Bolivia	P	SIM(5)	5	**14**
	RC	DWM(2), MFSIC(3), S(1), VC(1)	7	
Botswana	RC	DWM(1), P(14)	15	**15**
Brazil	P	AGM(15), PCI(3), UFM(4), WBT(1)	23	**212**
	RC	CM(1), DLSH(1), DWM(12), HGF(34), LSA(1), MMM(8), MR(1), MS(1), MSHR(16), OMI(14), R(38), S(4), SM(7), SPMS(21), SSC(13), SSHM(5), SSL(10), VC(2)	189	
Burkina Faso	RC	MA(1)	1	**1**
Burundi	RC	DMJ(1)	1	**1**
Cameroon	P	FPC(3), WBT(1)	4	**44**
	RC	DMJ(1), MHM(6), MSHR(21), SIJ(3), SJGS(5), SPMS(4)	40	
Canada	P	FPC(8)	8	**8**
Canary Islands	P	AGM(2)	2	**2**
Chile	RC	FMM(1), MHM(1), MSC(27), MSSC(11), PS(3), VC(2)	45	**45**
China	P	PCI(2)	2	**7**
	RC	MHM(1), MSC(3), MSSC(1)	5	

			Irish Missionaries by Country	
Country		Societies working in country	Total personnel	Grand total
Colombia	RC	DWM(1), MS(3), PL(1)	5	5
Comoro Islands	P	AIMI(1)	1	1
Costa Rica	RC	DO(1)	1	1
Djibouti	RC	FMOL(1)	1	1
Eastern Europe	P	ECM(11)	11	11
Ecuador	RC	AF(10), DWM(5), FMSJ(3), PS(8), S(1), SHC(2)	29	29
Egypt	P	CMSI(5)	5	20
	RC	GSS(4), MFSIC(11)	15	
El Salvador	RC	F(10), SJ(1), SSC(2)	13	13
Ethiopia	P	LM(1)	1	42
	RC	FMSA(8), GSS(5), HGF(7), LSA(3), MA(1), MMM(4), MSHR(10), SC(2), SM(1)	41	
Fiji	RC	MR(11), MS(9), MSC(25), SJCL(4)	49	49
France	P	BM(5), ECM(7)	12	12
Gambia	P	MMS(2)	2	29
	RC	CB(1), HGF(15), MS(2), SJAN(4), SJCL(5)	27	
Ghana	P	WBT(1)	1	74
	RC	AB(2), DMJ(6), DWM(5), FMM(2), HGF(16), MA(4), MSHR(4), MSLA(13), PRB(8), SAM(8), SSL(5)	73	
Grenada	RC	PB(3), SPMS(10), SJCL(2)	15	15
Haiti	P	MMS(3)	3	6
	RC	LCM(3)	3	
Hong Kong	P	OMF(1)	1	76
	RC	DWM(3), LSP(6), MB(1), MSC(2), MSSC(19), S(4), SJ(39), SSJB(1)	75	
India	P	BCMS(1), MMS(3), PCI(3)	7	182
	RC	CB(47), DO(1), DWM(2), FMM(5), GSS(13), LSP(4), PB(3), PS(13), R(7), RJM(3), S(1), SAM(1), SHFB(1), SJ(1), SJA(1), SJAN(3), SJC(2), SJCL(13), SL(51), VC(3)	175	
Indonesia	P	LM(1), OMF(2), PCI(2)	5	15
	RC	DWM(2), GSS(7), OMI(1)	10	
Irish Republic	P	BM(14), ECM(4), EMF(2)	20	20
Israel	P	CMJI(41), CMSI(2), PCI(2)	45	59
	RC	DO(2), MSLA(1), SJA(11)	14	
Italy	P	ECM(10), EMF(1)	11	11
Ivory Coast	P	MMS(1), WBT(5)	6	6
Jamaica	P	PCI(6)	6	14
	RC	MSC(8)	8	
Japan	P	OMF(2)	2	80
	RC	DWM(2), MR(2), MSC(58), S(1), SHC(5), SIJ(5), SJ(4), SSH(1)	78	
Jordan	RC	FMDM(4), SJA(3)	7	7

Irish Missionaries by Country

Country		Societies working in country	Total personnel	Grand total
Kenya	P	AIMI(6), BCMS(2), CMSI(3), FPC(1), PCI(8), WBT(4)	24	**419**
	RC	BS(3), CD(1), CO(1), DWM(3), FB(9), FMM(1), FMSA(27), FMSJ(6), GSS(3), HGF(62), LSP(3), MB(1), MHM(19), MMM(26), MSHR(22), OSC(2), P(1), PB(6), PL(3), RF(1), SJ(4), SL(32), SM(55), SMR(2), SPMS(86), SSH(1), UIUU(11), VC(1), VMM(3)	395	
Korea	P	OMF(1)	1	**116**
	RC	CF(4), FMM(1), MSC(76), MSSC(28), SJGB(6)	115	
Lesotho	RC	OMI(1), S(1), SHFB(2), SSJB(3)	7	**7**
Liberia	RC	CB(6), FMM(4), HGF(1), MMM(2), S(2), SAM(16), SJC(1), SJP(1), VC(1)	34	**34**
Macao	RC	FMM(1), S(1)	2	**2**
Madagascar	RC	GSS(3)	3	**3**
Malawi	P	PCI(13), USPG(1)	14	**57**
	RC	CM(1), FMSA(1), HGF(6), MA(1), MM(2), MMM(12), MRN(1), SPMS(19)	43	
Malaysia	P	OMF(1)	1	**25**
	RC	DLSB(13), FMM(1), LSP(1), MHM(2), SIJ(7)	24	
Mali	P	WBT(1)	1	**1**
Mauritius	RC	DLSB(2), HGF(5), SL(15)	22	**22**
Mexico	RC	BS(3), DWM(5), HGF(2), MS(3), VC(2)	15	**15**
Middle East	P	IS(2)	2	**2**
Namibia	P	AIMI(2)	2	**4**
	RC	CF(2)	2	
Nauru	RC	DLSH(1)	1	**1**
Nepal	P	CMSI(4), IS(1), MMS(2), PCI(9)	16	**16**
New Caledonia	RC	LSP(1)	1	**1**
Nicaragua	RC	DWM(1)	1	**1**
Nigeria	P	QIF(15), SIM(2)	17	**477**
	RC	AF(35), B(5), CD(4), CO(1), CS(4), DC(21), DHS(7), DLSB(6), FB(1), FMDM(5), HGF(5), MA(2), MMM(47), MSLA(45), R(3), SAM(106), SC(12), SHCJ(4), SIJ(3), SM(12), SPMS(65), SSL(20), V(8)	460	
North Africa	P	CMSI(1)	1	**1**
Norway	P	EMF(1)	1	**1**
Pakistan	P	IS(2), SIM(2), WBT(2)	6	**101**
	RC	FMM(6), HGF(9), MHM(5), MSC(12), MSSC(3), PS(36), RJM(15), SHFB(3), SJC(1), SJGS(4), SM(1)	95	
Papua New Guinea	RC	DLSH(3), DWM(7), HGF(6), MFSIC(3), MR(3), PN(1), PS(2), SHM(3), VC(2), VMM(2)	32	**32**
Paraguay	RC	CB(3), DWM(5), FB(1), P(1), SHFB(1), SJ(1)	12	**12**
Peru	P	BCMS(3), BM(13)	16	**85**
	RC	BSSP(8), CD(1), MSC(22), MSSC(10), SHF(4), SHFB(1), SIJ(1), SJAP(2), SJCL(1), SL(2), SM(15), VC(2)	69	

Irish Missionaries by Country

Country		Societies working in country	Total personnel	Grand total
Philippines	P	OMF(12)	12	**245**
	RC	CD(3), DWM(4), GSS(1), MHM(2), MR(1) MSC(150), MSSC(19), OMI(3), PS(7), R(36) S(1), SAM(2), SHFB(1), SJGB(1), SSH(1), VC(1)	233	
Portugal	P	AGM(4)	4	**4**
Reunion	RC	GSS(1)	1	**1**
Senegal	P	WBT(2)	2	**6**
	RC	GSS(1), SJA(3)	4	
Seychelles	P	FEBA(16)	16	**30**
	RC	SJ(10), SJCL(13)	14	
Sierra Leone	RC	DC(4), HGF(28), MSHR(25), SJCL(15) VC(4), VMM(1)	77	**77**
Singapore	P	CMSI(1). OMF(4), PCI(2)	7	**26**
	RC	DLSB(5), GSS(2), LSP(2), MB(1), SIJ(4), SJ(5)	19	
Solomon Islands	RC	MR(3)	3	**3**
South Africa	P	CMJI(2)	2	**757**
	RC	BC(1), CB(30), CD(1), CF(15), DLSB(17) DLSH(9), DS(132), F(38), FMM(7), FMSA(3) GSS(12), HGF(2), LCM(30), MA(1), MB(4) MSA(64), MSHR(34), OMI(37), P(4), PSN(37) S(18), SAM(7), SCPA(13), SF(8), SHC(72) SHF(1), SHFB(45), SHM(34), SL(58), SM(6) SPMS(8), SSJB(4), VC(1), VMM(2)	755	
Spain	P	ECM(10), EMF(1), FPC(5), PCI(2), UFM(1)	19	**19**
Sri Lanka	P	MMS(2)	2	**15**
	RC	BC(3), GSS(10)	13	
St Lucia	RC	PRB(5), SJCL(6)	11	**11**
St Vincent	RC	SJCL(1)	1	**1**
Sudan	RC	GSS(1), MA(1), MHM(4), MMM(3), MSLA(2) SHM(1), SPMS(6)	18	**18**
Swaziland	RC	DS(4), HGF(1), S(11)	16	**16**
Syria	RC	SSJB(1)	1	**1**
Taiwan	P	OMF(1)	1	**13**
	RC	MSC(12)	12	
Tanzania	P	AIMI(5), BCMS(4), CMSI(9), LM(2)	20	**93**
	RC	HGF(3), MA(2), MMM(26), OSC(1), PL(13) RF(18), SAM(7), VC(3)	73	
Thailand	P	OMF(2)	2	**5**
	RC	SJA(2), VC(1)	3	
Trinidad & Tobago	RC	DO(30), HGF(4), PRB(5), SHF(8), SJCL(15)	48	**48**
Turkey	RC	DLSB(1)	1	**1**
Uganda	P	CMSI(12)	12	**79**
	RC	CM(2), CO(1), DMJ(16), FMSA(24), HGF(1) MA(2), MHM(6), MMM(10), SMR(1), SSH(3) VMM(1)	67	
United Kingdom	P	PCI(4)	4	**4**
United States of America	P	CMJI(3), FPC(4)	7	**7**
Uruguay	RC	CB(5)	5	**5**

Irish Missionaries by Country

Country		Societies working in country	Total personnel	Grand total
Vanuatu	RC	MR(1)	1	**1**
Venezuela	RC	RF(1), SC(4), SHM(9), VC(2)	16	**16**
Virgin Islands	RC	R(1)	1	**1**
Zaire	P	AIMI(2), CMSI(2), UFM(5)	9	**10**
	RC	LSP(1)	1	
Zimbabwe	P	BCMS(1), MMS(4), USPG(2)	7	**139**
	RC	CB(4), CD(23), F(13), FMDM(18), FMSA(7) LCM(18), PS(25), PSN(5), SHC(3), SHCJ(1) SM(2), SPMS(4), VC(8), VMM(1)	132	

MISSIONARY SUPPORT ORGANISATIONS

Name & Magazine	Location	Chief Officer & Staff	Work & Income
Aid to the Church in Need (1972; Roman Catholic) *Mirror* 600,000 worldwide	☎ Dublin (353) 01 377516 151 St Mobhi Road Glasnevin, Dublin 9	Rev Joseph O'Donoghoe *National Director* n/a	To aid where the Church is persecuted or hindered in performance of its mission n/a
Christian Concern for Freedom of Conscience (n/a; interdenominational) *Church in Chains* Quarterly	☎ Dublin (353) 01 688781 28 South Lotts Road Dublin 4	Mr David Turner *Secretary* No full-time staff	n/a n/a
Christian Mission to the Communist World (*CC*; 1975; interdenominational) *Voice of the Martyrs* 2,000 quarterly *Eastern Europe* 2,000 quarterly	☎ Belfast (08) 0232 301697 Glenburn House Glenburn Road South Dunmurry Belfast BT17 9JP	Mr David Thompson *Irish Representative* Mr Brian D Loader *General Secretary, UK* Other staff 2	Evangelism in communist countries n/a
Churches Commission on Mission (*CC*; 1990; interdenominational) *Bulletin* Every four months	☎ London (0044) 071 620 4444 Inter-Church House 35 Lower Marsh London SE1 7RL	Rev Donald W Elliott *Commission Secretary, UK* n/a	Relating concern for mission in Britain and Ireland with that in the wider world n/a
Dublin University Far Eastern Mission (1886; Anglican) *Annual Report* 150 annually	☎ Dublin (353) 01 772941 Ext 1402 📠 Fax (353) 01 772694 Trinity College, Dublin 2	Mr George Clarke *Chairman* No full-time staff	Supporting Christian education and clergy training in the Far East £7,500 – Oct 90
Dublin University Mission to Chota Nagpur (1890; Anglican) No magazine	☎ Dublin (353) 01 289 3135 Tullon Rectory Carrickmines, Dublin 18	Rev K A Kearon *Chairman of Committee* No full-time staff	Supporting missionary work in India n/a
Evangelize China Fellowship (1947; non-denominational) *ECF News* 4,500 quarterly	☎ Bangor (08) 0247 465783 72a Ballymacormick Road Bangor Co Down BT19 2AB	Mr Roger Lyons *Hon Secretary* Dr Paul C C Szeto *General Director USA* No full-time staff	Missionary outreach to the Chinese; orphans schools; churches leadership training £15,000 – Mar 87

Missionary Support Organisations

Name & Magazine	Location	Chief Officer & Staff	Work & Income
Irish Missionary Union (1970; Roman Catholic) *IMU Report* 2,500 bi-monthly	☎Dublin (353) 01 965433 📠Fax (353) 01 965029 Orwell Park Rathgar, Dublin 6	Rev Enda Watters *Executive Secretary* Executive staff 1 Other staff 6	Association of Catholic Missionary organisations to co-ordinate the work of its members. Provides research, training and personnel to Third World n/a
Jerusalem and the Middle East Church Association (*CC*; 1887; Anglican) *Bible Lands* 3,500 half-yearly	☎Whitehead (08) 09603 73300 St Patrick's Rectory 74 Cable Road, Whitehead Carrickfergus Co Antrim BT38 9SJ	Rev K Ruddock *Hon Secretary* No full-time staff	Enabling/recruiting organisation serving the Anglican province Episcopal Church in Jerusalem and Middle East n/a
National Mission Council of Ireland (n/a; Roman Catholic) n/a	☎Dublin (353) 01 689674 Secretariate 54 Wellington Road Dublin 4	Rev Enda Watters *Acting Secretary* n/a	Co-ordinates the activities of all national missionary bodies and acts as a forum for discussion on matters related to national mission policy n/a
Pontifical Mission Aid Societies (1822; Roman Catholic) *Missions Today* Every four months *Children Helping Children* Every four months	☎Dublin (353) 01 972035 64 Lower Rathmines Road Dublin 6	Rev Seamus Galvin *National Director* Executive staff 3 Other staff 4	Umbrella organisations covering missionary animation and appeals to children, teenagers, adult laity, clergy and religious £2,229,000 – Feb 91
Survive – MIVA (*CC*; 1974; Roman Catholic but interdenominational) *Awareness* Half-yearly	☎No telephone The Grove, Celbridge Co Kildare	Mr Willie Walsh *Administrator* Mr Terry Hardy *Director, UK* n/a	Providing essential transport to missionaries working in the developing world n/a
Waldensian Church Missions Irish Committee (n/a, Waldensian)	☎Craigavon (08) 0762 881862 The Manse 61 Moygannon Road Donacloney, Craigavon Co Armagh BT66 7PN	Rev T J Hagan *Convener* No full-time staff	n/a n/a
*****Worldwide Missionary Convention** (1937; non-denominational) No magazine	☎Bangor (08) 0247 460868 15 Ranfurly Avenue Bangor Co Down BT20 2SN	Mr Raymond J Pitt *Hon Secretary* No full-time staff	Annual convention held in Bangor during last week in August £100,000 – Dec 90

Table 26

The ten Countries with the largest Irish Protestant Missionary Activity

By total number of Irish personnel

1	Kenya	24
2	Brazil	23
3=	Irish Republic	20
3=	Tanzania	20
5	Spain	19
6	Nigeria	17
7=	Nepal	16
7=	Peru	16
7=	Seychelles	16
10	Malawi	14

Table 27

The ten Countries with the largest Irish Roman Catholic Missionary Activity

By total number of Irish personnel

1	South Africa	755
2	Nigeria	460
3	Kenya	395
4	Philippines	233
5	Brazil	189
6	India	175
7	Zimbabwe	132
8	Korea	115
9	Pakistan	95
10	Japan	78

Table 28

The five largest Protestant Societies

By total number of Irish serving members

1	Presbyterian Church in Ireland Overseas Board	52
2	The Church's Ministry among the Jews — Ireland	49
3	Church Missionary Society Ireland	42
4	Baptist Missions	32
5	Overseas Missionary Fellowship	28

Table 29

The five largest Roman Catholic Societies

By total number of Irish serving members

1	Missionary Society of St Columban	415
2	St Patrick's Missionary Society	239
3	Holy Ghost Fathers	217
4	Missionary Sisters of the Holy Rosary	195
5	Society of African Missions	164

Services

	Page
Audio-Visual, Film and Video Producers and Suppliers	109
Benevolent Organisations	110
Counselling and Information Organisations	110
Educational Agencies	112
Musical and Theatrical Services	112
Professional Christian Groups	112
Radio and TV Programme Producers	113
Reconciliation Groups	113
Relief and Development Agencies	115
Social Service and Welfare Organisations	116
Theological Colleges and Bible Schools	
By Denomination	118
Northern Ireland	118
Overseas	119
Republic of Ireland	119
Training Centres and Services	120
Youth Organisations	121

AUDIO-VISUAL, FILM AND VIDEO PRODUCERS AND SUPPLIERS

Name & Magazine	Location	Chief Officer & Staff	Work & Turnover
Callister Communications Ltd (1990; interdenominational) No magazine	☎Lisburn (08) 0846 673717 ✉Fax (08) 0846 673652 88 Causeway End Road Lisburn Co Antrim BT28 2ED	Mr John Callister *Director* Executive staff 1 Other staff 2	Producing 16mm film and video to broadcast standard for Christian organisations and charities First year of operation
Christian Communication Network (1989; interdenominational) *CCN News Journal* 1,000 quarterly	☎Belfast (08) 0232 853997 ✉Fax (08) 0232 365536 646 Shore Road Whiteabbey Newtownabbey Co Antrim BT37 0PR	Pastor Roy Kerr *Missions Director* Executive staff 2 Other staff 7	Production of Christian television programmes for cable television and video £343,200 – Dec 90
Evangelical Outreach Ltd (*CC*; 1966; non-denominational) No magazine	☎Ballyclare (08) 09603 52470 11 Old Ballybracken Road Doagh, Ballyclare Co Antrim BT39 0SF	Mr James D Murphy *Executive Director* No full-time staff	Film and video production, family film festivals, video sales and film rentals £15,000 – Dec 90
Light and Life Films (*CC*; 1970; non-denominational) No magazine	☎Belfast (08) 0232 241550 4 Pandora Street Donegall Road Belfast BT12 5PR	Mr H E Johnson *Manager* Executive staff 2	Distributing as many films as possible for evangelism n/a

BENEVOLENT ORGANISATIONS

Name & Magazine	Location	Chief Officer & Staff	Work & Income
Catholic Women's Federation (1937; Roman Catholic) No magazine	☎ Dublin (353) 01 761594 4 Lower Abbey Street Dublin 1	n/a	Promoting rights of women, educational and social improvements, establishing relations with organisations, denominational and non-denominational n/a
Pioneer Total Abstinence Association of the Sacred Heart (n/a; Roman Catholic) No magazine	☎ Dublin (353) 01 749464 27 Upper Sherrard Street Dublin 1	Rev John C Smyth *Central Director* n/a	Promotion of temperance and sobriety n/a
Protestant Aid (n/a; interdenominational) No magazine	☎ Dublin (353) 01 684298 72 Upper Leeson Street Dublin	Mr Robin George *Executive Director* Other staff 2	Assisting old people and the unemployed throughout Ireland n/a
Society of St Vincent de Paul (1833; non-denominational) *Bulletin* Quarterly	☎ Dublin (353) 01 384164/384167 8 New Cabra Road Dublin 7	Mr Frank Cox *National President* Executive staff 3 Other staff 4	Alleviation of poverty IR£8,500,000 — Mar 89

COUNSELLING AND INFORMATION ORGANISATIONS

Name & Magazine	Location	Chief Officer & Staff	Work & Income
Catholic Communications Institute (n/a; Roman Catholic) *Intercom* Monthly	☎ Dublin (353) 01 288 7311 169 Booterstown Road Blackrock, Co Dublin	Rev Martin Tierney *Director* n/a	Advises Episcopal Commission on matters related to communications n/a
Church's Ministry of Healing (1932; Church of Ireland) *Christian Healing* 12,000 quarterly	☎ Dublin (353) 01 776078 St Andrews Church Suffolk Street Dublin 2 **Also at:** ☎ Belfast (08) 0232 457853 11 The Mount Belfast BT5 4NA **And:** ☎ (08) 0504 352396 St Peters Church Derry	Rev James A Farrar *Warden* n/a	Counselling, prayer service to the sick £43,000 — Dec 89
CURA (*CC*; 1977; Roman Catholic but serves all denominations) No magazine	☎ Dublin (353) 01 710598 30 South Anne Street Dublin 2 **And:** ☎ Athlone (353) 0902 74272 Shalom, St Mary's Place Athlone, Co Westmeath ☎ Cork (353) 021 277544 34 Paul Street, Cork ☎ Derry (08) 0504 268467 CURA Centre 164 Bishop Street Londonderry BT48 6UJ	Miss Anne Rowayne *Co-ordinator* Executive staff 14	Confidential telephone information, counselling and referral service for women with problem pregnancies; fourteen centres n/a — Dec 90

(continued on Page 111)

Counselling and Information Organisations

Name & Magazine	Location	Chief Officer & Staff	Work & Income
CURA (continued)	☎ Dundalk (353) 042 37533 CURA Office St Joseph's Home Seatown Place Dundalk, Co Laois ☎ Ennis (353) 065 29905 Harmony Row Ennis, Co Clare ☎ Galway (353) 091 61077 Arus de Brun Newtownsmith, Galway ☎ Kilkenny (353) 056 22739 Waterford Road, Kilkenny ☎ Letterkenny (353) 074 23037 c/o Jack O'Herlihy Bogay, Letterkenny Co Donegal ☎ Limerick (353) 061 318207 Social Services Centre Henry Street, Limerick ☎ Sligo (353) 071 43659 Social Services Centre Charles Street, Sligo ☎ Tralee (353) 066 27355 Ozanam House Day Place, Tralee, Co Kerry ☎ Waterford (353) 051 76452 Roseville College Street, Waterford ☎ Wexford (353) 053 27355 St Bridget's Centre Roches Road, Wexford		
Foundation Ministries (*CC*; 1979; interdenominational) *Prayer Update* 500 quarterly	☎ Armagh (08) 0861 525282 The Armagh Pastoral Centre 35 Charlemont Gardens Armagh BT61 9BB	Rev David H Greer *Director* Executive staff 5	Christian counselling and Bible teaching organisation £16,000 – Dec 90
Pilot Trust (*CC*; 1976; interdenominational) (Previously Pilot Counselling Service) No magazine	☎ Belfast (08) 0232 230743 Shankill Road (Presbyterian) Mission 116 Shankill Road Belfast BT13 2BD	Mr F Geoffrey Percival *Counselling Director* Executive staff 1	Phone-in "help line" for people struggling with homosexual problems throughout UK £6,614 – Dec 89
PrayerWatch (1987; interdenominational) *PrayerWatch News* 300 monthly	☎ Dublin (353) 01 517920 713 Virginia Heights Dublin 24	Mr Aidan Conway *Co-ordinator* Other staff 1	Facilitating and encouraging informed prayer for revival in Ireland and abroad n/a
Unison (n/a; Roman Catholic) No magazine	☎ Dublin (353) 01 785758 23 Merrion Square Dublin 2	Sr Katherine Curtin *Directress* No full-time staff	To foster women's vocations to the religious life; information service to young women interested in the religious life n/a

EDUCATIONAL AGENCIES

Name & Magazine	Location	Chief Officer & Staff	Work & Turnover
The Teresian Association (1911; Roman Catholic) No magazine	☎ Dublin (353) 01 269 1376 The Teresian School 12 Stillorgan Road Dublin 4	Miss R Doherty *Secretary* n/a	Promotion of Christian values in education and culture. Runs The Teresian School n/a
Irish Christian Study Centre (*CC*; 1977; non-denominational) *Journal of the Irish Christian Study Centre* 350 annually	☎ Belfast (08) 0232 602264 Glenburn House Glenburn Road South Dunmurry Belfast BT17 9JP	Mrs Janet Morris *Librarian* No full-time staff	Encouraging Christian scholarship and the practical application of Biblical Christianity to society £5,000 – Sept 90
National Bible Study Club (*CC*; 1963; Christian Brethren) *Crossroads* 1,500 every two months	☎ No telephone Lower Glenageary Road Dun Laoghaire Co Dublin	Mr Eric C Davis *Full-time Missionary* Executive staff 2	Bible correspondence school for adults and children £5,000 – Dec 87

MUSICAL AND THEATRICAL SERVICES

Name	Location	Chief Officer & Staff	Work
Irish Church Music Association (n/a; Roman Catholic) *Hosanna* Quarterly	☎ (353) 0503 42942 Irish Institute of Pastoral Liturgy College Street, Carlow **Correspondence to:** 28 Broadford Rise Dublin 14	Mr Sean Boylan *Secretary* n/a	Publication of music, regional meetings of church musicians, annual summer school n/a
Other Hand Music (1983; non-denominational) (Previously Other Hand Ministries) No magazine	☎ Portadown (08) 0762 337668 21 Tandragee Road Portadown, Craigavon Co Armagh BT62 3BQ	To be appointed *Director* No full-time staff	Music publishing and recording company n/a

PROFESSIONAL CHRISTIAN GROUPS

Name & Magazine	Location	Chief Officer & Staff	Work & Income
Catechetical Association of Ireland (n/a; Roman Catholic) *Newsletter* Quarterly	☎ Roscommon (353) 0903 7277 The Pastoral Centre Donamon Roscommon	Sr Kathleen Glennon *Secretary* n/a	Organisation for those involved professionally in the ministries of religious formation and education n/a
Central Council of Catholic Adoption Societies (n/a; Roman Catholic) No magazine	☎ Ennis (353) 065 28178 O'Connell Street Ennis, Co Clare	Rev Brian Geohegan *Chairman* n/a	To enable adoption workers to meet and discuss problems; to help societies maintain high standards. To negotiate with the Adoption Board and Depts of State n/a
International Hospital Christian Fellowship in Ireland and Scotland (*CC*; 1964; interdenominational) *Newsletter* (Ireland) 700 quarterly	☎ Belfast (08) 0232 453595 349 Beersbridge Road Belfast BT5 5DS **Also at:** ☎ Dublin (353) 01 298 6970 149 Meadow Grove Dundrum, Dublin 16	Miss Ann Houston *British Isles Promoter* Executive staff 6	Bringing Christians into fellowship and equipping them to be effective witnesses to staff and patients n/a

(continued on Page 113)

Professional Christian Groups

Name & Magazine	Location	Chief Officer & Staff	Work & Income
International Hospital Christian Fellowship in Ireland and Scotland (continued)	*And:* ☎ Stirling (0044) 0786 62809 55 Chattan Avenue Causewayhead Stirling FK9 5RF		
Protestant Adoption Society (n/a; interdenominational) No magazine	☎ Dublin (353) 01 906438 71 Brighton Road Rathgar, Dublin 6	Ms H Douglas *Senior Social Worker* Other staff 1	Single parent counselling, adoption, tracing n/a

RADIO AND TV PROGRAMME PRODUCERS

Name & Magazine	Location	Chief Officer & Staff	Work & Turnover
Commission (Christian Programmers For Radio) (1975; non-denominational) No magazine	☎ Belfast (081) 0232 830604 17 Millar Street Belfast BT6 8JZ	Mr J Noel Speers *Executive Secretary* All voluntary staff	Preparing programmes for missionary, hospital and local radio. Also assisting in AV soundtracks £8,000 – June 90
Let the Bible Speak (*CC*; 1973; Free Presbyterian Church of Ulster) No magazine	☎ Ballymoney (08) 026 56 62039 55 Market Street Dervock Road, Ballymoney Co Antrim BT53 6ED	Rev Leslie Curran *Programme Director* No full-time staff	Broadcasting the Gospel in United States of America, Canada, India and Africa £40,000 – Mar 90

RECONCILIATION GROUPS

Name & Magazine	Location	Chief Officer & Staff	Work & Income
Charismatic Renewal Movement (n/a; Roman Catholic) No magazine	☎ Dublin (353) 01 685223 "Emmanuel" House of Prayer 3 Pembroke Park Dublin 4	n/a	To foster spiritual renewal under the inspiration of the Holy Spirit. Over 500 prayer groups n/a
Christian Renewal Centre (1974; interdenominational) *Prayer Letter* 5,000 half-yearly	☎ Rostrevor (08) 069 37 38492 Shore Road Rostrevor, Newry Co Down BT34 3ET	Rev Cecil Kerr *Leader* Community members 16	Centre for prayer, renewal and reconciliation (accommodation for 15 people) £100,000 – Apr 90
Columbanus Community of Reconciliation (*CC*; 1983; interdenominational)	☎ Belfast (08) 0232 778009 683 Antrim Road Belfast BT15 4EG	Rev Michael Hurley *Leader* Full-time staff 2	Study centre for reconciliation, ecumenical Bible week and quiet days (residential accommodation for 19 people) £35,000 – Dec 90
Community of the Peace People (*CC*; 1976; non-denominational) *Peace by Peace* 800 monthly	☎ Belfast (08) 0232 663465 Peace House 224 Lisburn Road Belfast BT9 6GE	Mrs Ann McCann *Administrator* Executive staff 6 Other staff 4	Working to bring a just and peaceful society by non-violent means £55,000 – June 90

Reconciliation Groups

Name & Magazine	Location	Chief Officer & Staff	Work & Income
Co-operation North (1979; interdenominational)	☎ Belfast (08) 0232 321462 7 Botanic Avenue Belfast BT7 1JJ *Also at:* ☎ Dublin (353) 01 610588 37 Upper Fitzwilliam Street Dublin 2	Mr Brian O'Neill *Chief Executive* Other staff 40	Promoting understanding and co-operation between Northern Ireland and the Republic n/a
Cornerstone Community (1982; ecumenical) *Newsletter* 1,000 half-yearly	☎ Belfast (08) 0232 321649 443 Springfield Road Belfast BT12 7DL	Rev Sam Burch *Director* Executive staff 1	Reconciliation, peace work, prayer growth, retreat groups, social action; community building £35,000 – Dec 90
The Corrymeela Community (*CC*; 1965; interdenominational) *Corrymeela News* 2,300 quarterly	☎ Belfast (08) 0232 325008 8 Upper Crescent Belfast BT7 1NT	Rev J W Morrow *Leader* Full-time staff 26 Other staff 10	Christian community of reconciliation in Northern Ireland, responsible for resource centres in Belfast and residential centre in Ballycastle £371,000 – Mar 90
Cross Group (n/a; non-denominational) No magazine	☎ Dundonald (08) 0232 483952 6a Cumberland Park Dundonald Belfast BT16 0AY	To be appointed *Director* No other full-time staff	A social support group for those bereaved through violence in Northern Ireland n/a
Dublin Mennonite Community (1979; Mennonite) (Previously Irish Mennonite Community) No magazine	☎ Dublin (353) 01 309384 4 Clonmore Villas 92 Ballybough Road Dublin 3	Mr J Liechty *Leader* Other staff 5	Evangelical community committed to reconciliation between Protestants and Catholics and seeing God's kingdom in Ireland n/a
Evangelical Contribution on Northern Ireland (ECONI) (1988; non-denominational)	☎ Belfast (08) 0232 327231 📠 Fax (08) 0232 235826 City of Belfast YMCA 12 Wellington Place Belfast BT1 6GE	Mr Ivor Mitchell *Deputy Executive Director* n/a	Promoting a greater understanding and application of Biblical principles in the Northern Ireland situation n/a
Glencree Centre for Reconciliation (n/a; non-denominational) No magazine	☎ Dublin (353) 01 896802 Glencree Co Wicklow	Mr James McLoughlin Mrs Sarah McLoughlin *Co-ordinators* n/a	To encourage reconciliation between various faiths and political creeds; conflict resolution and meditation training; north-south exchange; farm education and work camps n/a
Nexus Ireland (n/a; Presbyterian)	☎ Dublin (353) 01 628 0393 📠 Fax (353) 01 628 0770 Lucan Youth Centre Primrose Lane Lucan, Co Dublin	Ms Gwen Montgomery n/a n/a	Evangelical reconciliation initiative for education and training of young people, residential courses n/a
Pax Christi (Irish Section) (n/a; Roman Catholic) No magazine	☎ No telephone 52 Lower Rathmines Road Dublin 6	Rev Ray Maher *National Director* n/a	To work with all people for peace and witness to the peace of Christ n/a

Reconciliation Groups

Name & Magazine	Location	Chief Officer & Staff	Work & Income
Protestant & Catholic Encounter (*CC*; 1968; interdenominational) *PACE* 1,400 every four months	☎ Belfast (08) 0232 232864 103 University Street Belfast BT7 1HP	Mr David McKittrick *Field Officer* n/a	Protestant/Catholic encounter for peace and justice; arts projects, inter-church activity, discussion, conferences £19,000 – Mar 90

RELIEF AND DEVELOPMENT AGENCIES

Name & Magazine	Location	Chief Officer & Staff	Work & Income
Christian Aid (*CC*; n/a; interdenominational) No magazine	☎ Belfast (08) 0232 381204 Inter-Church Centre 48 Elmwood Avenue Belfast BT9 6AZ **Also at:** ☎ Dublin (353) 01 966184 Rathgar Road Rathgar, Dublin 6	Rev I S McDowell *National Secretary* Mrs M Boden *Area Secretary* n/a	Operating in most Third World countries largely through national councils of churches and their members n/a
Concern (*CC*; 1968; Roman Catholic) *Concern* 35,000 quarterly	☎ Dublin (353) 01 681237 1 Upper Camden Street Dublin 2 **Also at:** ☎ Belfast (08) 0232 23156 47 Frederick Street Belfast BT1 2LW	Rev Aengus Finucane *Chief Executive* Executive staff 7 Other staff 7	Third World relief agency operating through its own volunteers in the developing world £2,400,000 – Dec 83
Dr Tom Dooley Fund (1961; non-denominational) No magazine	☎ No telephone Cuala, Greenfield Road Sutton, Dublin 13	Dr J Barnes *President* n/a	Medical aid (personnel mainly) to Third World n/a
Tear Fund (The Evangelical Alliance Relief Fund) (*CC*; 1976; interdenominational) *Tear Times* 8,000 quarterly	☎ Belfast (08) 0232 324940 10 Wellington Place Belfast BT1 6GE **Also at:** ☎ Dublin (353) 01 298 4858 92 Landscape Park Churchtown, Dublin 14	Mr Cliff Kennedy *Irish Co-ordinator* Mr David W Adeney *Executive Director UK* Executive staff 1 Other staff 4	Helping meet the spiritual and material needs of people throughout the world (UK & Ireland) £14,439,000 – Mar 90
Trócaire (*CC*; 1973; Roman Catholic) n/a	☎ Dublin (353) 01 288 5385 ✆ Fax (353) 01 288 3577 169 Booterstown Avenue Blackrock, Co Dublin	Mr Brian McKeown *Director* Executive staff 3 Other staff 3	Assisting medium and long term development projects in the Third World n/a
World Vision (*CC*; 1979; interdenominational) *Window on the World* Distributed quarterly	☎ Belfast (08) 0232 739348 The Kings Building 152 Albertbridge Road Belfast BT5 4GS	To be appointed *Regional Manager* n/a	Christian relief and development agency serving the poor and needy in over 80 countries
World Vision Ireland (*CC*; 1986; interdenominational) *Window on the World* 5,000 quarterly	☎ Dublin (353) 01 283 7800 ✆ Fax (353) 01 283 7673 10 Main Street Donnybrook, Dublin 4	Ms Ingrid Knapp *Director* Executive staff 1 Other staff 3	International relief and development agency assisting the needy worldwide n/a

SOCIAL SERVICE AND WELFARE ORGANISATIONS

Name & Magazine	Location	Chief Officer & Staff	Work & Income
174 Trust (*CC*; 1983; non-denominational) *Saltshaker* 500 every two months	☎Belfast (08) 0232 747114 Saltshaker Centre 174 Antrim Road Belfast BT15 2AJ	Mr Derek McCorkell *Director* Executive staff 7 Other staff 65	Caring Christian witness and practical service to the people of north Belfast £300,000 – Sept 90
Apostleship of the Sea (Ireland) (n/a; Roman Catholic) No magazine	☎Cork (353) 021 505833 Anchor House Penrose Quay, Cork **Correspondence to:** Stella Maris Seafarers' Club 3 Beresford Place, Dublin 1	Rev Edmund O'Brien *National Director* Mrs Rose Kearney *President* n/a	Care and welfare of all seafarers and their families n/a
*****Belfast City YMCA** (*CC*; 1850; interdenominational) *Y's Moves* Quarterly	☎Belfast (08) 0232 327231 🖷Fax (08) 0232 235826 12 Wellington Place Belfast BT1 6GE	Mr Gerald Clarke *Executive Director* Executive staff 7 Other staff 34	Caring for young people, both practically and spiritually; striving for reconciliation in the community £650,000 – Mar 90
Catholic Protection and Rescue Society of Ireland (n/a; Roman Catholic) No magazine	☎Dublin (353) 01 779664 30 South Anne Street Dublin 2	Miss Hilda Cassidy *Secretary/Senior* *Social Worker* n/a	Services for single mothers; counselling, arranging accommodation, medical care, ante- and post-natal care, fostering, adoption and assistance n/a
Christian Family Movement (n/a; interdenominational) No magazine	☎Dublin (353) 01 902284 14 Rossmore Drive Templeogue Dublin 6	Mr Brendan Moroney Mrs Nellie Moroney *President couple* No full-time staff	Promoting the Christian way of life in the family, community and institutions afffecting the family n/a
Clifton Street Social Witness Club (1986; Presbyterian) No magazine	☎Belfast (08) 0232 245569 🖷Fax (08) 0232 332019 Room 220 Church House Fisherwick Place Belfast BT1 6DW	Mr Eric Lennon *Director* Executive staff 3	Employment, government funded workforce; drop-in centre; residential alcohol unit £325,000 – Jan 90
Focus Point Project Limited (*CC*; 1985; non-denominational) No magazine Regular publications of reports	☎Dublin (353) 01 712555 14a Eustace Street Dublin 2	Mr Stanislaus Kennedy *Director* Executive staff 6 Other staff 30	Works to help homeless people or those who are threatened by homelessness to find, create and make a home n/a
Irish Episcopal Commission for Emigrants (1957; non-denominational) No magazine	☎Dublin (353) 01 966880 🖷Fax (353) 01 966388 The Cottage 63 Harold's Cross Road Dublin 6	Rev John Gavin *Executive Secretary* Executive staff 3 Other staff 2	Responds to the needs of Irish emigrants in Britain, mainland Europe and major US cities n/a
Muintir Na Tire (n/a; interdenominational)	☎Tipperary (353) 062 51163 Canon Hayes House Tipperary	Mr Tom Fitzgerald *Administrative Officer* No full-time staff	To promote welfare of Irish people through community development based on Christian principles n/a

Social Service and Welfare Organisations

Name & Magazine	Location	Chief Officer & Staff	Work & Income
National Catholic Chaplaincy for the Deaf (n/a; Roman Catholic)	☎ Dublin (353) 01 305744/301057 40 Lower Drumcondra Road Dublin 9	Rev Diarmuid O'Farrell *Director* n/a	Pastoral service to the deaf community n/a
Order of Malta (1174; Roman Catholic)	☎ Dublin (353) 01 684891/685768 St Johns House 32 Clyde Road, Dublin 4	Comdt Richard F Hearns *Executive Officer* n/a	Ambulance corps, day care centres, sheltered workshops, overseas volunteers; regional organisations throughout Ireland n/a
Protestant Orphan Society (*CC*; 1828; Protestant)	☎ Dublin (353) 01 762168 28 Molesworth Street Dublin 2	Mr Desmond Hourie *Secretary* Other staff 1	To support orphans, one of whose parents was/is a Protestant n/a
Salvation Army Social Services (*CC*; 1884; Salvation Army) *Social Services News and Views* (internal)	☎ Belfast (08) 0232 351900 Thorndale Centre Duncairn Avenue Antrim Road Belfast BT14 6BP **Also at:** ☎ Dublin (353) 01 743762 Lefroy House 12 Eden Quay, Dublin 1	Major Alan Hart *Divisional Commander* n/a	Meeting human need through professional caring services n/a
W J Thompson House (1984; Presbyterian Church in Ireland) No magazine	☎ Belfast (08) 0232 370923 428 Antrim Road Belfast BT15 5GA	Mr Sydney McCormick Executive staff 6 Other staff 2	Hostel accommodating 11 ex-offenders; rehabilitation for the whole person £120,000 – Mar 91
Walkinstown Social Service Centre (1974; Roman Catholic)	☎ Dublin (353) 01 505881 Mt St Annes Milltown, Dublin 6	n/a	Day care centre for the elderly n/a

THEOLOGICAL COLLEGES AND BIBLE SCHOOLS BY DENOMINATION

Anglican
Church of Ireland Theological College

Baptist
Irish Baptist College

Roman Catholic
All Hallows College
Dublin Diocesan Seminary
Irish College
Irish Institute of Pastoral Liturgy
Mater Dei Institute of Education
Pontifical Irish College
St John's College
St Kieran's College
St Patrick's College
St Patrick's College
St Patrick's College
St Peter's College

Free Presbyterian Church
Whitefield College of the Bible

Interdenominational/ Non-denominational
Audio Visual Ministries
Bible Centred Ministries
ICI (International Correspondence Institute)
Irish Bible School
Irish School of Ecumenics

Methodist
Edgehill Theological College

Presbyterian
Union Theological College

Reformed Presbyterian
Reformed Theological College

NORTHERN IRELAND

Name	Location	Chief Officer & Staff	Course
Audio Visual Ministries (1974; interdenominational)	☎ Dundrum (08) 0396 75388 Fax (08) 0396 75388 PO Box 1, Newcastle Co Down BT33 0EP	Mr Keith Gerner *Principal* No full-time staff	1 year Correspondence course and tape/video training
*Belfast Bible College (CC; 1943; interdenominational)	☎ Belfast (08) 0232 301551/301655 Fax (08) 0232 301523 Glenburn House Glenburn Road South Dunmurry Belfast BT17 9JP	Rev Graham Cheeseman BD, MPhil, ALBC *Principal* Lecturers 5 Other staff 8	3 years; 18 men, 12 women + 40 men 30 women non-residential £2,475 pa residential
Edgehill Theological College and Christian Education Centre (1926; Methodist)	☎ Belfast (08) 0232 665870 9 Lennoxvale Belfast BT9 5BY	Rev Dr Dennis Cooke *Principal* Executive staff 2 Other staff 6	Biblical, theological, historical and evangelical studies
Irish Baptist College (1892; Baptist)	☎ Belfast (08) 0232 471908 67 Sandown Road Belfast BT5 6GU	Dr Hamilton Moore *Principal* Executive staff 5 Other staff 1	Biblical/theological with pastoral/missionary training, Diploma in theology, Batchelor of Divinity and Post-graduate theological studies recognised by Queen's University, Belfast
Reformed Theological College (1854; Reformed Presbyterian) (Previously Reformed Presbyterian Theological Hall)	☎ Belfast (08) 0232 660689 Cameron House 98 Lisburn Road Belfast BT9 6AG	Dr A Loughridge *Principal* Other staff 3	Diploma in theology. Certificate in Biblical studies

Theological Colleges and Bible Schools

Name	Location	Chief Officer & Staff	Course
Union Theological College (1853; Presbyterian but open to students of any denomination) (Previously the Presbyterian College)	☎Belfast (08) 0232 325374 108 Botanic Avenue Belfast BT7 1JT	Rev R Finlay Holmes *Principal* Executive staff 5	4 years (Primary BD) 3 years for graduates (BD)
Whitefield College of the Bible (1979; Free Presbyterian Church of Ulster)	☎Gilford (08) 0820 662232 117 Banbridge Road Gilford, Craigavon Co Armagh BT63 6DL	Dr John Douglas *Principal* Executive staff 13 Other staff 4	2 year college course 4 year ministerial and theological course

OVERSEAS

Name	Location	Chief Officer & Staff	Course
Irish College (1578; Roman Catholic)	☎Paris (010 or 00) 33 1 45355979 5 Rue des Irlandais Paris 5, France	Very Rev Brendan Devlin *Rector* n/a	The college is at present on lease to the Polish hierarchy
Pontifical Irish College (1628; Roman Catholic)	☎Rome (010 or 00) 39 6 7315697/737295 Via Dei 55, Quattro I Rome, Italy 00184	Rt Rev Mgr John Brady *Rector* Executive staff 4	Training of priests for the Irish Diocesan priesthood

THE REPUBLIC OF IRELAND

"PUM affiliation" indicates that the theological college or Bible school in question is affiliated to the Pontifical University (St Patrick's College, Maynooth).

Name	Location	Chief Officer & Staff	Course
All Hallows College (1842; Roman Catholic)	☎Dublin (353) 01 373745/373741 Drumcondra, Dublin 9	Very Rev Kevin Rafferty *Rector* Executive staff 9	Degree in theology and religious studies (PUM affiliation) n/a
Bible Centred Ministries (1965; interdenominational) (Previously Bible Club Movement)	☎Naas (353) 045 33166 Shalom, Roseberry Newbridge, Co Kildare	Ms Alice Lloyd *Senior Missionary* Other staff 5	n/a
Church of Ireland Theological College (n/a; Anglican)	☎Dublin (353) 01 975506 Braemor Park Rathgar, Dublin 14	Rev Canon J R Bartlett *Principal* n/a	Three or four year professional course to degree level or Professional Diploma in Theology
Dublin Diocesan Seminary (n/a; Roman Catholic)	☎Dublin (353) 01 375103/375104 Holy Cross College Clonliffe, Dublin 3	Rev Peter Briscoe *President* Executive staff 8 Other staff 38	Full degree course in theology and philosophy
Institute of Theology and Philosophy (n/a; interdenominational)	☎Dublin (353) 01 269 7257 Milltown Park Dublin 6	Very Rev James McPolin *President* n/a	n/a
ICI (International Correspondence Institute) (1980; interdenominational)	☎Dublin (353) 01 280 3227 6 Queens Park Monkstown, Blackrock Co Dublin	Rev John Mayo *Director* Executive staff 2 Other staff 2	Four programme levels: (1) Christian life (2) Christian service (3) Christian ministry (4) BA degree in Bible theology

Theological Colleges and Bible Schools

Name	Location	Chief Officer & Staff	Course
Irish Bible School (1982; interdenominational)	☎Clonmel (353) 052 54306 Coalbrook, Thurles Co Tipperary	Mr Warren Nelson *Registrar* Executive staff 2 Other staff 8	1 year Certificate 3 year Diploma Cambridge Diploma in Religious Studies
Irish Institute of Pastoral Liturgy (1974; Roman Catholic)	☎Carlow (353) 0503 42942 College Street, Carlow	Rev Sean Collins *Director* n/a	1 year residential course in pastoral liturgy (PUM affiliation)
Irish School of Ecumenics (1970; interdenominational)	☎Dublin (353) 01 269 8607 or 8819 Milltown Park Dublin 6	Rev Alan D Falconer *Director* Executive staff 4 Other staff 5	1 or 2 year full or part-time courses in ecumenical studies and peace studies
Mater Dei Institute of Education (n/a; Roman Catholic)	☎Dublin (353) 01 376927/376028 Clonliffe Road Dublin 3	Sr Eileen Randles *President* n/a	4 year Degree course for BRelSc, Post-graduate course for MRelSc (PUM affiliation)
St John's College (1807; Roman Catholic)	☎Waterford (353) 051 74199 Waterford	Very Rev Michael N O'Connor *President* Executive staff 6 Other staff 18	2 year Diploma in Arts and Philosophy 4 year Diploma in theology (PUM affiliation)
St Kieran's College (1782; Roman Catholic)	☎Kilkenny (353) 056 21086 Kilkenny	Rev Martin Campion *President* Executive staff 7 Other staff 47	6 year Diploma in theology (PUM affiliation)
St Patrick's College (1795; Roman Catholic)	☎Dublin (353) 01 628 5222 ☎Fax (353) 01 628 6583 Maynooth, Co Kildare	Rt Rev Mgr Micheál Ledwith *President* Executive staff 15	The National Seminary, Pontifical University and recognised college of the National University of Ireland
St Patrick's College (1793; Roman Catholic)	☎Carlow (353) 0503 31114 Carlow	Very Rev John McDonald *President* Executive staff 5 Other staff 26	Seminary: 6 year integrated course in theology, philosophy and humanities Institute: 1 year residential diploma course
St Patrick's College (n/a; Roman Catholic)	☎Thurles (353) 0504 21201/21882 Thurles Co Tipperary	Very Rev William Lee *President* Executive staff 7 Other staff 11	2 Year National Certificate in philosophy 4 year Diploma in theology (PUM affiliation)
St Peter's College (n/a; Roman Catholic)	☎Wexford (353) 053 42071 Wexford	Very Rev Laurence O'Connor *President* Executive staff 5 Other staff 11	5 year degree in theology

TRAINING CENTRES AND SERVICES

Name & Magazine	Location	Chief Officer & Staff	Work & Income
Christian Life Communities (n/a; Roman Catholic) No magazine	☎Dublin (353) 01 767321 36 Lower Leeson Street Dublin 2	Rev Alan Mowbray SJ *Secretary* n/a	To practice the spiritual exercise of St Ignatius, to unite human life in all its dimensions n/a

Training Centres and Services

Name & Magazine	Location	Chief Officer & Staff	Work & Income
Christian Training Centre (1980; Presbyterian Church in Ireland) No magazine	☎ Belfast (08) 0232 248424 Magee House 7 Rugby Road Belfast BT7 1PS	Rev A Harold Graham *Director* Executive staff 2 Other staff 12	Training courses for ministers and lay leaders £70,000 – Dec 90
Edgehill Christian Education Centre (1984; Methodist) *Edgehill College Annual* 2,000 annually	☎ Belfast (08) 0232 665870 9 Lennoxvale Malone Road Belfast BT9 5BY	Rev Dr Dennis Cooke *Director* Lecturers 2 Other staff 9	Methodist lay training centre for 20 residential and 100 non-residential students n/a
* **Project Evangelism** (*CC*; 1969; interdenominational) *Newsletter* 1,000 quarterly	☎ Portrush (08) 0265 822775 Project House 38 Mark Street, Portrush Co Antrim BT56 8BT	Mr John Moxen *Director* Executive staff 2 Other staff 5	Training in church-based and outreach evangelism; short-term Bible school; provision for the unemployed £25,000 – Dec 90

YOUTH ORGANISATIONS

Name & Magazine	Location	Chief Officer & Staff	Work & Income
Baptist Youth (Baptist Union of Ireland) (*CC*; 1977; Baptist) No magazine	☎ Belfast (08) 0232 663108 ✆ Fax (08) 0232 663616 117 Lisburn Road Belfast BT9 7AF	Mr Mike Ewan *Baptist Youth Secretary* Other staff 1	Promoting all aspects of youth and children's work leadership training and evangelistic outreach £55,000 – Jan 90
Catholic Boy Scouts of Ireland (n/a; Roman Catholic)	☎ Dublin (353) 01 761598 19 Herbert Place Dublin 2	Mr Michael Hassett *Chief Commissioner* n/a	Affiliated to World Scout Conference, organised on a regional and parish basis n/a
Catholic Young Men's Society (n/a; Roman Catholic)	☎ Dublin (353) 01 744264 29 North Frederick Street Dublin 1	Mr Michael Shortall *President* n/a	Spiritual, intellectual, social and physical development of members, organised at national and diocesan level n/a
Church of Ireland Youth Council (n/a; Anglican)	☎ Belfast (08) 0232 671659 217 Holywood Road Belfast BT4 2DH *Also at:* ☎ Dublin (353) 01 607122 74 Upper Leeson Street Dublin 4	Rev David Chillingworth *Chairman* Other staff 6	Training, resource material, support and advice for youth leaders and young people n/a
The Churches' Youth Service Council (*CC*; 1943; interdenominational) No magazine	☎ Belfast (08) 0232 731458 Kings Building 152 Albertbridge Road Belfast BT5 4GS	Miss Lynda Gould *Training & Development Officer* Other staff 2	Training and service agency for those working with young people n/a
Covenant Christian School Society (1982; interdenominational)	☎ Belfast (08) 0232 854734 4 Abbeyville Place Whiteabbey, Newtownabbey Co Antrim BT37 0AQ	Mr Raymond Stewart *Secretary* Other staff 2	A parent-controlled Christian school providing Christian education, recognised by NI Department of Education n/a

Youth Organisations

Name & Magazine	Location	Chief Officer & Staff	Work & Income
EYM Ministries (1965; interdenominational) *In Contact* 2,000 quarterly	☎ Belfast (08) 0232 455158 Fax (08) 0232 450780 285 Newtownards Road Belfast BT4 1AG	Mr David Millen *Director* Executive staff 6 Office staff 3	Seminars on evangelism and discipleship; youth outreach; women's ministry n/a
Frontier Youth Trust (*CC*; 1964; interdenominational) *Frontline* 70 every four months	☎ Belfast (08) 0232 454806 183 Albertbridge Road Belfast BT5 4PS	Mr Joe Campbell *Development Officer* n/a	Associating, servicing and training Christians working with alienated young people mainly in urban/industrial missionary areas; "envisioning" churches and running camps n/a
International Catholic Girls' Society (1908; Roman Catholic) No magazine	☎ Dublin (353) 01 761594 4 Lower Abbey Street Dublin 1	n/a	Advice and information to girls working away from home, relating to hostel accommodation, employment agencies, etc n/a
Irish Methodist Youth Department and Irish Methodist Association of Youth Clubs (n/a; Methodist)	☎ Belfast (08) 0232 327191 Aldersgate House University Road Belfast BT7 1NA	Rev David Neilands *General Secretary* n/a	Training and resources for youth work, caring for young people n/a
National Council of the YMCAs of Ireland (1844; interdenominational) *Hope in Action* 200 quarterly	☎ Belfast (08) 0232 327757 St George's Buildings 37 High Street Belfast BT1 2AB	Mr Stephen Turner *National Secretary* Executive staff 14 Other staff 70	Catering for young people, body, mind and spirit, to bring them to wholeness in Christ £730,000 – Mar 90
Public and Preparatory School Camps (The West of Ireland Camps) (*CC*; 1919; interdenominational) No magazine	☎ Sligo (353) 071 43528 Hill House Loughanelteen, Sligo **Contact:** Brampton Lodge, Newcastle Staffordshire ST5 0QW	Mr John Caddick-Adams *Secretary & Treasurer* Other staff 2	Christian adventure centre providing outdoor activity holidays for boys and girls 8-18 years from independent schools n/a
Young Christian Workers (n/a; Roman Catholic) No magazine	☎ Dublin (353) 01 788484/788091 Cardijn House 15 Talbot Street Dublin 1	Rev Denis Laverty *Secretary* n/a	Calling, forming and sustaining young workers who will be apostles in their own environment n/a
Young Life (1925; non-denominational) *Young Life* Every two months	☎ Belfast (08) 0232 231133 Room 511 Scottish Provident Buildings 7 Donegall Square West Belfast BT1 6JG	Mr Steve Wright *Irish Organiser* Staff 2	Youth evangelism, follow-up, teaching, in-service training and resources n/a

Table 30: Summary of Christian Organisations

Category	Number	Estimated total number of full-time staff[1]	Average number of staff in organisations with full-time people	Percentage with no full-time staff	Percentage with Fax phone	Religious Affiliation - Roman Catholic	Percentage who are Anglican	Inter[2]	Other
				%	%	%	%	%	%
Accommodation									
Conference Centres NI	8	100	13	0	0	13	0	87	0
Conference Centres RI	22	145	7	0	5	59	0	36	5
Retreat Houses NI	7	28	4	0	0	57	14	29	0
Retreat Houses RI	24	166	7	0	0	88	0	8	4
TOTAL ACCOMMODATION	61	439	7	0	2	64	2	31	3
Books									
Bookshops NI	28	97	4	4	4	0	7	72	21
Bookshops RI	23	71	3	4	17	43	13	44	0
Libraries	3	7	2	0	0	33	33	0	34
Publishers	18	124	8	17	33	11	11	67	11
TOTAL BOOKS	72	299	4	7	15	18	11	59	12
Churches and Evangelism									
Church Headquarters	81	181[3]	2	1	6	33	16	0	51
Church and Other Organisations	5	26	7	20	20	20	0	60	20
City and Town Missions	11	66	6	0	0	0	9	27	64
Evangelistic Agencies	30	176	8	27	7	7	7	69	17
TOTAL CHURCHES AND EVANGELISM	127	449	3	8	6	23	13	21	43
Overseas									
Missionary Societies (Protestant)	31	n/a	n/a	n/a	16	0	39	48	13
Missionary Societies (Roman Catholic)	93	n/a	n/a	n/a	4	100	0	0	0
Missionary Support Organisations	14	45	6	43	14	36	21	43	0
TOTAL OVERSEAS	138	45	6	43	8	71	11	15	3
Services									
Audio Visual, Film and Video Producers and Suppliers	4	14	5	25	50	0	0	100	0
Benevolent Organisations	4	28	7	0	0	50	0	50	0
Counselling and Information Organisations	22	26	1	5	0	73	5	22	0
Educational Agencies	3	4	2	33	0	33	0	34	33
Musical and Theatrical Services	2	n/a	n/a	50	0	50	0	50	0
Professional Christian Groups	6	24	4	0	0	33	0	67	0
Radio and TV Programme Producers	2	0	0	100	0	0	0	0	0
Reconciliation Groups	14	166	12	0	7	14	0	72	14
Relief and Development Agencies	10	73	7	0	20	30	0	70	0
Social Service and Welfare Organisations	20	427	24	10	15	25	0	55	20
Theological Colleges and Bible Schools NI	7	52	9	14	29	0	0	29	71
Overseas	2	8	4	0	0	0	0	100	0
RI	16	283	18	0	0	63	6	31	0
Training Centres and Services	4	40	10	0	0	25	0	50	25
Youth Organisations	14	218	16	0	14	29	0	57	14
TOTAL SERVICES	130	1363	10	7	9	36	2	51	11
TOTAL ALL ORGANISATIONS 1992	528	2595	4	16	8	43	8	33	16

[1] Many organisations did not report part or all of their non-executive staff
[2] Interdenominational/Non-denominational/Ecumenical
[3] Excluding serving ministers

INDEX — ORGANISATIONS AND PERSONNEL

174 Trust	116	
26.3 Trust	83	

A

Acre Gospel Mission	88
Adeney, Mr David W	115
Africa	
see St Patrick's	
Missionary Society (SPS)	98
Africa Inland Mission	
International	88
African Missionary	
see Society of African	
Missions	100
Agapé (Ireland)	84
Agape Fellowship	84
Agger, Very Rev George	93
Aid to the Church in Need	106
AIM International	
see Africa Inland Mission	
International	88
Alcorn, Mr R W	81
Alderdice, Rev Duncan	77
Alexian Brothers (CFA)	91
Alford, Rev Timothy G	88
All Hallows College	119
Allen, Mr William	69
Ambassador Productions Ltd	68
Anderson, Rev R T	79
APCK Book Centre:	
Cork	66
see also:	
Belfast Cathedral	
Book Centre	63
The Lisburn Bookshop	65
St Ann's Book Centre	66
Apostleship of the Sea	
(Ireland)	116
Ard Mhuire, Capuchin	
Franciscan Friary	59
Ardfert Diocesan Retreat	
Centre	59
Ards Evangelical Bookshop	65
Arklow Rock	56
Armstrong, Rev David H S	64
Armstrong, Rev Canon R C	90
Armstrong, Rev Samuel	81
Arnould, Miss Nicole	68
Association for Promoting	
Christian Knowledge	68
Audio Visual Ministries	118
Augustinian Fathers (OSA)	91
Awareness	
see Survive — MIVA	107
Aylward, Very Rev Eamon	97

B

Bain, Rev Desmond C	83
Baker, Mr Wilfred	76
Ball, Rev Canon John M	88
Baptist Missions	88
Baptist Union of Ireland	71
Baptist Youth	121
Barnes, Dr J	115
Bartlett, Rev Canon J R	119
Baxter, Rev Derek	88
Baxter, Sister Hilda	99
BCMS Crosslinks	88
Bedlow, Mrs Norah	66, 69
Beere, Mr Ian	56
Belfast Bible College	118
Belfast Cathedral Book Centre	63
Belfast Central Mission	82
Belfast City Mission	83
Belfast City YMCA	116
Bell, Mrs Betty	64
Bell, Mr Charles Wesley	85
Bellinter Adult Education Centre	56
Benburb Conference &	
Retreat Centre	55
Benedictines (OSB)	91
Berean Books	68
Bergin, Sister Mary E	99
Best, Rev Kenneth	77, 83
Bestseller — NBSI Bookshop	66
Bethel	64
Beulah Bookshop	65
Bible Centred Ministries	119
Bible Lands	
see Jerusalem & the	
Middle East Church	
Association	107
Bible Society	68
Biblio	
see Central Catholic Library	68
Birmingham, Rev Kieran	98
Bleakley, Rt Hon David W	82
Blowick Conference Centre	56
Boden, Mrs M	115
Boland, Mrs Heather	85
Bon Secours Sisters of Paris	91
Bookends	64
Bothwell, Ian	84
Boylan, Mr Sean	112
Brady, Rt Rev Mgr John	119
Breen, Mrs A	68
Brennan, Very Rev Dermot	57
Breslin, Very Rev Eamon	57
Briathar De Newsletter	
see National Bible Society	
of Ireland	69
Bridcut, Rev W J	83
Brigidine Sisters	91
Briscoe, Rev Peter	119
Brooks, Most Rev Francis	73
Brothers of Charity	91
Brown, Rev Brian	81
Bru Na Mona	56
Bryne, Mr John	68
Buchanan, Rev William T	83
Burch, Rev Sam	114
Burns, Brother Felan	93
Burrell, Mr Walter & Mrs Mary	86
Byrne, Mrs Barbara	66
Byrne, Very Rev Brendan	62
Byrne, Rev Thomas	60

C

Caddick-Adams, Mr John	122
Caird, Most Rev Donald	76
Callanan, Rev John	61
Callister Communications Ltd	109
Callister, Mr John	109
Campbell, Mr Joe	122
Campbell, Mrs Mary	63, 65
Campbell, Rev W M	83
Campion, Rev Martin	120
Cantwell, Mr Jim	71
Capuchin Franciscans	
(OFM Cap)	91
Carey, Mr Joe	84
Caritas	
see St John of God	
Brothers (OH)	97
Carmelite Book Service	66
Carmelite Conference &	
Retreat Centre	59
Carmelites (Discaled OCD)	92
Carmelites (OCarm)	91
Carrick, Miss Gwen	65
Carrig Eden	56
Cashen, Sister Sebastian	98
Cassidy, Miss Hilda	116
Cassidy, Most Rev Joseph	74
Castle Erin Christian Hotel &	
Conference Centre	55
Castlewellan Castle Christian	
Conference Centre	55
Catechetical Association of	
Ireland	121
Cathedral Books Ltd	66
Catholic Boy Scouts	
of Ireland	121
Roman Catholic Church:	
Archdiocese of:	
Armagh	71
Cashel	73
Dublin	73
Tuam	74
Diocese of:	
Achonry	74
Ardagh & Clonmacnois	71
Clogher	71
Clonfert	74
Cloyne	73
Cork & Ross	73
Derry	71
Down & Connor	71
Dromore	73
Elphin	74

Ferns	73	
Galway, Kilmacduagh & Kilfenora	74	
Kerry	73	
Kildare & Leighlin	74	
Killala	74	
Killaloe	73	
Kilmore	73	
Limerick	73	
Meath	73	
Ossory	74	
Raphoe	73	
Waterford & Lismore	73	
Catholic Communications Institute	110	
Catholic Press & Information Office	71	
Catholic Protection & Rescue Society of Ireland	116	
Catholic Women's Federation	110	
Catholic Young Men's Society	121	
Cavanagh, Captain K J	84	
CCN News Journal see Christian Communication Network	109	
The Cenacle Christian Bookshop	68	
Cenacle Retreat House	59	
Central Catholic Library	68	
Central Council of Catholic Adoption Societies	112	
Centre for Parish Development	69	
Charismatic Renewal Movement	113	
Charismatic Renewal Services	66	
Cheeseman, Rev Graham	118	
Children Helping Children see Pontifical Mission Aid Societies	107	
Chillingworth, Rev David	121	
Christian Aid	115	
Christian Book Centre:		
Ballyclare	63	
Monaghan	68	
Randalstown	65	
Christian Bookshop, Craigavon	65	
Christian Brothers (CFC)	92	
Christian Businessmen's Committee of Great Britain & Ireland	84	
Christian Communication Network	109	
Christian Concern for Freedom of Conscience	106	
Christian Family Movement	116	
Christian Healing see Church's Ministry of Healing	110	
Christian Irishman Magazine see Irish Mission	85	
Christian Life Communities	120	
Christian Literature Distributors (Wholesale)	63	
Christian Mission to the Communist World	106	
Christian Programmers For Radio see Commission	113	
Christian Publication Centre	66	
Christian Renewal Centre	55, 113	
Christian Training Centre	121	
Christian Vision see International Gospel Outreach	85	
Chrysalis	57	
Church Army	84	
Church Missionary Society Ireland	88	
Church in Chains see Christian Concern for Freedom of Conscience	106	
Church of Ireland	74	
Archdiocese of:		
Armagh	74	
Dublin	76	
Diocese of:		
Cashel & Ossory	76	
Clogher	74	
Connor	76	
Cork, Cloyne & Ross	76	
Derry & Raphoe	76	
Down & Dromore	76	
Kilmore, Elphin & Ardagh	76	
Limerick & Killaloe	76	
Meath & Kildare	76	
Tuam, Killala & Achonry	76	
Church of Ireland Gazette see Church of Ireland	74	
Church of Ireland Jews Society see The Church's Ministry among the Jews	88	
Church of Ireland Theological College	119	
Church of Ireland Youth Council	121	
The Church's Ministry among the Jews	88	
Church's Ministry of Healing	110	
Churches Commission on Mission	106	
The Churches' Youth Service Council	121	
Cistercian Order (OCSO)	92	
Cistercian Sisters	92	
Clar Ellagh	57	
Clarke, Mr George	106	
Clarke, Mr Gerald	116	
Clarke, Rev Martin	56	
Clarke, Miss Vanessa	57	
Clarkson, Rev Eugene	61	
Cleary, Very Rev J Bernard	96	
Cleary, Rev Hilarion	96	
Cleary, Sister M James	99	
Clifford, Most Rev Dermot	73	
Clifton Street Social Witness Club	116	
Cluain Mhuire Retreat Centre	60	
Clune, Sister Maura	56	
Co-operation North	114	
Coffey, Mr Bertie	86	
Coles, Rev Malcolm	77	
Collins, Sister Morag	99	
Collins, Rev Sean	120	
Columba	66	
Columba Press	69	
Columbanus Community of Reconciliation	59, 113	
Comboni Missionaries (MCCJ) (Verona Fathers)	92	
Comiskey, Most Rev Brendan	73	
Commission (Christian Programmers For Radio)	113	
Community Lending Library	68	
Community of the Peace People	113	
Concern	115	
Congregational Union of Ireland	77	
Congregationalist see Congregational Union of Ireland	77	
Connell, Most Rev Desmond	73	
Considine, Sister Mona	93	
Contact see Sacred Heart Fathers (SCJ)	97	
Contend for the Faith see South East Antrim Reformation Movement	86	
Conway, Mr Aidan	111	
Conway, Most Rev Dominic	74	
Cooke, Rev Dr Dennis	118, 121	
Cooke, Mr William H	83	
Cooney, Very Rev Thomas F	91	
Cordner, Rodney	84	
Cornerstone Community	114	
Corry, Sister Catherine	61	
Corrymeela Centre	55	
The Corrymeela Community	114	
Country Antrim Reformation Movement: see: North Antrim Reformation Movement	86	
or: South East Antrim Reformation Movement	86	
Courtney, Rev Herbert	79	
Covenant Christian School Society	121	
Covenanter Bookshop	64	
Covenanter Witness see Reformed Presbyterian Church of Ireland	77	
Cox, Mr Frank	110	
Coyle, Sister Mary	61	
Crean, Very Rev Maurice	95	
Cross Group	114	

Crossfire Trust
  see Ian Bothwell 84
Crossroads
  see National Bible Study
  Club 112
Cullen, Rt Rev Celestine 91
Cullen, Mr Michael &
  Mrs Annette 60
Cummings, Mr David 91
Cunningham, Mr Chris 66
Cunningham, Rev H G 64
CURA 110
Curran, Rev Leslie 113
Curtin, Sister Katherine 111

D

Daly, Most Rev Cathal B 71
Daly, Most Rev Edward 71
Darling, Rt Rev Edward 76
Daughters of Charity (DC) 92
Daughters of Mary & Joseph 92
Daughters of Our Lady of the
  Sacred Heart 92
Daughters of the Holy Spirit 92
Davey, Rev J I 81
Davis, Mr Eric C 112
Day Star in Africa
  see Franciscan Missionary
  Sisters for Africa 94
De la Salle Brothers (FSC) 93
Deane, Mrs Eva 66
Dennison, Mr J 68
Devlin, Very Rev Brendan 119
Dickinson, Rev J R 79
Dillon, Rev Sister Therese 95
Dispatch
  see Qua Iboe Fellowship 90
Divine Word Missionaries (SUD) 93
Doctrine & Life
  see Dominican Order (OP) 93
Dodd, Sister Brendan 95
Doherty, Miss Ann 55
Doherty, Miss R 112
Dolly, Sister Sheila 97
Dominican Order (OP) 93
Dominican Pastoral Centre 57
Dominican Retreat &
  Pastoral Centre 60
Dominican Sisters (OP) 93
Doran, Sister Mary 98
Douglas, Mr Edward 63, 64, 65
Douglas, Ms H 113
Douglas, Dr John 76, 119
Doyle, Sister Nora 99
Dr Tom Dooley Fund 115
Dromantine 59
Dublin Central Mission 83
Dublin Christian Mission 83
Dublin Diocesan Seminary 119
Dublin Mennonite Community 114
Dublin University Far Eastern
  Mission 106

Dublin University Mission
  to Chota Nagpur 106
Duffy, Most Rev Joseph 71
Dunlop, Rev Robert 85
Dunne, Ms Ann Maria 57
Dwyer, Sister Catherine 95

E

Eames, Most Rev Robin 74
Earle, Mr Michael 55
East Asia Millions
  see Overseas Missionary
  Fellowship 89
East Belfast Mission 83
Eastern Europe
  see Christian Mission to the
  Communist World 106
ECF News
  see Evangelize China
  Fellowship 106
ECONI
  see Evangelical Contribution
  on Northern Ireland 114
Edgehill Christian Education
  Centre 121
Edgehill College Annual
  see Edgehill Christian
  Education Centre 121
Edgehill Theological College &
  Christian Education Centre 118
Egan, Mr Thomas W 66
Elim Pentecostal Church 77
Elliott, Rev Donald W 106
Elsdon, Dr Ron 88
Emmanuel House of Providence 60
Emmaus Retreat Centre 60
Empey, Most Rev Walton N F 76
Erskine, Very Rev Samuel 96
Europe's Millions
  see European Christian
  Mission 88
European Christian Mission 88
European Missionary
  Fellowship 89
Evangelical Alliance 82
The Evangelical Alliance
  Relief Fund
  see Tear Fund 115
Evangelical Bookshop:
  Belfast 64
  Enniskillen 65
Evangelical Contribution on
  Northern Ireland (ECONI) 114
Evangelical Outreach Ltd 109
Evangelical Presbyterian
  see Evangelical Presbyterian
  Church 77
Evangelical Presbyterian
  Church 77
Evangelical Protestant Society 84
Evangelical Youth Movement
  Ministries
  see EYM Ministries 84, 122

Evangelize China Fellowship 106
Every Home Crusade 69
Ewan, Mr Mike 121
EYM Ministries 84, 122

F

Fahy, Mother Frances I 98
The Faith Mission 84
Faith Mission Bookshop:
  Ballymena 63
  Bangor 63
  Belfast 64
  Cookstown 64
  Craigavon 65
  Lisburn 65
  Londonderry 65
Faithful Companions of Jesus 93
Falconer, Rev Alan D 120
Familybooks 64
Far East
  see Missionary Society of
  St Columban (SSC) 96
Far East Broadcasting
  Association
  see FEBA Radio 89
Farragher, Rev Martin 91
Farrar, Rev James A 110
Farrelly, Dr Adrian 60
Fay, Mr Patrick 85
FEBA Radio 89
Feheny, Brother Matthew 61
Fergus, Sister Evelyn 94
Ferguson, Mr A C 89
Ferguson, Mr Laurence 88
The Festivals of Male Voice
  Praise 84
Finlay, Rev S A 81
Finneghan, Most Rev Thomas 74
Finucane, Rev Aengus 115
Fitzgerald, Mrs C 68
Fitzgerald, Mr Tom 116
Flynn, Very Rev James 97
Flynn, Most Rev Thomas 74
Focus Point Project Ltd 116
Foheney, Brother Matthew 97
Foley, Rev William 59
Forristal, Most Rev Laurence 74
Forward
  see Sandes Soldiers' &
  Airmen's Centres 86
Foundation Ministries 111
Franciscan Brothers (OSF) 93
Franciscan Missionaries of
  Mary (FMM) 93
Franciscan Missionaries of
  Our Lady (FMOL) 93
Franciscan Missionaries of the
  Divine Motherhood (FMDM) 93
Franciscan Missionary Sisters
  for Africa (OSF) 94
Franciscan Missionary Sisters
  of St Joseph (FMSJ) 94

Franciscans (OFM)	93	
Free Presbyterian Church of Ulster	77	
Free Presbyterian Church of Ulster Mission Board	89	
Frontier Youth Trust	122	
Frontline *see* Frontier Youth Trust	122	

G

Gabriel, Mother Joseph	96
Gallagher, Rev Louis	66
Gallagher, Very Rev Raphael	97
Galvin, Sister Marie	96
Galvin, Rev Seamus	82, 107
Gavin, Rev John	116
Geddis, Dr T H	88
Geohegan, Rev Brian	112
George, Mr Robin	110
Geraldine, Sister	94
Gerner, Mr Keith	118
Gill & Macmillan	69
Gill, Mr Michael	69
Gillett, Mr James W	85
Gleeson, Very Rev Timothy	97
Glen River YMCA National Centre	55
Glenada YWCA	55
Glencree Centre for Reconciliation	114
Glenday, Rev David	92
Glennon, Sister Kathleen	112
GO *see* INTERSERVE	89
Good Shepherd Sisters	94
Gordon, Rev James	79
Gould, Miss Lynda	121
Grace Dieu Retreat House	60
Graham, Rev A Harold	121
Graham, Miss Elaine	89
Graham, Very Rev Paul	59
Graham, Rev R C	79
Grant, Rev J R	71
Gray, Mr Ian	91
Greave, Mr Frank	67
Greenow, Rev D J	85
Greer, Rev David H	111
Grier, Mr John	64
Griffin, Mr Tom	69

H

Hagan, Rev T J	107
Haine, Mr W R	68
Halpin, Sister Ailbe	99
Halyburton, Mrs Netta	55
Hanly, Very Rev William	96
Hannon, Rt Rev Brian D A	74
Hardy, Mr Terry	107
Harnett, Very Rev Philip	100
Harper, Mr Herbert	58
Harrington, Very Rev Joseph	98
Harrington, Very Rev P	100
Harrison, Mrs Ann	64
Hart, Major Alan	82, 117
Harty, Most Rev Michael	73
Hassett, Mr Michael	121
Hay, Rev Dr Ian M	90
Heaney, Most Rev Seamus	73
Hearns, Comdt Richard F	117
Helmsman *see* Seamen's Christian Friend Society	86
Herron, Rev Walter	81
Higgins, Sister M Angela	98
Hodges, Mr Alan	82
Hodnett, Mr Tim	55
Holmes, Rev R Finlay	119
Holy Family Convent	57
Holy Ghost Fathers (CSSP)	94
Honan, Sister M Brid	57
Honeghan, Brother J J	92
Hope in Action *see* National Council of the YMCAs of Ireland	122
Hosanna *see* Irish Church Music Association	112
Hourie, Mr Desmond	117
Houston, Miss Ann	112
Hughes, Ms Amanda	67
Hughes, Rev Louis	61
Hunsdale, Mr Robert	84
Hunter, Mr Frank	64
Hunter, Rev W I	79
Hurley, Mrs Anne	68
Hurley, Rev Michael	59, 113
Hutchinson, Rev Samuel	79
Hyndman, Rev C Knox	82

I

Ian Bothwell (Crossfire Trust)	84
ICI (International Correspondence Institute)	119
IDEA *see* Evangelical Alliance	82
IMU Report *see* Irish Missionary Union	107
In Contact *see* EYM Ministries	84, 122
Info-Mission *see* Baptist Missions	88
Insight *see* Irish Missionary Fellowship	85
Institute of Theology & Philosophy	119
Inter-Church Relations Board	82
Intercom *see* Catholic Communications Institute	110
Interlink *see* Festivals of Male Voice Praise	84
International Catholic Girls' Society	122
International Correspondence Institute *see* ICI	119
International Gospel Outreach	85
Internation Hospital Christian Fellowship in Ireland & Scotland	112
INTERSERVE	89
Iona Carmelite Retreat House	59
Ireland Outreach	85
Irish Baptist *see* Baptist Union of Ireland	71
Irish Baptist College	118
Irish Bible School	57, 120
Irish Christian Study Centre	112
Irish Church Missions	83
Irish Church Music Association	112
Irish College	119
Irish Council of Churches	82
Irish Ecumenical News *see* Irish Council of Churches	82
Irish Episcopal Commission for Emigrants	116
Irish Evangelistic Band	85
Irish Gospel Outreach	85
Irish Institute of Pastoral Liturgy	120
Irish Messenger *see* Society of Jesus (SJ)	100
Irish Methodist Association of Youth Clubs *see* Irish Methodist Youth Department	122
Irish Methodist Youth Department	122
Irish Mission	85
Irish Missionary Fellowship	85
Irish Missionary Union	107
Irish Missionary Union Institute	57

J

J & M Dowds Bible & Bookshop	64
Jameson, Rev Canon D	56
Jeffreys, Mr Mark	56
Jerusalem & the Middle East Church Association	107
Jesuits & Friends *see* Society of Jesus (SJ)	100
Johnson, Mr H E	109
Johnston, Mr Denis	90
Johnston, Rev T W D	79
Jones, Ms Angela	65
Jones, Mr Billy & Mrs Martha	86
Jordan, Very Rev Thomas	93
Joy & Light *see* Lord's Day Observance Society	86

K

Kairos *see* Divine Word Missionaries	93

Entry	Page
Kavanagh, Brother Aongus	96
Kearney, Mrs Rose	116
Kearns, Brother Laurence	97
Kearon, Rev K A	106
Keating, Rev Brother J C	92
Kelly, Rev A N	90
Kennedy, Mr Cliff	115
Kennedy, Sister Loretta	55
Kennedy, Mr Morris	57
Kennedy, Mr Niall	85
Kennedy, Mr Stanislaus	116
Kenny, Sister Patricia	93
Kerr, Rev Cecil	55, 113
Kerr, Rev David J	77, 82
Kerr, Pastor Roy	109
Kilbride, Sister Paula	100
Kilbroney Conservation Centre	56
Kilroy, Sister Phil	100
Kingston, Rev Paul	77
Kirby, Most Rev John	74
Knapp, Ms Ingrid	115
Knights of St Columbanus	85
Knox, Mr David	86
Knox, Miss Hazel	86
Kolvenbach, Very Rev Peter	100

L

Entry	Page
La Retraite	60
Advertisement	60
Langan, Sister Patricia	95
Lausanne Committee for Evangelism in Ireland	85
Laverty, Rev Denis	122
Leach, Rev William E	90
Leamy, Sister M A	91
Ledwith, Rt Rev Mgr Micheal	120
Lee, Sister M Dominic	92
Lee, Very Rev William	120
Leech, Mr Walter W	84
Legion of Mary	85
Lennon, Mr Eric	83, 116
Lennon, Sister Kathryn	93
The Leprosy Mission International	89
Let the Bible Speak	113
Lewis, Mr Gordon	83
Lewis, Rev Howard	82
Lewis, Mr Philip	64
Liechty, Mr J	114
Life Indeed *see* The Faith Mission	84
Light & Life *see* UFM Worldwide	90
Light & Life Films	109
Limerick Christian Bookshop	67
Advertisement	67
The Lisburn Bookshop	65
Little Company of Mary	94
Little Sisters of the Assumption	94
Little Sisters of the Poor	94
Lloyd, Ms Alice	119
Loader, Mr Brian D	106
Londonderry City Mission	83
Looney, Rev Tom	59
Lord's Day Observance Society	86
Loughridge, Dr A	118
Lowry, Mr Samuel	68
Lucan Youth Centre	57
Lynas, Very Rev Dr R V A	79
Lynch, Brother Anthony	56
Lyons, Mr Roger	106

M

Entry	Page
McAdam, Mr James	63, 65
McCann, Mrs Ann	113
McCarthy, Father Gabriel	57
McCarthy, Rt Rev Dom Justin	92
McCarthy, Very Rev Michael F	94
McCarthy, Sister Ursula	94
McCausland, Mr Nelson	86
McCloskey, Sister Dorothy	99
McComb, Rev E	77
McConnell, Mr G	65
McConnell, Mr George	69
McCorkell, Mr Derek	116
McCormack, Sister Assumption	61
McCormack, Brother Matthew	93
McCormick, Rev J B	81
McCormick, Mr Sydney	117
M'Coubrey, Mr Richard	65
McCullough, Mr Fergus	66
McDermott, Mr Stanley	64
McDermott, Sister Ursula	100
McDonald, Very Rev John	120
McDonnell, Very Rev Colum	98
McDougald, Mrs Sheila	57
McDowell, Rev I S	115
McElhone, Sister Eileen	59
McGail, Mr Tony	89
McGarry, Sister Brendon	93
McGill, Sister Margaret	99
McGonagle, Very Rev William	96
McIlven, Rev David	89
McIlvenna, Mr John	69
McKelvey, Rev Canon R S J H	66, 69
McKeogh, Very Rev Stephen	59
McKeown, Mr Brian	115
McKiernan, Most Rev Francis	73
McKittrick, Mr David	115
McLoughlin, Mr James & Mrs Sarah	114
MacMahon, Sister Bernadette	92
McMullan, Rt Rev Gordon	76
McMullan, Rev R J T	90
McPolin, Very Rev James	119
McSorley, Rev Gerard	58
McSweeney, Very Rev Eustace	91
MacThomais, Brother M P	60
Magee, Most Rev John	73
Maguire, Very Rev Salvian	59
Maher, Rev Ray	114
Mairs, Mr Richard	64
Manning, Miss Maureen	82
Manresa House	61
MARC Europe *Advertisement*	67
Maria Legionis *see* Legion of Mary	85
Marianists	94
Marie Reparatrice Retreat House	61
Marinella Pastoral Centre	57
Marist Brothers (FMS)	94
Marist Sisters	95
Marists (SM)	95
Martin, Rev A V	81
Mater Dei Institute of Education	120
Mawhinney, Rev Edmund T I	77
Mawhinney, Miss Esther	66
Mawhinney, Mr Stanley	85
Maxwell, Sister Elizabeth	61
Mayes, Rev J C D	90
Mayes, Ven M H G	91
The Maynooth University Bookshop	68
Mayo, Rev John	119
Medical Missionaries of Mary	95
Mehaffey, Rt Rev James	76
Mercy Conference & Retreat Centre	61
Messenger *see* Reformed Presbyterian Church of Ireland	82
Methodist Bookroom	64
Methodist Church in Ireland Districts:	
Belfast	77
Down	77
Dublin	77
Enniskillen & Sligo	77
Londonderry	77
Midlands & Southern	77
North East	77
Portadown	78
Methodist Missionary Society (Ireland)	89
Methodist Newsletter *see* Methodist Church in Ireland	77
Mill Hill Missionaries	95
Millen, Mr David	84, 122
Milligan, Mr Seamus	84
Minehan, Sister Rita	91
Mirror *see* Aid to the Church in Need	106
Mission *see* BCMS Crosslinks	88
Missionaries of Africa (White Fathers)	95
Missionary Franciscan Sisters of the Immaculate Conception	95
Missionary News *see* Acre Gospel Mission	88

Entry	Page
Missionary Newsletter *see* Free Presbyterian Church of Ulster Mission Board	89
Missionary Sisters of Our Lady of Apostles	95
Missionary Sisters of St Columban (SSC)	96
Missionary Sisters of the Assumption	95
Missionary Sisters of the Holy Rosary (MSHR)	95
Missionary Society of St Columban (SSC)	96
Missions Today *see* Pontifical Mission Aid Societies	107
Missionwide *see* Holy Ghost Fathers (CSSP)	94
Mitchell, Mr Ivor	114
Mizpah Bible & Bookshop	64
Moloney, Sister Margaret	92
Montfort House	61
Montfort Missionaries (SMM)	96
Montgomery, Ms Gwen	114
Moore, Dr Hamilton	118
Moore, Canon T R	74
Moroney, Mr Brendan & Mrs Nellie	116
Morris, Mrs Janet	112
Morrow, Rev J W	114
Mount St Anne's	61
Mount St Joseph Guest House	57
Mount St Joseph Retreat & Conference Centre	61
Mourne Missionary Trust	69
Mowbray, Rev Alan	120
Moxen, Mr John	86, 121
Moynan, Mrs Elsie	68
Muintir Na Tire	116
Muldoon, Sister Margaret	99
Mulrennan, Sister Madeleine	100
Murdoch, Rev J F	81
Murphy, Very Rev Cornelius	100
Murphy, Mr James D	109
Murphy, Most Rev Michael	73
Murphy, Very Rev Patrick	96
Murray, Very Rev J	61
Myross Wood House	61

N

Entry	Page
National Bible Society of Ireland	69
National Bible Study Club	112
National Catholic Chaplaincy for the Deaf	117
National Council of the YMCAs of Ireland	122
National Mission Council of Ireland	107
Neilands, Rev David	122
Neill, Rt Rev John R W	76
Nelson, Rev Dr J W	79
Nelson, Mr Warren	57, 120
Nesbitt, Rev David	82
New Day *see* The Leprosy Mission International	89
Newton, Most Rev Jeremiah	73
Nexus Ireland	114
Non-subscribing Presbyterian *see* Non-subscribing Presbyterian Church of Ireland	79
Non-subscribing Presbyterian Church of Ireland	79
Noonan, Very Rev Mark	100
North Antrim Reformation Movement	86
North Belfast Mission	83
North-West Books	65
Northern Publishing Belfast	64

O

Entry	Page
O'Boyle, Mr Sean	66, 69
O'Brien, Rev Edmund	116
O'Brien, Sister Marie	94
O'Brien, Sister Nuala	94
O'Ceallaigh, Rev Fiachra	93
O'Cleirigh, Miss Kate	60
O'Connell, Very Rev James	95
O'Connell, Rev John	57
O'Connell, Mr Timothy	67
O'Connor, Mrs Helen	67
O'Connor, Very Rev Laurence	120
O'Connor, Sister Maura	93
O'Connor, Very Rev Michael	120
O'Dalaigh, Rev Tadgh	97
O'Donoghoe, Rev Joseph	106
O'Driscoll, Sister Bernadette	98
O'Driscoll, Sister Eileen	59
O'Driscoll, Mr P	71
O'Farrell, Sister Catherine	95
O'Farrell, Rev Diarmuid	117
O'Ferrall, Dr Fergus	66, 68, 69
O'Flynn, Rev Sylvester	59
O'Gorman, Brother Stephen	97
O'Hara, Very Rev Vincent	92
O'Neill, Mr Brian	114
O'Neill, Sister Eileen	61
O'Reilly, Most Rev Colm	71
O'Sullivan, Most Rev Dermot	73
O'Sullivan, Sister Josepha	100
O'Sullivan, Sister Maria Rosa	98
O'Sullivan, Sister Marian	93
Oblate Lourdes Messenger *see* Oblates of Mary Immaculate	96
Oblates of Mary Immaculate (OM)	96
Order of Malta	117
Order of St Camillus	96
Other Hand Music	112
Our Lady of Apostles Guest & Retreat House	59
Our Lady of Sion Adult Education Centre	57
Advertisement	58
Our Lady's Retreat House	61
Outlook *see* Holy Ghost Fathers (CSSP)	94
Outlook on Ireland Outreach *see* Ireland Outreach	85
Overseas Missionary Fellowship	89

P

Entry	Page
PACE *see* Protestant & Catholic Encounter	115
Pallotines (SCA)	96
Pantoglini, Rev Antonio	97
Parker, Brother Colman	94
Passionists (CP)	96
Patrician Brothers (FSP)	96
Paul of the Cross, Mother	96
Pax Christi (Irish section)	114
Payne, Mr Brendan & Mrs Barbara	58
Peace by Peace *see* Community of the Peace People	113
Peden, Mr James	86
Penfold, Mr Michael J	64
Peppard, Sister Elma	56
Percival, Mr F Geoffrey	111
Pickard, Mr David	89
Pickett, Rev John H	90
Pilot Trust	111
Pioneer Total Abstinence Association of the Sacred Heart	110
Pitt, Mr Raymond J	107
Pontifical Irish College	119
Pontifical Mission Aid Societies	107
Pontifical Missionary Union of Priests & Religious	82
Poor Sisters of Nazareth	96
Porter, Rev D C	81
Porter, Mr W J	84
Poyntz, Rt Rev Samuel	76
Prayer & Praise Circular *see* Irish Evangelistic Band	85
Prayer Update *see* Foundation Ministries	111
PrayerWatch	111
The Presbyterian Church in Ireland	79
Presbyteries:	
Ards	79
Armagh	79
Ballymena	79
Belfast East	79
Belfast North	79
Belfast South	79

Carrickfergus	79
Coleraine	79
Derry & Strabane	79
Donegal	79
Down	79
Dromore	79
Dublin	79
Foyle	79
Iveagh	79
Monaghan	79
Newry	79
Omagh	79
Route	79
Templepatrick	79
Tyrone	79
Presbyterian Church in Ireland Overseas Board	90
Presbyterian Herald	
see Presbyterian Church in Ireland	79
Prescott, Mr Kingsley	67
Presentation Brothers (FPM)	97
Presentation Sisters (PBVM)	97
Project Evangelism	86, 121
Protestant Adoption Society	113
Protestant Aid	110
Protestant & Catholic Encounter	115
Protestant Orphan Society	117
Public & Preparatory School Camps (West of Ireland Camps)	122

Q

Qua Iboe Fellowship	90

R

Rabey, Mr George P	90
Rafferty, Very Rev Kevin	119
Randles, Sister Eileen	120
Rea, Rev W James	83
Reality	
see Redemptorists (CSSR)	97
Reaume, Rev Michael	94
Recover	
see Order of St Camillus	96
Redemptorists (CSSR)	97
Refausse, Dr Raymond	68
Reformed Presbyterian Church of Ireland	82
Reformed Theological College	118
Reilly, Ms Anne	101
Religious Press Association	82
Religious of Jesus & Mary	97
Renaud, Very Rev Etienne	95
Renewal Publications	69
Representative Church Body Library	68
Revivalist	
see Free Presbyterian Church of Ulster	77
Reynolds, Rev William	61
Rizzo, Rev Pio	66
Roberts, Mr H R	68
Roddie, Rev Robert	77
Rodney Cordner	84
Roman Catholic	
see under Catholic	
Ronzani, Rev Rinaldo	92
Rooney, Rev Michael	96
Rosminian Fathers (IC)	97
Rosser, Rev John C W	85
Rowayne, Miss Anne	110
Ruddock, Rev K	107
Russell, Most Rev Michael	73
Ryan, Brother Felim	96
Ryan, Most Rev Laurence	74
Ryan, Sister M Vincent	95

S

Sacred Heart Fathers (SCJ)	97
Sacred Heart Missionaries (MSC)	97
Sacred Hearts Community (SSCC)	97
St Ann's Book Centre	66
St Clements Retreat House	59
St Dominic's Retreat & Conference Centre	61
St John of God Brothers (OH)	97
St John of God Holiday & Retreat House	61
St John of God Sisters	97
St John's College	120
St Joseph's Advocate	
see Mill Hill Missionaries	95
St Kieran's College	120
St Patrick's College:	
Carlow	120
Maynooth	120
Thurles	120
St Patrick's Missionary Society (SPS)	98
St Patrick's Purgatory	58
St Patrick's Retreat	59
St Paul's Book Centre	66
St Peter's College	120
Salesian Sisters of St John Bosco	98
Salesians (SDB)	98
Saltshaker	
see 174 Trust	116
Salvation Army: Northern Ireland Division	82
Salvation Army Social Services	117
Sandes Soldiers' & Airmen's Centres	86
Scoble, Mr Gordon	88
Screene, Very Rev Michael	60
Scripture Gift Mission Inc	69
Scripture Union Adventure Centre	58
Scripture Union Book Centre:	
Dublin	67
Dun Laoghaire	67
Scripture Union Resource Centre	64
Seamen's Christian Friend Society	86
Searle, Rev Bob	85
Semple, Mr Roy	63
Servite Friars (OSM)	98
Servite Missions	
see Servite Friars (OSM)	98
Seventh-day Adventist Church	82
SGM News	
see Scripture Gift Mission Inc	69
Shankill Road Mission	83
Share	
see South American Missionary Society	90
Sheehy, Brother Peter	91
Sherwood, Mr R H	74
Shortall, Mr Michael	121
SIM Now	
see SIM UK	90
SIM UK	90
Sinnott, Sister Monica	97
Sisters of Charity	98
Sisters of Charity of St Paul the Apostle	98
Sisters of Loreto (IBVM)	98
Sisters of Marie Reparatrice	98
Sisters of Mercy	98
Sisters of St Clare	99
Sisters of St Joseph of Annecy	99
Sisters of St Joseph of Chambery	99
Sisters of St Joseph of Cluny	99
Sisters of St Joseph of Peace	99
Sisters of St Joseph of the Apparition	99
Sisters of St Louis	99
Sisters of the Holy Cross	99
Sisters of the Holy Faith	99
Sisters of the Holy Family of Bordeaux	99
Sisters of the Infant Jesus	100
Sisters of the Sacred Heart of Mary	100
Smith, Rev Declan	88
Smith, Most Rev Michael	73
Smyth, Rev John C	110
Society for International Ministries	
see SIM UK	90
Society of African Missions (SMA)	100
Society of Jesus (SJ)	100
Society of St Vincent de Paul	110
Society of the Holy Child Jesus (SHCJ)	100
Society of the Sacred Heart	100
South American Missionary Society	90
South East Antrim Reformation Movement	86

Southern Association of
   Irish Baptist Churches   71
Southey, Rt Rev Dom Ambrose   92
Speer, Mr Alan   67
Speers, Mr J Noel   113
Spense, Brother Francis   91
Spotlight
   see Dublin Christian Mission   83
Starkon, Sister Elizabeth   97
Stella Maris   61
Stevenson, Mr David   84
Stewart, Mr Raymond   86, 121
Stracey, Mr A   88
Sunday School for Ireland
   Religious Resource Centre   66
Survive — MIVA   107
Szeto, Dr Paul C C   106

T
Tabor House   61
Tarbett, Mr Aidan   66
Taylor, Mr Dale   68
Taylor, Rev Richard H   77
Teach Bridge House of
   Welcome for Young People   62
Tear Fund   115
Tear Times
   see Tear Fund   115
Teggin, Mr Jack   89
Temple, Rev David J   85
The Teresian Association   112
Thompson, Mr David   106
Tierney, Rev Martin   110
Timoney, Very Rev Charles   95
Todd, Rev S Kenneth   79
Together
   see Agapé (Ireland)   84
Toner, Sister Mary   59
Transmission
   see Church Missionary
      Society Ireland   88
Trocaire   115
Troubador
   see Franciscans (OFM)   93
Truth for Youth
   see Free Presbyterian
      Church of Ulster   77
Turner, Mr David   106
Turner, Mr Stephen   122

Twomey, Miss Una   100
Tyrell, Sister A Patricia   61

U
UFM Worldwide   90
Union Theological College   119
Unison   111
United Beach Missions   86
United Society for the
   Propagation of the Gospel   90
The Upper Room   67
Ursulines (Irish Ursuline Union) 100
USPG
   see United Society for the
      Propagation of the Gospel   90

V
Veritas Bookshop:
   Blackrock   66
   Cork   66
   Dublin   67
   Ennis   67
   Letterkenny   67
   Sligo   68
Veritas Publications   69
Viatores Christi   100
Vigano, Very Rev Egidio   98
Vincentians (CM)   100
Vision of Europe
   see European Missionary
      Fellowship   89
VMM Newsletter
   see Volunteer Missionary
      Movement   101
Voice
   see Franciscan Missionaries
      of the Divine Motherhood   93
Voice of the Martyrs
   see Christian Mission
      to the Communist World   106
Volunteer Missionary
   Movement   101

W
W J Thompson House   117
Waldensian Church Missions
   Irish Committee   107
Walkinstown Social Service
   Centre   117

Wallace, Rev H B   81
Wallace, Rev S Leslie   89
Walpole, Rev Christopher G   77
Walsh, Most Rev Patrick J   71
Walsh, Mr Willie   107
Walshe, Rev Michael   97
Warke, Rt Rev Robert A   76
Waters, Very Rev Ignatius   96
Watson, Mr Jonathan   89
Watson, Rev Samuel   77
Watters, Rev Enda   107
Watts, Rev Dr Donald   79
Webber, Rev Daniel   89
Weir, Rev W D   81
Wesley House   62
Wheatley, Mr L John   89
Whisker, Mr Frank D   62
White Fathers/White Sisters
   see Missionaries of Africa   95
Whitefield College of the Bible 119
Whitley, Mr James   84
Wider World
   see Presbyterian Church in
      Ireland Overseas Board   90
Williams, Miss Olive   88
Willoughby, Rt Rev Noel V   76
Wilson, Rev Cecil   88
Wilson, Rt Rev William G   76
Window on the World
   see World Vision   115
Witherow, Mr Ronald   65
Word
   see Divine Word Missionaries 93
World Vision   115
World Vision Ireland   115
Worldwide Missionary
   Convention   107
Wright, Mr Steve   122
Wycliffe Bible Translators   91
Wycliffe News
   see Wycliffe Bible
      Translators   91

Y
Y's Moves
   see Belfast City YMCA   116
Young Christian Workers   122
Young Life   122
YWCA, Waterford   58